MC 10⁰

With blessings from the author

Father Gehring an

A Child of Miracles

The
Story
of
Patsy
Li

A
Child of
Miracles

by REV. FREDERIC P. GEHRING, C.M.
with MARTIN ABRAMSON

JEFFERIES and MANZ, INC. - PHILADELPHIA

This book is reverently dedicated to the Patsy Lis who never grew up—the children I knew in China who died at the hands of the Japanese and the Chinese Communists. It is dedicated, too, to the boys who never came home from Guadalcanal to hear the end of the Patsy Li story.

Contents

Illustrations appear at page 148 and page 180.

A Child of Miracles

Out
of
the
Jungle,
a
Child

1

On the night of October 13, 1942, in that bloody, parched, vermin-infested jungle called Guadalcanal, we gave up a life that was precious to us, and received a new one that came in a manner so strange and wondrous it seemed to defy all human explanation. Indeed, to this day, even the most cynical of us who were there can only explain the sequence of events that began that night by describing them as "miraculous"—a word that is often bandied about like a tired cliché, but in this case means everything it could possibly imply.

It was a night when the whole mystifying panorama

of human life spun around us like a pinwheel, confusing us and blurring our vision.

It was a party night, full of songs, laughter, and make-do refreshments. But this was a party like Cinderella's, because it had a midnight of tragedy.

It was a night that was memorable for one other reason—it was the only night I can remember when the worst bane of our existence, "Washing Machine Charlie," somehow failed to pay us a visit.

On Guadalcanal, the Japanese ran their war with both maniacal fervor and railroad-timetable precision. Each evening at dusk, Tokyo Rose would come on the radio with soft, dreamy music and a bewitching voice that spread propaganda like so much honeyed poison. Her English was perfect and she even knew how to make effective use of American slang. After Tokyo Rose finished her nightly session, we would get only a short respite before suffering the nightmare of "Charlie's" arrival.

"Charlie" was a twin-engined Japanese bomber whose engines were purposely kept out of synchronization in order to harangue our eardrums with a grinding, rasping noise. "Him sick bird," the natives on the island used to say of Charlie. Charlie wasn't at all sick, but its noise made *us* sick, particularly since it always came when we were trying to catch some shut-eye. Aside from acting as a sleep-wrecker, Charlie would hit us with a few scattered explosives, then end its aerial tour by dropping dazzling flares that lit up our positions like the neon marquees on Times Square. The flares were the signal for the Japanese naval armada that lay off our island to pound us with tons and tons of screaming shellfire.

At midnight, the shelling would stop to allow the Japanese infantry to come at us in their bloodthirsty banzai attacks. Sometimes, the Japanese planes would bomb us at the same time, but more often they waited with their raids to coincide with another infantry attack at noon, when the overhead glare of sunlight blinded our antiaircraft gunners and weakened our defenses.

This night, Tokyo Rose was particularly beguiling with her talk of mother and apple dumpling, and her description of all the pleasures that awaited us the minute we revolted against our Simon Legree commanders and left our miserable jungle hole for that paradise called America.

"Where are your wives and girl friends tonight?" Tokyo Rose asked us ever so softly. "Why, they're dining and dancing in beautiful, air-conditioned hotels with the slackers and the defense workers who are making two hundred dollars a week while you boys rot and die here of disease and Japanese bullets." Then she gave us a running commentary on how our favorite ball teams were doing back home and filled us in on the latest activities in Hollywood and on Broadway, all the while interspersing her "news reports" with reminders that if we continued our doomed cause on Guadalcanal, we would never live to savor again the good times of the American home front.

"Hey, Tokyo Rose, stop smoking so much opium," one Marine shouted loudly at the radio. "If you think we left nothing but palaces behind us, you should see the crummy shack where I used to live!"

"I'll bet your face could stop Big Ben," one of the Seabees wisecracked. "Send us a picture of yourself so you can scare us off the island!"

Other Seabees and Marines joined in the banter, but I knew that behind their gags and wisecracks, there were a lot of misty eyes and yearning hearts. Tokyo Rose's "soft sell" propaganda was not being countered by any stimulating programs from our side, or at least not by any programs that were reaching us. The Mata Hari of the airwaves had no competition for our attention or our interest. Though we naturally discounted most of what she told us, some of it couldn't help sinking in. And we had learned from bitter experience that many of the warnings she had given us about Japanese capabilities had proved devastatingly accurate.

Our Marines had been fighting with unbelievable courage and skill, but with Japanese power steadily increasing on the island,—and with our own supply of equipment and replacements dried up to a trickle— there was a gnawing fear among us that the home front was incapable of giving us the help we desperately needed.

"You are being forgotten like the men of Bataan and Corregidor were forgotten," Tokyo Rose would purr at us. And indeed our position seemed dishearteningly similar to that of the exhausted Americans who surrendered in the Philippines and were put through the torture of the "Bataan Death March." As Catholic chaplain to the Naval forces on Guadalcanal, who was supposed to act not only as spiritual counselor but also as all-round morale booster, I was worried about the spirit of valorous men who were beginning to feel that they, too, were expendable.

Oddly enough, Guadalcanal had seemed like an easy mission at first. When our 1st Marines landed in August on this strategic island northeast of Australia, they caught the corps of Japanese defenders by surprise. They found only token opposition at their landing site on Lunga Beach and advanced quickly to take over the island's important airfield, which they named Henderson Field.

Most of the Japanese scurried off to jungle hideouts and caves north of the field, leaving their rice breakfasts cooking in open pots for our men to finish. It looked like America's first offensive victory of the war could be achieved merely by marching on the squirrel-like roosts where the defenders had holed up and using dynamite charges to blast them out. But the picture changed radically when a strong force of Japanese heavy cruisers slipped past two U. S. destroyers patrolling the Slot—the narrow waters between Guadalcanal and Florida Island—and destroyed four of our cruisers. It was too risky for the remainder of our warships to stay in an area where the Japanese had sea supremacy, and they sailed away, leaving us helplessly exposed.

The Japanese navy and air force closed in on us, bombarding us by day and by night, until many of our men were turned into raving, wild-eyed shell shock cases. The burning heat of the daytime, the thirst, the torrential rains, the mud and dirt, the maddening assault by mosquitoes and other types of infectious insects, and the necessity of fighting through thick, tangled walls of ba-

nana trees, brambles, and jungle growth that stretched
as high as a hundred feet, were something our American
boys had never faced before. These were irritants that
constantly worked on their physical reserves and nervous
systems. More and more of them were wasting away
with malaria, dengue fever, and dysentery.

Most frightening of all was the manner in which the
Japanese were able to keep landing reinforcements on
the island. They maintained such a steady buildup that
our shoestring force of ten thousand men was soon outnumbered by perhaps three to one. Their control of the
sea lanes allowed them to bring soldiers and material in
on a fleet of transports that we sarcastically called the
"Tokyo Express." They were so arrogant and cocksure
of victory that they took to trumpeting just how many
new troops they intended to land each time—and even
where they would land them. The warnings always
came to us in the pearly tones of our favorite lady-ser-
pent.

"Tonight, three thousand more Japanese soldiers will
land south of Point Esperance," Tokyo Rose would announce. "They are very good soldiers, trained in jungle
fighting. They will kill many, many American boys.
Many of you listening to me must die unless you surrender or leave this island." Other times, Tokyo Rose
would pinpoint the landings as west of the field or north
of it, and dare our Navy to do what it could not do—
sink the Japanese transport ships, and bring us floods of
supplies and reinforcements. "Only a few American
ships were sent to help you, but they never got here,"
Rose would remind us. "Japanese ships sank them, and

all your supplies went to the bottom. Japanese sailors are much better than Americans. They are much better gunners; they laugh at the way your gunners miss them. Your Navy is a big joke. Soon the whole Pacific will see nothing but Japanese ships."

For this night, that was to make of me a principal in as fantastic a drama as one can conceive, Rose had promised us more bad news. There were to be no new troop landings, she told us, but the crescendo of shellbursts hammering our island base would reach a height of violence and devastation. This dire pronouncement was followed immediately by a sparkling recorded medley from Oscar Hammerstein's "Showboat." I wandered glumly away from both Rose and Oscar and headed for my tent. One needed one's rest before the carnage.

"Padre, where've you been; I've been looking for you," a booming voice called out to me. The man behind the voice was equally formidable. He was Sergeant Jim O'Leary, a tall, husky Marine with about fifteen years of service behind him. O'Leary was the kind of career serviceman one sees in the popular movies. He was an unmarried, girl-in-every-port type; a tough, salty-tongued noncom with the traditional soft heart hidden beneath the granite exterior.

"We're having a party and you're invited," he told me. "Plenty of laughs and jungle juice. Please bring your fiddle, Padre. We need some swingy music. Oh, if we only had some dames!"

"What's the occasion for a party?" I wanted to know. "Has Admiral Yamamoto decided to chuck everything, and is he coming down to surrender to you personally?"

"Padre, didn't anybody tell you? The Kid's wife had that baby. He's a father, God help him."

"The baby *came?*" I exclaimed. "Why, that's a wonderful blessing. It's a good omen for all of us. When did he find out about it?"

"This afternoon. One of the planes brought in some mail. I gave him a cigar from that box we scrounged from the last Navy supply ship. He's choking on it now."

"O'Leary, you must be the happiest man in the world about this, next to the Kid."

O'Leary looked stricken. "Now, Padre," he said. "You know what I think about marriage and babies and all that sort of guff."

"Sure, sure, I know. And I know how you tease the Kid whenever he talks about his little wife and how you pretend to be the world's No. 1 cynic. But you don't fool me. I know how you've protected the Kid like he was your own younger brother and how you're dying to see that new baby and have him call you 'Uncle Jim'!"

O'Leary held his hand up. "Padre, please, no speeches. This little blessed event is just an excuse for a wild party. So please come quick. And don't forget that Stradivarius."

I went into my tent to pick up the violin that had traveled with me to so many parts of the world. For the moment, the weariness that bit so deep into my bones fell away and along with it all the dark thoughts I had been harboring about our perils on Guadalcanal. If this jungle island to which we had been consigned by military order seemed like an outpost of Hades, at least the

Good Lord was still spreading His bounties to other parts of the world and had given us something to cheer about via V-Mail. For weeks now, the "Kid"—he was an apple-cheeked youngster named Eddie who had married his school sweetheart just before he joined the Marines —had been living on tenterhooks, waiting for the good word to reach him from across the endless miles of ocean. His air of tense anticipation had been contagious, and we had all become expectant fathers by a kind of osmosis. We had earned the right to celebrate. It was too bad, I reflected, as I hurried over to the sergeant's bivouac area, that it would have to be a quickie party. "Washing Machine Charlie" would be around soon to end the fun.

There was, as the sergeant promised, a proper quota of liquid refreshment. It was a mixture of some of the Navy's medicinal alcohol supply mixed with various native concoctions—hence the phrase "jungle juice." As I played and as the boys toasted the Kid as well as the Kid's kid, time and place fell away, and it was only after we'd been partying for an hour, that it suddenly dawned on us that our noisy, air-borne nemesis had, for some mys‚ terious reason, taken the night off.

"Isn't it wonderful?" I shouted over the din. "It looks like Charlie heard the good news too and has decided to give us a break."

Suddenly, there was a cataclysmic roar outside our tent and the ground beneath us began to heave and rock as if in an earthquake. We tore open the flap and rushed outside to see geysers of orange flame spurting upward from explosions east of Lunga Beach. Tokyo Rose had kept her deadly promise. The Japanese navy had discarded its usual formula for the night, and was shelling us even without the help of Charlie's usual flares. They were relying on close range and a full moon to make their cannonade effective.

"Get to the foxholes, blast you!" an officer screamed.

I raced with a group of Marines to the nearest vacant hole. A shell exploded only a few yards away, showering us with a mound of dirt and shrapnel. The Japanese ships, looking like strange, seaborne wraiths in the moonlight, hurled salvo after salvo across the water into our narrow perimeter. A few overshot the mark and landed close to the Japanese lines, but many more came dangerously close to our foxholes. The shells trailed dazzling paths of crimson as they rocketed out of their ships' cannons. Then they seemed to hang suspensefully in air before crashing down on us with terrifying impact.

Huge clouds of smoke billowed up around us, and the acrid fumes stung our eyes and throats and made us choke. The thunder of the shellbursts echoed so violently in our ears it was like being hit with a percussion hammer. One shell crashed into an ammunition truck, blowing it and its occupants into a thousand fragments and sending furnace-hot streams of flame racing down into our trench.

Alongside me, head bowed, there were Catholic boys reciting their rosaries, Protestants murmuring prayers, and Jewish boys, with closed eyes, fingering the holy *mezuzahs* they wore around their necks. The adage that there are no atheists in foxholes was already familiar to me. In moments of deadly peril, the human hand reaches out for help from above. Even those who hadn't uttered a word of prayer or been inside a house of worship for years before the war, were looking now for a Divine hand to shield them.

The cannonade from the sea was followed by a frenzied, all-out attack by Japanese infantry. They came in waves, screaming like deranged animals, and hurling themselves bodily against our front lines of Marines, who had to slash and tear at them with their bayonets when rifle fire couldn't stop them. During the early weeks on the island, our boys were so inexperienced in night fighting that they sometimes fired on one another in the confusion of the "banzai" attacks. But now the boys were battle-hardened, and if they had to give ground they made the Japanese pay a heavy price. We were unable to take many prisoners, because the Japanese clung to their code of Bushido which forbade their surrender in battle, no matter what the circumstances.

When the ground fighting and shelling let up a bit, I crawled out of my foxhole and went forward to help with the wounded and administer the Last Rites to those whose bodies were contorted in the agony of the dying. I had made several trips up and back to the field hospital when I passed an exhausted Marine who was wandering around in a daze, mumbling and moaning to himself. I put my arm around him and he turned toward me. I was shocked to look into a tear-drenched, ashen face and recognize O'Leary, the tough noncom.

He looked at me with blank eyes. It took a few moments before he began to focus, and he recognized me.

"The Kid's dead . . . he's gone," he shouted at me. "What the hell good are your prayers and your religion? Did they stop the shrapnel that tore half his head off!"

The news cut like a knife. I had learned to steel myself against the day-in, day-out reality of violent death, but the enormity of this particular tragedy was almost too much to bear.

O'Leary was beside himself. "Why wasn't it me instead of him?" he raged at me. "I don't have a family! If there is really a God and He had to have a human sacrifice, why couldn't He have been satisfied with O'Leary, instead of taking a kid with a young wife and a brand new baby who'll never see his father? Why should anyone believe and trust in Jesus or Mary when they've allowed a crime like this to happen? Why *did* it happen, Padre? Why? Why?"

In his hurt and bitterness, O'Leary had asked the question that is the most difficult of all questions to answer. "We must take God on faith," I said softly. "Everything that happens is always for good reason, even if we simple mortals find it hard sometimes to understand." O'Leary shook his head to show he wasn't buying my explanation. Angrily, he turned on his heel and walked away. But he was so bushed he nearly fell. I hurried after him, threw my arm around him, and guided him toward my chaplain's tent. Inside, I helped him into one of the cots, took off his shoes, and washed his face. "I'll send word to your company that you're over here," I told him.

He shook his head, but he was too exhausted to make

a real protest. He sprawled out on the bed, and in a few minutes was fast asleep.

I sat next to him in the darkness, watching him. I was overcome with a deep feeling of inadequacy. Here was a human being who had been so cruelly hurt he had impulsively renounced all faith, and I had been unable to comfort him or give him real understanding.

"Chaplain Gehring," a voice called out. A Marine burst into the tent. "There are three natives who've just come through the enemy lines and are calling for the 'priest-man,' " he said.

"All right, bring them right here," I told him.

"There's something else you ought to know, Padre," the Marine said. "They're carrying a child."

The
Padre's
Pet

2

It didn't make sense. I was sure it was some kind of a weird joke. Even when I stepped outside the tent and saw the three natives carefully picking their way toward me, escorted by another Marine, and carrying something in their arms, I kept shaking my head in disbelief. Why would anyone bring a tot to me at this hour of night, right in the middle of a war, daring the deadly fire that must have come at them from both sides of the battle lines?

But it *was* a child—a girl of about five or six. And when I looked at her, I felt a pang of horror. Her arm and her feet had been slashed with a bayonet, and she was bleeding in several places. Her head had been bashed with a blunt instrument, probably the butt end of a rifle. Her body was burning up with fever. I had her placed on my cot and sent the Marines rushing out for medical help. They brought back a corpsman who stemmed the flow of blood and bound the child's wounds. Shortly afterward, Dr. James Delaney, a Navy medical officer from Detroit, came in. He was even more shocked by the child's appearance than I was. He examined her quickly and gave her several injections. But she didn't seem to respond, and he looked at me sadly and said, "Pray hard for her. She needs the Great Physician. Only a miracle can keep her alive."

The three natives were Melanese who had been baptized into the Christian faith and whom I had been supplying with food to smuggle to French Marist missionaries. These missionaries were hiding in caves and huts behind the enemy lines. They had been living on the island when the Japanese first occupied it, and after being threatened, had taken to secret hideouts. The Japanese had found that the natives who were sheltering the missionaries, were sending us valuable intelligence. In reprisal, they had sacked one of the native villages just before launching their nighttime attack against our troops. Every villager had been brutally murdered, save for this unknown child who had been thrown into a rain-soaked ditch to die. My Melanese friends had come upon her wounded and battered body while combing the ruins of the village. Finding her still gasping, they had risked their lives to bring her to me.

I knelt by the child's bedside, placed a Miraculous Medal around her neck, and commended her to the Immaculate Heart of Mary and the Divine Physician. Then I began to pray, with my three friends joining me. We maintained our vigil throughout the night. Toward morning, she started to come out of her coma, and uttered a series of frightened moans. But then she lapsed back into unconsciousness, and when we called Dr. Delaney, he was no more encouraging than before. There was, he said again, very little hope for her. We continued our prayers and our vigil, hoping against all reasonable hope that this child of sorrows could hang on to her small spark of life. Suddenly, I heard someone whisper behind me, "Where'd the kid come from?" It was O'Leary, now wide awake. I told him the story of the child, and he joined us in our vigil.

During the day, she began to stir again. She opened one eye suddenly, stared at me, and closed it. Then she began to whimper. She was coming out of it! Through the second night, she still wavered fitfully on the line that marks the boundary between here and hereafter. The next morning, just as our fiery jungle sun was breaking through the early mist, we noticed that the child's fever seemed to be subsiding. Again, there was a hurry call to the medico. This time when he looked up from the patient, he seemed positively jubilant.

"I'm either a genius doctor, or you're a genius priest, but in any case, by golly, I think our girl is going to make it," he said.

Later that day, I walked slowly with O'Leary back to his company. All during our death-watch that had turned unexpectedly into a life-watch, he had been grimly silent. Now he wanted to tell me something, but I could see it was difficult for him.

"Padre, I was wrong," he said finally. "I'll never know just why the Kid had to die, but when that little girl came to us on the same night the Kid went, I realized it must have been some kind of omen. When I thought of how those natives had taken such terrible risks to bring her to us, I felt that God must have been directing them to bring us a new life to replace the one we'd lost. I think God was testing us to see if we considered the life of a little native girl worth caring about, and when we showed Him we'd give everything we had for her, He rewarded us by saving her.

"Like you said, we can't question God; we've got to take Him on faith. I know I wanted to throw that faith away, but I don't anymore. I'm gonna hang on to it, Padre, no matter what happens."

Now there existed on the island of Guadalcanal a strange phenomenon. We were ten thousand American males—and a nameless girl. The commanding officer told me that in our desperate situation, he couldn't think of diverting one of our meager supply of planes to ferry my little charge out of the battle zone. So the child who had been so cruelly orphaned by the Japanese massacre of her village had to be satisfied with a somewhat battle-weary chaplain as a makeshift father and mother. She seemed to know instinctively that I belonged to her because she clung to me constantly. We made a little pallet for her on which she slept. She hovered nearby when I celebrated Mass. I couldn't take a step outside the tent without feeling my shadow fall into step with me.

The little girl with the bandaged head soon had more admirers than any female can hope to cope with in a lifetime. The word spread quickly about her, and the Marines came flocking around. To them, the child was a symbol of love and hope, the prototype of all the little children playing peacefully on the front stoop back home. She was also a bright new experience in the jungle and something to take their minds off the day-to-day misery of combat.

When the first group of visitors came, the child became frightened and buried her face in my arms. I thought it was their appearance that disturbed her; they were mud-covered and unshaved, with eyes red-rimmed with fatigue. But when she pointed to a carbine one of the Marines was carrying, I realized it wasn't their faces, but their guns, which bothered her. She associated them with the brutal attack on her by the Japanese. So I gave an order to the boys: "Leave your weapons outside the tent when you come to visit . . . at least until the child gets used to them."

Each day, our quota of visitors increased. Never did a child have so many adopted fathers and not one mother. The Marines began bringing flowers and fruit they picked in the dense underbrush, as well as chocolate from their rations. Men from the 6th Seabee Battalion improvised wooden dolls for her. Some of the Marine fliers used torn or damaged parachutes as raw material from which they fashioned little silk sarongs.

A few Sailors from the Navy's Cub I Unit came with presents that weren't suitable for a little tyke, but rather for a siren of nineteen or twenty. They had been told that Chaplain Gehring had become the guardian of a beautiful South Seas creature, and the practical jokers who fed them the information conveniently forgot to tell them this creature was no more than six! One would-be swain even worked for days making a full-length evening gown out of parachute silk before discovering that his leg had been pulled.

I called the child "Pao-Pei." It meant "Little Pet" or "Little Treasure" in Chinese. It was a name I had learned when I was a missionary in China before the war. The Marines and Seabees picked up the name and called her "Pao-Pei" too, even though none of them had any idea what it meant.

The child herself puzzled me. I had picked up bits and pieces of the native language on the island, but she didn't understand any of the words I used. I decided that my accent or phrasing was wrong. Nor did she respond to the pidgin English used by some of the Melanese. I had learned the Mandarin language in China and tried some simple Mandarin phrases. The child appeared to be of Chinese descent, rather than Melanese, so I thought Mandarin might draw a reaction. It didn't—it drew a blank. At times the child looked so attentive when I spoke English that I was half-convinced that it was *our* language she understood. But then I decided this was impossible and dismissed the idea.

Another oddity was the delicate air she affected when she ate her food. She would sit prim and ladylike, waiting to be served. Then when she received her bowl or tin plate, she would use her utensils with what seemed like practiced skill and finesse. Having seen the primitive manner in which the natives on the island attacked their food, I couldn't imagine where the child's air of breeding came from. I decided that perhaps her parents had lived on another, more civilized, island before they came to Guadalcanal.

Now and again, the child murmured some words I couldn't understand, but most of the time she was completely silent. She wore an eternal expression of sadness that was heartbreaking to see. There was nothing we could do to get her to smile or laugh. Nobody worked harder at this job than Al Landes, a Jewish Seabee from Queens, New York, who served as my assistant. Al was famous as the best scrounger on Guadalcanal, and we also called him "Mr. Happy Times" because of his unfailing good cheer and bubbling personality. "I'm going to make this kid laugh if I have to stand on my head," he told me.

He made funny faces and goo-goo eyes, did crazy jigs, went through contortions, and devised magic tricks. He did everything he possibly could—and nothing worked. In the end, and after much huffing and puffing, he *did* stand on his head. Everybody around him howled, but Pao-Pei just refused to be amused. The veil of sorrow that enveloped her little being was too thick for us to pierce.

I played my violin for her whenever I could, and though this seemed to interest her, it still failed to bring any shine to her sad eyes. One afternoon, Buddy Brennan, who had been a pianist with Guy Lombardo's band, got together with me to do a routine of funny musical numbers. Some of the Navy boys had salvaged a little piano from an ammunition ship which the Japanese had torpedoed off Lunga Beach, and Brennan used that to accompany me. The boys lapped it up, but we won no jubilant applause from our female audience. "If we ever had to play a theater with people like her in the audience, we'd be stone cold dead in the market," Buddy decided.

One of the Marines who had come in as a combat replacement was Barney Ross, the former lightweight and welterweight champion of the world. Barney was over-age for the Marines—some of the boys laughingly called him "Grandpa"—but he had fought as hard as he did in the ring to get into combat service, and he finally persuaded the higher-ups in Washington to give him an age waiver. We had become very friendly, and when he came around to see my little orphan he decided we ought to entertain her with a boxing show. We put on heavy gloves and staged a mock fight. It wound up with both of us falling to the floor like dying swans, pretending to be counted out. But it was more wasted effort because it didn't get a rise out of Pao-Pei.

One of my biggest problems was trying to shield this haunted child from the effects of the war that raged around us. Each time enemy planes or ships attacked us, I would scoop her up and run with her to the foxhole. There some of the boys would join me in covering her with our bodies so that any flying shrapnel would strike us and not her. One bomb landed so close we were showered with debris, and one of the boys who was helping to cover the child had his face gashed open by a piece of flying steel.

The explosions made Pao-Pei hysterical, and we would sing every song we knew to soothe her. The louder the din from the bursting bombs, the louder we sang. We even forgot our own natural fear of being killed or maimed in our anxiety to protect our girl and keep her from a breakdown. My foxhole was four feet deep and extra-large in width so that I always had plenty of company. The Seabees had built it to accommodate fifteen men because the Japanese attacks sometimes came when I was holding services, and we would have to drop everything and run en masse for cover.

For the sake of little Pao-Pei, we would pretend these bombardments were all a game, and that the torrent of flame and smoke and steel that rained down on us was no more dangerous than Fourth of July firecrackers. We kept up a running line of chatter and banter and told Pao-Pei endless tales about the statues and medals that I had placed atop the coconut logs that rimmed the hole. We knew the child didn't understand what we were saying, but we felt the endless gabble would distract her from the realities. Sometimes we had to crouch in the damp hole for hours until the raids ended, so that our efforts to make this seem like playtime at a kiddie camp became a frantic chore. One of our worst times came when a Navy officer was strafed and wounded out in the open field by a low-flying Japanese plane. I ran out of the foxhole and dragged him in with us, but we had to minister to him and try to ease his pain for over an hour, while at the same time continue the charade with our little pet.

Another time, Gene Markey, a well-known Hollywood producer turned Navy intelligence officer, dived into my foxhole at the start of a raid. Gene's tent was not far from mine, but he had been away on a special mission and nobody had told him about the pocket-sized addition to the chaplain's family. When he saw her, his eyes popped. I explained how the natives had found her left for dead in a ditch, and he kept shaking his head. "If we made a movie about all this, people wouldn't believe it," he said. "They'd say it was just a lot of Hollywood fantasy."

Gene had been born and raised a Catholic, but his adventures in Hollywood's tinsel world had led him to stray a bit from the good Lord's orbit. I'd been gently trying to coax Gene back into the fold, but he'd been stalling me. "Give this old sinner a little more time," he used to say.

That night a shell exploded right on top of the foxhole that Gene normally used. Had he been there his name would have made a new addition to the casualty list. The near-miss came, understandably, as quite a shock. It left Gene breathless. "This little girl must be the guardian angel that God sent down in disguise to watch over His favorite chaplain," he told me. "When's the next Mass, Padre? After this, I'm with you!"

Gene was not only at the next Mass but at virtually every other one after that. It wasn't long before I had him serving my Mass and acting as altar boy. "The prodigal hath returned with a vengeance" was Gene's half-humorous, half-serious way of describing his "reformation." "If I ever live through this damned war, I'm going back to Hollywood—not as a producer, but as a missionary of the faith. I'm going to give Fulton Sheen competition."

We had another Hollywood expert on the island who agreed with Gene that our real-life saga of ten thousand fighting men and a girl would be deemed "too incredible" by the public if they saw it on the silver screen. This second expert was Navy Lieutenant Commander Robert Montgomery, who had been with the PT boats, then came to the Canal on a destroyer. Like everyone else, he was intrigued with Pao-Pei's presence. "She's cute enough to become a South Sea Island Shirley Temple, but she'll never make the grade if she doesn't learn to smile," was the way Montgomery sized her up.

There were times when I just couldn't keep Pao-Pei with me, and I worked out a kind of hide-and-seek game to get her out of the way without frightening her into thinking she had completely lost me. For instance, I didn't want her along when I made the rounds of the hospital tents where boys lay moaning in agony, with limbs blown off or faces horribly scarred. I naturally could not take her when the tactical situation made it necessary for me to crawl to the front lines to hear the confessions of Marines and bring them Holy Communion. At these times, I would leave her with Al under the pretense that I had gone into hiding and wanted her to find me. Then Al would take her on a long walk and go poking through different tents, presumably to find me and flush me out.

We did the same thing when I had to carry out an almost daily assignment of conducting services for the dead. Each morning following a night attack by the enemy, Marine trucks would come by my tent loaded with the bodies of our casualties. I would then accompany the bodies to our island cemetery and recite the final prayers for their souls. We always had two hundred to three hundred graves that had been dug in preparation for this painful ordeal. Obviously, I didn't want to subject my little girl to any of this, so we made sure to start our hide-and-seek game even before the trucks arrived.

Of course, there were some scenes of brutality and terror to which the child inevitably had to be exposed. The dogfights that our heroic Marine pilots like Joe Foss, Bob Smith, Bob Galore, Major Dobbins and the rest fought with the better-armed, faster, and much more numerous Japanese Zeroes, simply could not be hidden behind any screen. Nor could the sight of planes shot down and exploding near us or pilots' bodies being incinerated in sheets of crackling flame be lightly dismissed even from a child's mind and heart.

The coolness our fliers displayed in dangerous emergencies was evident on the ground as well as in their more familiar habitat of the sky. I used to say Mass for the Marine air wing in a bivouac area we had carved out of jungle ground close to Henderson Field. When Pao-Pei was with me, she would stand slightly to the right of me, eyes fixed on the altar stone I used. One morning, just as I had begun the service, two shots rang out. A Japanese sniper with a high-powered rifle was in one of the trees and had drawn a bead on us.

The Latin words I was reciting died in my mouth. I looked anxiously at the child, but she didn't seem aware of what was happening. I thought of taking her and running for cover, but there were no protective bushes close by. The fliers betrayed not a tremor of nervousness —they remained in a kneeling position. Only one of them moved. He was a young lieutenant who left us very quietly. A few moments later we heard a burst of fire, and then the sniper's body toppled from his roost. I let out a deep sigh and resumed the Mass.

One day Foss, who was rapidly becoming the ace of our theater of war, was shot down by a swarm of Zeroes. He escaped by parachuting out of his plane, and landed in the water. A Navy crash boat rushed to pick him up. Just as the sailors got Foss into the boat, a Japanese pilot whose plane had gone out of commission also bailed out and landed in the water. The boat went over to save him too. Standing on shore, we watched Foss gallantly lean over the edge of the craft to pull his enemy to safety. Then we froze in horror as the pilot whipped a pistol from his pocket and fired at Foss's head. Luckily, the gun jammed. Before he could shoot again, a sailor on the boat smashed his head with a boat handle, killing him instantly.

The action went so fast we were numbed into silence. But suddenly there was a piercing cry behind me. In the excitement of the moment, I had forgotten to send Pao-Pei off somewhere with "Mr. Happy Times," and she had been an eyewitness to this tableau of violence. The fatal blow on the head of the pilot may have conjured up memories of the vicious beating she herself had suffered only too recently. In any event, I had a difficult time trying to calm her and to convince her that nobody meant her any harm. She kept screaming and sobbing pitifully for more than two hours.

Our most harrowing experience occurred one evening when a Naval surgeon called me into the hospital tent to anoint some wounded Marines before he operated on them. I told Al to take care of my little charge, but she insisted on scooting after me, and it took a bit of effort on Al's part to keep her outside the tent while I ducked inside. The surgeon, Commander William Knowland, began to operate on his first case when a Japanese warship unexpectedly opened fire on the island. All our lights were quickly doused, and the nurses set up an emergency spotlight with the help of a kerosene lamp. Suddenly there was a terrific crash which nearly knocked us flat. A shell had torn right through the side of our enclosure and ploughed into wooden boards only a few feet from where the surgeon was at work.

Horrified, I tried to cry out but couldn't. The corpsmen and nurses were also petrified, but as we all gaped with morbid fascination at the shell protruding from the floor, it slowly dawned on us that it was a dud. Otherwise, it would have exploded instantly, shattering us to pieces. Dr. Knowland's face remained imperturbable, and I noted with amazement that his hands had never stopped working skillfully and effortlessly over his anesthetized patient. His only acknowledgment that there had been a disturbance came when he quietly told a corpsman to look for the mine disposal officer. The shell, he observed wryly, might be nursing a slow fuse.

Remembering that Pao-Pei was close at hand, I hurried outside. I found that Al had not been able to get her into a trench. They were so close to the hospital tent that they would surely have been doomed, along with those of us inside the enclosure, if the shell had behaved as shells normally do.

It was a few nights later that we found a new name for Pao-Pei. A midnight attack sent us scurrying to our foxholes and we were soon following our usual ritual of humming and singing to our frightened little girl. We sang a number of songs that had girls' names as titles— songs like "Ida," "Margie," "Sweet Adeline," and "If You Knew Susie." At this point, a Marine named O'- Sullivan decided he was tired of the Chinese pet name I had been using.

"What do you say we get a new name for this kid?" he suggested. "She's one of us now, so how about an American name for her?"

It was, on the face of it, a trivial request. Not one of the ten or twelve of us huddled in that hole that night could possibly imagine that this request would be the first ripple in a series of waves that would flow across thousands of miles of sea and link together lost fragments of an incredible human story. We did not think that night of things astounding or strange. We thought only of the obvious and the simple. An American name, O'Sullivan had suggested. Well, why not? The first name was settled very quickly. "I've called her 'Pao-

Pei' and the nearest common American name to that is 'Patsy'," I said. "Shall we make it Patsy?" The boys all nodded agreement.

"Now what about the last name?" a Marine named Richardson wanted to know. "Shall we make it Smith or Brown or Jones, or a long name like Collingwood or Shuttleworth?"

"How about Shaughnessy?" someone chimed in.

"Patsy Hasenpfeffer," remarked one kidder.

"Let's name her after the Admiral," somebody else suggested. "We'll call her Patsy Halsey."

"How about giving her the general's name—Patsy Vandegrift?" (General Alexander A. Vandegrift commanded the Marine forces on the island.)

"Look, she's the Padre's girl, and if we name her after anybody on this island it's got to be after him," one Marine insisted. "Patsy Gehring is a good name for this little tyke."

"Well, boys," I said, "I'd like to give little Patsy my name, but I think I'll give her my Chinese name, which is Li."

"How do you spell that—L-E-E?" one of the boys asked.

"L-I is the way the Chinese usually spell it," I explained. "But it's pronounced exactly like the name L-E-E."

"How'd you ever get that name?" Richardson wanted to know.

"I don't know if you fellows know this, but I was a missionary in China for several years before the war," I told them. "When I first got over there, a Chinese teacher at the mission who was supposed to teach me the language couldn't pronounce the name Gehring very well. He happened to notice that I was wearing a hat which had the Lee label. So he said, 'Lee, or Li, is a good Chinese name, and it's very easy to pronounce. So from now on, I will call you Father Li.' The name stuck, and pretty soon all the Chinese people and children that I met were calling me by that name."

"Okay, now it's official; this little girl is Patsy Li of the U. S. Navy and Marine Corps," Al Landes announced. "She's homeless, but not nameless. How about it, boys—let's give three cheers for Patsy Li!"

We all gave three cheers. Then a shell exploded not far away. We ducked deep into the foxhole. The child in my arms began to cry.

"New name or no new name, she still bawls the same way she always did," one Marine muttered.

The next night, in the same foxhole, the talk reverted again to my Chinese name and my Chinese past.

"Were you in one of the cities, Padre, or the interior?" O'Sullivan wanted to know.

"The interior," I told him.

"Pretty rugged."

"I'll say it was. And we had our war there, too, before America ever dreamed she was going to get involved. In fact, the poor Chinese have been up to their necks in two wars—with the Japanese *and* with the Communists."

"What made you interested in going to China?" a Navy man wanted to know.

"Well, the truth is, I've been fascinated with China

ever since I was three or four years old," I said. "There was a Chinese laundryman I knew in Brooklyn who used to fill my head with the wonders of his old country. Going to that strange, distant land became the ambition of my life. I'm glad he did such a fine selling job on me. It was rugged there, as O'Sullivan says, and we had our share of danger and terror. But I had experiences and adventures—and an education—I'll never forget."

"Let's hear the whole story," a Seabee demanded.

"Oh migosh, that would take days and days and days. You don't want that."

"Sure, we do. Besides, you've got plenty of time. It looks like a long war. Why don't you start with that Chinese laundryman?"

3

His name was Charlie Wong, I told the boys. Chinese laundrymen in America are usually described as being short, fat, and silent. Well, maybe many of them are, but certainly Charlie didn't fit the pattern. He was tall and slim and exuded so much effervescence that he was known in the neighborhood as "Jolly Charlie" or "Jolly Wong." I never learned about the squalor that dogged the lives of China's teeming millions from "Jolly Charlie." He had happily forgotten all that, once he found passage on the ship that took him from the Orient to America. His stories were all about China's breathtaking spectacles—its great mountains and valleys; its strange rivers which had acquired a yellow color; its Grand Canal; its Great Wall which had been built by human hands and which stretched for more than 1,500 miles; its pagodas and temples; its colorful costumes and pageantry; its festivals, and its fleets of little houseboats which served as homes for people who didn't want roots on shore.

Charlie's memory and his imagination were both extremely vivid. His store was decorated in correspondingly exotic style, so that you almost felt you were in Little Nanking or Shanghai when you walked in. I was always volunteering to take my dad's shirts and cuffs to Jolly Charlie so that I could steep myself in the excitement he created. I was amazed at the way he could tell stories even while he was swishing water out of his mouth and onto the shirts for ironing. Once I voiced my admiration of his skill, and he rewarded me with a handful of Chinese rice cakes. I was very free with my compliments after that!

Although I was only one of several youngsters who became part of Jolly Charlie's circle, I was his favorite and the one he always singled out as the boy who would surely grow up to explore his homeland. According to Charlie, he had discerned in me "the spirit of Marco Polo." From time to time, Charlie and I would dicuss the possibility of my becoming an importer when I grew up, so I could go to China on matters of trade. At various other times we agreed I would go to China as a sea captain, a salesman of American goods, a teacher of English and German, a musician in a wandering gypsy orchestra, or simply as a stowaway and a vagabond. Charlie had a deck of fortune cards, but although he consulted them to try to get a clear image of what was going to happen to me, somehow the picture they gave him was always blurred and confused.

"Never mind fortune cards. You smart boy. You find right way to get there yourself," he finally decided. He never held out the possibility that he himself would return to his old country. "I busy make living here, I no can go, you go for me," was the way he summed it up.

My father, Louis Gehring, had a store and factory at 137 Manhattan Avenue, in the German section of Greenpoint, Brooklyn, where he manufactured the wax candles and artificial flowers that were popular in the early 1900's. We lived above the factory. My brother, Louis, Jr., was born in 1902 and I came a year later, to be followed in due course by my sister Marietta. I also had a half-brother, George, and a half-sister, Phyllis, who were by then at boarding schools. They were the children of my father's first marriage. Dad was a widower when he met my mother, Marie, twenty-five years his junior. Dad was a native of Bavaria and had come to America as a boy. He lived first with relatives in Philadelphia, then went to Washington, where, at the age of fifteen, he was apprenticed to a confectionery and bakery shop. A few years later, he made his way to Brooklyn and began to ply the trade of wax-making. He had received some training in this craft in Bavaria, as a youngster in knee pants. After some fits and strains the business prospered. More and more children making their First Communion and Confirmation began to approach the altar with decorative wax candles. Wax orange blossoms and wreaths became popular with brides. Dad also had a genius for making wax figures of the infant Jesus that looked so natural and lifelike it was difficult to conceive they were made of paraffin and wax.

Soon after I was born, Dad's business spurted to the point where he had fifty girls working for him, mostly young immigrants who were newly arrived from Germany. He then decided to follow other residents of the community who were moving to the more fashionable Bushwick section. Here, on Willoughby Avenue, he and Mother bought a spanking new, three-story brownstone home. We were directly across from St. John the Baptist's Church and from St. John's Prep School and College run by the good Vincentian fathers.

The love of music, so treasured in Bavarian families, was an integral part of our lives. Mother played the piano and Dad's proud boast was that he owned one of the first gramophones ever to come on the market. From this somewhat battered instrument there issued forth constantly the mellifluous melodies of Johann Strauss and Victor Herbert.

In our home, musical education commenced simultaneously for Marietta, Louis, and myself. Marietta was assigned to Mother's piano and Louis and I were presented with violins. Dad arranged for an Italian musician who owned a shop nearby to give us lessons twice a week and also set up a rigid schedule of daily practice. One of Dad's first questions when he came home from the factory each day was, "How was your practice?" He held the clock on us weekends too.

I continued my music lessons all through my tenure at the neighborhood parochial school, and Marietta, Louis, and I formed a family trio which performed at all the local dances and parties. We called ourselves immodestly "Gehring's Gala Orchestra." Augmented by other local talent, and utilizing mostly violins and mandolins, we would go from house to house on the days before Christmas, playing the carols and expressing our season's greetings in song. In summer we would bring our instruments down to Coney Island and play serenades, first on the beach and later in front of Nathan's Famous, where the crowds assembled for their Coney Island red-hots and orange drinks.

My decision to become a Vincentian was not made until my last semester at St. John's Prep School, but it had been building in the back of my mind for several years. The thread of deep religious conviction had run through the entire history of the Gehring clan, and one of Dad's proudest possessions was a fragment of the True Cross which had been carried in the Crusades, and which had been handed down from generation to generation. I had been inspired, too, by the kindly Vincentians ever since they began visiting my folks on Willoughby Avenue. When the priests asked me if I wanted to wear the cassock of an altar boy, I jumped at the opportunity. I soon found myself learning the Latin and getting up at five A.M. to serve two, sometimes three, Masses each morning. The seminarians at the Diocesan

Seminary attached to St. John's would frequently congregate on our front stoop to chat with Dad. Their wonderful spirit and sense of dedication stirred in me the desire that someday I would wish to be one of them.

When our country was forced into World War I, I was heartsick at the way the beautiful ideal of "peace on earth" had been gutted by human failings. It seemed to me that more recruits than ever were needed to spread the gospel of "good will toward men."

All this time, I had kept up my visits to the "Little Nanking" oasis of Jolly Charlie. My obsession with China remained as strong as ever, but I now found I had to adjust my childhood ambition to my growing conviction that I belonged in the Church. It was my Vincentian teachers who showed me how I could reconcile my two drives. I could steer my course to the Orient, not as a sea captain, a vagabond, an importer or an exporter— but as a missionary!

The original missions in China had been established by the French, but their ranks were dwindling fast. The war, which began for France in 1914, had depleted their seminaries, and they lacked new blood to replace the old. My teachers anticipated that when the war ended there would be a call to America to fill the gap. "We've grown out of the frontier class and we've got to shoulder some of the responsibilities the Europeans can't handle any more," they explained.

One evening, Dad brought home a story in a Catholic publication which described the work of the old French missionaries in China. We were busy discussing it when we heard pounding on our front door. It was our neighbor, Mr. Blum, red-faced and strangely agitated. "Come quickly, Louis, your place is on fire," he cried.

When we got to the factory, the firemen were there, too, but the blaze was already raging out of control. Someone had left a pile of paper decorations in a hallway adjoining the factory, and then someone else had carelessly tossed a lighted cigarette on top of them. The flames had spread to cardboard cartons and to the mounds of wax in the factory. By the time the firemen's hoses had doused the last few cinders, the building and everything in it—representing a lifetime of work—was in total ruin. The only thing we found later, strangely unharmed, was a figure of the Holy Mother.

It was a devastating financial blow, because Dad carried no insurance. It also came at a time when Dad's general business outlook was declining due to the fact that interest in wax bridal wreaths and wax flower displays had fallen off. In addition, when Dad managed to get another little factory started again, he suffered a bad fall and was laid up for three years. During this time, his business ground to a standstill.

My father had always been the tower of strength in our family, but this double-barreled misfortune left him stunned. Luckily, our frail little Mother rose to the occasion. She convinced Dad to save expenses by moving his business to the extension of our house. She also spurred him to fresh effort with the admonition that it could have been worse, and that, though we would now live with tightened belts, the good Lord would somehow spare us the spasms of starvation. Mother began to help Dad with the molds, while Louis and I both helped out after school, soliciting orders and delivering them. When I saw a bowl of fruit in a Loft's window wilting from the sun one day, I convinced the manager he ought to order a wax fruit display from my father. This led to other orders for wax fruit displays that helped cushion the loss of interest in our regular wax products. It also caused me to take a hard, new look at my own future. For the family's sake, I thought I should now devote myself full time to Dad's business and give up my hopes for the priesthood. Louis had shown great aptitude and interest in an art career, and I felt it wouldn't be fair to take him away from it.

My folks, however, wouldn't even listen to my suggestion. "You follow the kind of life that's closest to your heart," they said. "We'll make out somehow." When Dad died at the age of eighty in 1925, Mother insisted that she would handle our little family business on her own. Louis and I were to keep right on doing what we'd been doing, she said, and she made it plain she would brook no arguments on this subject.

In 1921, my last year at St. John's Prep, the Holy Father asked for American priests and sisters to volunteer for the Chinese missions just as my teachers had predicted. During the following four years, which I spent at St. Joseph's Preparatory Seminary in Princeton, New Jersey, I met a number of pioneer missionaries who were heeding the call to the East. As each one left, it seemed to bring me a few giant steps closer to the realization of my own dream. The province of Kiangsi had been earmarked for the Vincentian missions, but others were going over too. The Jesuits had been given

North China. The Dominican Fathers had been assigned to Fukien Province and the offshore islands; the Franciscans were heading for Hupeh, and the Passionists for Hunan. The Maryknoll Fathers were taking Kwantung, a strip of southern China, where the first American foreign mission seminary was established.

Father Lennon, the president of St. Joseph's, was a bug on horticulture, and he had developed a large-scale fruit and vegetable patch, which we used to tend, along the edge of Carnegie Lake, across from the bailiwick of the Roaring Princeton Tigers.

"All future priests should have a knowledge of the good earth," he used to say. When he heard of my interest in China, he complimented me, then reminded me that China was a backward agricultural land. "You have a responsibility to learn more about the soil than anyone else," he said. So I found myself spending the early mornings before class planting seed, spacing endless rows of asparagus shoots, spraying the apple trees, and picking strawberries. (The berry-picking, at least, had its compensations, for dear old Brother John in charge of the kitchen promised a shortcake to the student who brought in the most berries. I gained thirty pounds in my first year at St. Joseph's, probably from the shortcake alone.)

After my graduation in 1925, I began my novitiate and seminary studies at the Vincentian headquarters in Germantown, Pennsylvania. My preoccupation with the Orient and my fervid interest in every morsel of Chinese gossip and news—whether it was news of the new missions there or of the internal strife that plagued the country—soon earned me the nickname of "China Boy." I lived up to the name in earnest in my final year of study. I was allowed to take a special course in elementary Chinese. Together with a classmate of Prep days named Freddie McGuire, I started a Crusade Society to help the missions in China. Our headquarters was in the basement of our chapel in Germantown.

I was ordained in May, 1930, and was promptly assigned to the Vincentian Mission in China headed by Bishop John A. O'Shea. But then we received alarming news. The Chinese Communists, who had been engaged in guerrilla warfare against the coalition government of General Chiang Kai-shek, had burst through Chiang's defenses in Kiangsi and had occupied virtually the entire province. They had sealed off the province to "foreigners," meaning that no new missionaries could get in. And with the Communists' known hatred for Americans and for the Church, the Vincentians who were already there were in mortal danger.

So Jolly Charlie's homeland would still have to wait for me a bit. In company with Freddie McGuire, my fellow "China Boy," I went to Georgetown University to take a medical missionary course and learn how to run a clinic—something that would be infinitely important in a primitive country with few doctors.

We then spent two years traveling through the eastern states, preaching for the missions and soliciting funds for them. Late in 1932, when we were in Connecticut, the word came through that the situation in Kiangsi had eased and that missionaries would soon be sent there again. Freddie and I promptly brushed up on our horseback riding, for we knew that much of our traveling in Kiangsi would have to be done by horse or mule. I considered myself a connoisseur of the saddle from my early riding days in Prospect Park, and I'm afraid I boasted too much about my prowess to the inexperienced Freddie. The good Lord served me my just desserts. My horse reared and I was thrown bodily. For some reason, I kept my hands glued to the reins as I fell. The horse promptly started running again, and I was dragged along the ground after him until my companion finally rode up and stopped him.

When I reached St. Vincent's Hospital, they told me I had a badly wrenched leg. Two weeks later, Father Freddie McGuire left for China without me. From shipboard he scribbled a good-by note. "A Hopalong Cassidy you're not," he joshed. "But cheer up, China will eventually be motorized and then we'll be able to accommodate all you tenderfeet!"

The early winter months of 1933 were a grand episode in frustration for me. But then came the spring—and sunshine. From Germantown came word that I would leave on the night of May 9 for San Francisco. There, I would board the *President Coolidge,* which was to be my "slow boat to China." Two other missionaries would accompany me. One of them, Father George Erbe, was a veteran of the Orient who was returning to his mission after a period of sick leave in the States. The other was Father Frank Melvin, a raw recruit like myself.

On the evening of May 9, there was a party in the

house at 795A Willoughby Avenue the likes of which
Bushwick had never seen before. More food was con-
sumed, more Rhine wine imbibed, more toasts toasted,
and more songs sung (gloriously loud and gloriously
off-key) than even the oldest resident could recall.
There were also more people crowded into one house
than seemed physically possible.

We went right from the house to Grand Central
Terminal and the final good-bys. Mother, though holding up like a redoubtable missionary mother should,
couldn't help shedding a few tears. There was also, I
must confess, a slightly damp trickle from the eyes of a
certain Orient-bound traveler. The real heaving sobs
came, however, not from any of us in the family, but
from good old Jolly Charlie. Said brother Louis very
cogently, "What are *you* bawling for? You're the one
who started the whole thing!"

On Friday morning, May 19, we clambered aboard
the President Lines' *President Coolidge* and nearly
swooned at the opulence in which we were going to float
for the next twenty-three days. The trade ships that
Jolly Charlie had talked about as plying the sea lanes
between California and the East were nothing but ugly
little scows compared to this eight-million-dollar sea-
going castle that the mission headquarters had—through
some colossal but happy mistake, we were sure—booked
us on. Awe-struck, we inspected the brilliantly decorated ballrooms, the specially-tiled pools, the gymnasium, the elegant dining rooms, and the lavish Oriental
rugs and furnishings that had been provided for the

luxury trade that formed the backbone of the ship's passenger list.

Promptly at noon, we nosed our way out of the harbor amid shrilling blasts, the shouting of farewells, and the waving of thousands of hankies. The words of Sir Walter Scott kept humming in my ears—"Breathes there the man, with soul so dead, who never to himself hath said, This is my own, my native land!" Good-by Brooklyn, good-by America. Hello, Jolly Charlie's world!

Then Father Erbe said, "Let's go for a stroll on deck and meet some of the people."

We donned our black clerical suits—which had been pressed to a fine crease by an obliging ship's valet—and put on our black hats. I took so much time adjusting mine that my two companions laughingly derided me as the "dude." I explained that I'd been given three spanking new Lee hats by an official of the Lee hat company whom I'd met during my mission tour in Connecticut, and that I'd promised the official that I would always do right by his present. "I've got to wear his hats properly or I'll be a poor advertisement for the good man's company," I pointed out.

Up on deck, we found a glorious sunshine bathing the *President Coolidge* and an even more glorious view of shimmering blue water stretching out of sight. The cool breezes made the weather just right for a constitutional, and we were sauntering briskly along when we were brought up short by a smiling, red-haired Irishman of forty-odd who stepped in front of us and said, "Aha, here are the Three Black Crows!"

The remark struck a chord of laughter across the deck, for in our garb we did indeed resemble not only the crows who go flapping around the air but also the "Three Black Crows" trio, who were a popular vaudeville and radio singing team of that era. We joined in the chorus of merriment, and the smiling Irishman said he was happy his remark hadn't offended us. When we exchanged introductions, he gave us a bit of a turn, for he was Frank Murphy, the distinguished former Mayor of Detroit who had just been appointed Governor General of the Philippine Islands by President Roosevelt. And we were soon to learn that he was every bit as informal and as "regular" as our first meeting with him indicated.

Murphy introduced us to his official party, which included his sister Marguerite Teahan, who was to act as the Governor General's First Lady in the Philippines (Murphy was a bachelor); her husband, Bill Teahan; Ed Kemp, Joe Mills, and Norman Hill, who were among the members of his staff; a lively girl named Emma, the family maid; and a handsome, bright, blond young woman named Eleanor Bumgardner, who was the Governor General's secretary. Eleanor, I discovered, was just out of college when she answered an ad for a secretarial position in Detroit. The advertiser was, of all people, the Mayor of Detroit, who was looking for a much more experienced hand, but who allowed the cheery Miss Bumgardner to talk herself into the job.

Murphy, I learned, admired his secretary, not only because of her competence and ability to handle people, but also because she had the same easy-going demeanor, no-nonsense attitude, and irreverent wit that he possessed. During this voyage, she acquired the nickname of "Lady"—a name she is identified with to this day. Mrs. Teahan, a charming lady but one inclined to become panicky at the thought of all the new responsibility she was to assume, was issuing a stream of orders at Miss Bumgardner one morning, including the assignment of some clean-up chores. Whereupon Miss Bumgardner announced very pointedly that her job was to act as the Governor's secretary and not to serve as Lady-in-Waiting to the whole Murphy Royal Family!

When the Governor heard of this rejoinder, he got a laugh out of it and began to call his secretary, jokingly, "Lady Eleanor." Soon we were all calling her by that name.

The Governor invited us "Three Crows" to become part of his party on the "Coolidge," and thus began a friendship which for me, personally, became a very warm and meaningful one over the years that were to follow.

In addition to getting to know Governor Murphy and his entourage, I made a number of other lasting friendships on the trip. As a matter of fact, some of us on this voyage later got into the habit of calling ourselves the "Coolidge Family."

After five days of sailing, we found ourselves approaching the Isle of Paradise—Hawaii. The soul-stirring strains of "Aloha" welcomed us as we docked. Smiling Hawaiians were standing by in Honolulu harbor laden with their traditional leis. Most of them quickly became garlands around Frank Murphy's neck as he stepped down, for he was the central figure for whom the reception committee had been waiting. The reception committee had enough wreaths left over for some of us lesser lights too.

We bowed out of beautiful Honolulu at dusk, with the band this time playing its good-by song, "Farewell to Thee." We had ten days to go before we would sight Japan, and we went right into a routine of deck sports and swimming, evening entertainment and all-round socializing. The heat had become tropical by now, and so the "Three Black Crows" transformed themselves into the "Three White Wings." We wore white pants and white soft shirts all day although we had to observe the formalities and dress formal-style for dinner.

We had only one day to see Japan and we rushed around town trying to cram in every sight we could. I expected to see paperlike houses and Japanese lanterns, but instead found both Tokyo and Yokohama to be thriving, bustling cities—as modern as any of those we'd left behind us in the States. Our driver explained that the earthquake of some years back had effected the radical change in Japanese architecture. The paperlike houses of the ancient cities had crumbled in the quake, and the new ones that went up in their place were patterned on the modern American metropolis. Were it not for the doll-like kimonoed women strutting about, we would have had difficulty identifying the country we were in as Japan.

We had one day's sail to Kobe, then we wove through the Inland Sea with its picturesque panorama of green islands and twinkling lighthouses. Leaving Japan, we spent three days steaming through the Yellow Sea. I found the waters appropriately named, for they were dank and discolored by the soil dumped into them by a series of wandering Chinese rivers. Shanghai lay ahead —sure sign that we were coming to the last stages of our glorious odyssey.

The
Walled
City

4

We arrived in Shanghai harbor on the morning of June 11, 1933, and I raced Frank Melvin up the deck to see which of us would get the first look at a Chinese city. Hawaii had been fascinating and Japan exotic, but China was where we were going to live and work—and what a sight it was! If an artist had splashed his canvas with every known color, it might have matched the riot of hues that glinted at us from the city's shoreline. And as startling as the rainbow that greeted us was the sight of rickety buildings pressing so close to the edge of the waterfront that it seemed they were ready at any moment to tumble into the sea.

While Melvin and I stood at the rail, fascinated, "Old Hand" Erbe moved alongside us and watched us watch the city. He was so quiet I didn't even notice him until I turned suddenly and nearly walked into him.

"Well, Fred," he smiled, "how do you like this leg of your free world tour?"

"Utterly fascinating," I told him. "But save me from ever living in one of those waterfront houses. I'd be afraid to go to sleep at night for fear that I'd wake up ten feet below the surface."

"You won't have to worry about waterfront living where you're going," he assured me. "You'll be up in mountain country, and you'll have to do so much climbing you may beg for reassignment to a seashore spot." The Vicariate I was headed for was in one of the deepest inland walled cities in South China. The city was Kanchow, in Kiangsi Province.

As we waited for our ship to dock, Father Erbe began to chat about his early experiences in China. He had been one of the first American missionaries to heed the Pope's call to the American community in 1921 to provide a transfusion for the dying French missions. For eleven years, Erbe had labored in Kiangsi Province, transforming a small village into a Christian community of more than three thousand souls. With his own hands he had laid the foundation stone for a school and a flourishing church. He still refused to talk at length about the great odds he had been up against and about the attacks by bandits and Communists. He was very modest about what he had accomplished. It would be a little while before Frank Melvin and I would find out just how much these accomplishments had cost him.

"There is so much to be done in China that it almost scares one to think about it, and so the best thing is not to think about it but just to go ahead and do it," Father Erbe told us. China, he explained, could be equated with a giant that had been restlessly tossing in his sleep for centuries. Its ancient philosophers had been brilliant men, among the first on earth to preach the beauty of peace and good fellowship. Yet its soil seemed almost never to have known any peace. For centuries, tribal wars had bathed its almost infinite landscape in red. Then, when it seemed to be achieving some semblance of unity and harmony, it had been torn apart by new civil wars and by the nightmare of aggression by Japan. The best of China's old customs had been uprooted, and it was in a state of ferment. It badly needed the missionary spirit and zeal to bring it new faith in ancient values and beliefs.

"Incidentally, Shanghai is not really a Chinese city," Father Erbe pointed out.

"What then do you call it?" Father Melvin wanted to know.

Erbe smiled broadly and pointed to the crowded shoreline. "I call it Babel," he said.

And Father Erbe was right. For Shanghai, China's most "westernized" city, was, in fact, a modern city of Babel where many worlds clashed violently. Narrow, crooked streets, jammed with people on foot or riding in rickshaws, gave way to broad boulevards crowded with automobiles and lined with motion-picture houses, modern department stores, neon signs, apartment houses, and hotels several stories high.

There was a French Concession, and an International Settlement where businessmen from a dozen Western nations lived with their families behind steel gates protected by concrete blockhouses. More blockhouses studded the Avenue du Roi Albert, the main street leading to Shanghai's "Times Square." There was not much contact, I was told, between the western enclaves of Shanghai and the teeming, all-Chinese neighborhoods of this many-faceted city.

Father Erbe told us that armed violence had become so common in Shanghai that the pillboxes had been erected by the police in a desperate effort to keep the situation from getting completely out of hand. Kidnapings and assassinations were so frequent that wealthy residents traveled in bulletproof cars with armed bodyguards.

Only a few blocks from the center of the city we skirted a dismal district known as "Blood Alley"—a street lined with cheap cabarets, beer parlors, and clip joints. Nearby was a row of opium dives—filthy little places shrouded with a heavy sweetish odor unmistakable a block away.

"The police pick up a hundred or more bodies on the streets of Shanghai each day," Father Erbe said. "A considerable percentage of these are opium addicts who have literally starved to death. Many of the coolies who visit these places don't earn enough to pay for their day's food as well as the opium that gives them a few moments relief from a life of hunger and sweat.

"The slaughter inflicted by the Japanese here was terrible," he said. "Residents of the International Settlement were not molested, but I am told that they could hear the screams of wounded and dying Chinese for days."

At that time, Father Melvin and I had been studying for our missionary work at the Vincentian Seminary in Germantown, Pennsylvania. We had naturally read about the Japanese attack in the newspapers, but it had somehow seemed unreal. We could not believe that a "civilized" nation like Japan could be guilty of such atrocities.

But the horror of the Shanghai Incident suddenly became vivid to us as Father Erbe called our attention to the fresh bullet scars on some of the stone buildings. As we walked wearily back to the waterfront, he also pointed out newly patched holes in the surface of the street. Here, Japanese artillery shells had landed. A little further on, we passed the charred remains of a row of buildings. "This must be the area where the main assault took place," I said.

"Yes," said Father Erbe. "The Japanese marines came ashore after a heavy bombardment by their ships lying inside Shanghai harbor. Chiang Kai-shek's Nineteenth Army was taken by surprise by the suddenness of the attack and was pushed back with heavy casualties. It hung on to a defense line in the eastern suburbs, but it couldn't prevent the Japanese from pillaging whatever sections they occupied. For more than a week, a good part of the city was at the mercy of the Japanese. Then they withdrew."

The Shanghai Incident was a follow-up of the Japanese occupation of Manchuria in 1931, Father Erbe pointed out. Manchuria had been considered part of China for more than a century, but the Japanese simply walked in on it. Chiang Kai-shek had protested, but since he was facing civil war with the Communists, he lacked the strength to throw the Japanese out.

"The militarists who have been calling the tune in the Japanese government may exploit Chiang Kai-shek's problems by making other warlike moves. There's a danger that these extremists will plunge all Asia into war."

We spent a few more days in Shanghai, then continued on to Hong Kong, where we boarded a square-sailed, swiftly moving junk that carried us overnight to Canton, a city crowded with thousands of Nationalist soldiers. Many of them looked barely seventeen or eighteen years old, wearing uniforms that were too large for their small-boned frames. Father Erbe studied the insignia on their jackets and informed us that these were veterans of the famous 19th Division that had fought so bravely at Shanghai.

In Canton we bought a thick loaf of bread and a bottle of wine to take on the train that was to carry us 150 miles inland to Shiuchow, the end of the line.

"Miserere nobis!" exclaimed Father Melvin as he caught sight of the train awaiting us in the Canton station. The locomotive itself was imposing—a fairly modern model stamped with the imprint of the Baldwin locomotive works in Philadelphia. But the passenger

cars looked like nothing so much as a string of trolleys out of the horse-drawn era of the eighteen-hundreds.

We climbed aboard one of these boxlike affairs to find that the seats had been constructed of wooden boards specially treated, apparently, to provide the hardest possible surface. In behind us poured a veritable flood of humanity—Chinese merchants, dealers, soldiers, and peddlers. It seemed likely that the overloaded train would be unable to start, but the whistle sounded a deafening blast, there was a series of bone-jarring jerks, and the car lurched into motion. It swayed disconcertingly as it picked up speed.

As the hours dragged on, the heat became unbearable. Feet and arms dangled out of the tiny windows. The passengers ate fruit and threw the refuse on the floor, smoked, chewed, spat. It was difficult for us to breathe.

After nine hours of torment, just when we had given up hope of relief, there was a sudden squeal of brakes, and the train shuddered to a stop. We gazed about and found ourselves on the outskirts of Shiuchow (later Kukong). Our journey was at an end.

A young priest whose cassock identified him as one of the Salesian Fathers of the Blessed John Bosco emerged from the crowd. Gently, he led us to the Salesian mission—a lofty stone building with a balcony overlooking the narrow streets of the village.

The Salesian Bishop himself greeted us warmly. Smiling, he led us into the sparsely furnished, but immaculately clean, guest quarters.

"I can see that you are tired," the Bishop said, "but permit me a moment before you rest."

With a flourish, he drew out three large documents marked with the red wax seal of the governor of the province. As he handed one of the documents to me, I was surprised to find that my photograph had been attached beneath a long series of Chinese characters. "Oh, oh," I quipped, "here I've just arrived and already you've got me in the Rogue's Gallery!"

"Call this Rogue's Gallery if you wish, but you'll need it to stay alive," the Bishop said. "From this point on, you'll be journeying deep into the heart of China. Without this kind of identification, one of these over-zealous soldiers might shoot you as a spy."

I held the document in my hand while Father Erbe translated the Chinese characters for me. They gave my name and identified me as a *shen-fu,* or priest. The remaining characters said: "This is to guarantee the safe and unmolested journey of the Shen Fu throughout the Province. Under no condition whatsoever is the Shen Fu to be hindered in his journey. And it is the desire of the Governor that whatever help can be given to the Shen Fu, it be given graciously and willingly. . . ."

I gazed at the paper with its red seal. Somehow it reminded me of a high school diploma, Chinese style. I remembered that I had once mislaid one of my school diplomas and it had taken my mother two weeks to find it. "Better not lose this diploma," I told myself. "Lose this, and you may lose your hide."

It was three in the morning when the Bishop woke

us up. "If you don't hurry," he said, "you will miss the bus!" By the light of a single flickering lamp, we groped for our cassocks and stumbled about the dim room, hastily stuffing our trunks and jamming the lids down. Then, still half asleep, we joined the Bishop in the mission yard. "Let us say Mass and have our breakfast," he said. "There is still a little time before you must leave. While we eat, I will tell you about the miracle."

Shortly afterward, we were sitting around the mission table with a plate heaped with scrambled eggs before each of us.

"There is a new China in the making," the Bishop said. "You will see the first sign of it shortly, but perhaps only Father Erbe will be able to appreciate what he sees. In the few short months that have passed since he left his mission, changes have taken place in this country the like of which have not been seen for a thousand years."

The Bishop's eyes sparkled as he leaned toward us across the table. "The miracle I am speaking of is a road," he said. "It is such a road as we missionaries have never before dreamed of. It is being built by thousands and thousands of coolie laborers. They have no modern machines as we have in the West, but they are building this miraculous road with their bare hands. All the stone and dirt is hauled by the coolies, each carrying a load of up to eighty pounds balanced on his shoulders for a distance of six or eight miles. Then the stones are piled together and hammered down with huge handmade weights. Soon, for the first time in the history of China, there will be wide automobile highways reaching into the interior. Already, you can travel a hundred miles from Shiuchow along a smoothly flowing highway. The first stage of your trip—which Father Erbe well knows would require five or six days by foot—will be accomplished in just four hours!"

Father Erbe furrowed his brow. "But what about the Communist bandits?" he asked. "If they are still as active as they were when I was last in China, they'll try desperately to sabotage the road."

"I don't see why," said Father Melvin. "Why should the bandits bother about a road?"

"There is an easy answer to your question," the Bishop said. "Ever since 1927, when Chiang Kai-shek began fighting the Communists, rebel bands have had a perfect hideout in the inaccessible mountain country of Kiangsi. Chiang drove the Reds from Nanking, Canton, and Shanghai, but his troops have never been able to penetrate their stronghold in Kiangsi Province. Right now, there are about eighty thousand Reds infesting the Kiangsi mountains. Several times a year, they swoop down to terrorize the countryside, burning, killing, and looting. They have brazenly proclaimed the capital of what they call 'Soviet China' in Kiangsi."

Father Melvin and I lowered our forks and exchanged worried glances. Suddenly, I found that I had lost my hearty appetite. So this was our assignment—to be Catholic missionaries in the heart of Soviet China!

Our dismay did not escape the Bishop's notice.

"I'm sure our confreres will be happy to know that the same road they travel to Kanchow is also being used to bring up Nationalist troops for a major campaign against the Reds," he said, with a wink at Father Erbe. "Doubtless, the Kanchow Vicariate will soon be as peaceful as any parish in Brooklyn, U. S. A."

"Some of those Brooklyn parishes are pretty lively," I replied, managing a wan smile. "But it's nice to know that Chiang's offensive is sure to succeed."

"The thought is encouraging," Father Erbe agreed. "I remember feeling very hopeful when Chiang launched his last offensive."

"You mean the Nationalists have tried unsuccessfully before this?"

"Oh, yes. If I recall correctly, this campaign will be Chiang's fifth. There is a lot of shooting, of course, and sometimes the Reds get so mad that they launch a little offensive of their own, which makes life a bit difficult for the missionaries. But you can get used to anything after a while. The first attack generally seems the worst."

"I am beginning to suspect," said Father Melvin, "that one still needs more than a white cassock and a bus ticket to be a missionary in China!"

It was still dark when we arrived at the tiny corrugated iron shack that served as a bus station. We soon realized why the Bishop had been intent on making sure that we got an early start. Although the bus was not scheduled to leave for two hours, there was already a big crowd of Chinese waiting. Had we come any later, it would have been impossible for us to get aboard. As it was, we three shen-fus were jammed into a tiny corner of the vehicle with our luggage.

We passed a gang of coolies shouldering hoes, then two columns of soldiers in gray cotton uniforms jogging along the road with their Enfield rifles at port arms. Small, narrow paths jigsawed around the irrigated rice fields where the first tender shoots of the summer crop had just begun to emerge. Finally, in the distance we could distinguish the outline of the Kiangsi hills. They looked so serene it was difficult to believe that they could be alive with Red bandits.

When we arrived in Nananfu that afternoon, we were tired, stiff, and dirty, but elated by the knowledge that we were finally approaching our mission in China. There was a small mission in Nananfu where we were to spend the night, but when we arrived at the low-lying building, we found the compound swarming with dusty Nationalist troops.

"I pity the poor priest who has to stay here," I said to Father Erbe. "He can't have much privacy."

A shadow passed over Father Erbe's thin face, and he bowed his head slightly. "I, too, pity the priest," he said, "but not because of the soldiers. Several years ago, when there were no soldiers, a veteran missionary named Father Young was the priest here. He was an old friend of mine, and he had spent many years working to build this mission. Then one night the Communist bandits raided Nananfu. The villagers tried to protect Father Young, but they could not stop the Reds from smashing into the mission and dragging him away."

Silently, we threaded our way through the crowded compound, occasionally stepping over the prostrate form of some exhausted Nationalist soldier who lay sprawled out sleeping. Judging from their condition, I assumed that these soldiers had just returned from a patrol in the nearby mountains.

The suspicion was confirmed when we reached the building that had once served as the mission school. There, we found that the Nationalists had set up a crude field hospital where several freshly wounded soldiers were lying. One man whose jaw had been shattered by a bullet was softly moaning as the doctor bent over him.

The Nationalist commander had set up his headquarters in the priest's house. He greeted us warmly after Father Erbe addressed him in Chinese. As they talked, my eye drifted to the heavy wooden door of the building. With a shudder I noticed that the door had recently been patched, but some of the original wood still bore the marks of Communist rifle butts.

"Captain Yi-cheng has graciously consented to let us spend the night here in his quarters," Father Erbe said. "He apologizes for the presence of his troops and hopes the shen-fus will not be disturbed."

That night there was a continual clatter of equipment as soldiers moved about in the compound, and twice Chinese officers came into our room, turned on the lights, and then left after lengthy apologies. But after what Father Erbe had told us about Father Young, I found such interruptions more of a comfort than an annoyance.

The next morning we arose at five, said Mass, and then began the last stage of our journey on horseback. Leaving Nananfu behind, we began to ascend the Kiangsi foothills. Far up on the mountain sides, the farmers were working in their tiny rice fields, standing calf-deep in the flooded paddies.

Suddenly, we came to a bend in the trail and Father Erbe raised his arm. We checked our horses and found ourselves facing a group of Chinese who stood in the center of the road, blocking our passage. I drew a sharp breath. Bandits!

Father Erbe calmly dismounted and began speaking to the leader of the group. They talked seriously for a few moments and then the Chinese began to smile, nodding and jabbering enthusiastically. These were not bandits but Christians. They had heard that three shen-fus were passing through the countryside, and they had been waiting patiently for hours in the hope of meeting us. It had been a year since they had seen a priest.

Father Erbe heard confessions in a little mud-walled hut that served as the home of one of the Christian families. We slept in the house that night, with the family huddled in another corner of the room. The beds were narrow and made of wood, with a wooden block for a pillow, but we were so tired that we slept soundly. In the morning, when we rose and said Mass, I was astonished to find fifteen Chinese devoutly kneeling to receive Holy Communion.

After Mass we had a real Chinese breakfast—a bowl of rice and fried eggs, cooked over a small stone stove, washed down with some rice wine—then once more we were on the road. This time we had light hearts, for we were to arrive that afternoon in Taoli, the small village about twenty miles from Kanchow where Father Erbe had his mission.

Five miles from Taoli, the shrill blast of a bugle broke the silence of the countryside. It was the sign that an advance party from the mission had sighted us. There were porters to take our baggage on their backs, Chinese boys who took care of our horses, and three chairs mounted on bamboo poles and carried on the shoulders of coolies. Like an imperial procession, we wound in and out of the rice fields. Soldiers and Chinese peasants gaped as we marched by. Then we crossed a narrow bridge and began to ascend a small hill.

At the top of the hill a delegation of Chinese Christians met us with firecrackers sizzling and popping, bugles blasting a greeting. The jubilant crowd streamed behind us to the mission compound, where we found hundreds of other Chinese with drums beating and flags flying.

Father Erbe could not hold back any longer. Tears streamed down his cheeks. He had come home.

Shortly after lunch the next day, Father Melvin and I said our good-bys to Father Erbe. We left our friend with genuine regret, yet we were impatient to get on with the final leg of a long journey. Once we left Taoli, we urged our horses westward, trotting along the twisting mountain paths and breaking into a gallop on the infrequent straight stretches. As we approached Kanchow after four hours in the saddle, the sun began to dip down into the Kiangsi hills.

Suddenly, Father Munday, a priest from Kanchow

who had been sent out to Taoli to guide us on the final stage of our trip, reined his hard-breathing horse to a halt. We looked down on a huge valley and saw the glistening rooftops of Kanchow encircled by the dark shadow of a massive stone wall. The last golden daylight shimmered over the city, seemingly trapped in the valley like water at the bottom of a bowl. The whole scene reflected a beauty that kept Father Melvin and me staring with mouths agape.

Our reverie was broken by an exclamation from Father Munday: "Hurry! We've got to reach the city before nightfall! Otherwise we'll find the gates closed and we'll be locked out for the night."

The custom of closing the city gates in China dates back to ancient times, when the country was ravaged by warring tribes. The towering walls, built with parapets for watchmen armed with bows and arrows, now offered Kanchow residents protection against the modern arms of marauding Communists. Since these attacks were most likely to come at night, it was a rule of the city fathers that the gates must remain closed between the hours of darkness and daylight. To be locked outside was not just a matter of inconvenience, but a peril that might cost a traveler his life.

A wide river crossed our path to the city, but fortunately we had arrived just in time to board the last ferry—a flat-bottomed boat already crowded with farmers and travelers seeking the safety of the city. As we drew close to the city, I could make out immense, ugly shell holes splattered across the forty-foot walls. At intervals the snouts of heavy machine-guns protruded from slits in the parapet, and soldiers with drawn sabers and bayoneted guns stood guard near the ponderous iron gate. These grim signs forcibly reminded us that only a year had passed since Kanchow had withstood a siege by a force of sixty thousand Red soldiers, mostly renegades.

After crossing the river we were able to enter the city by way of a heavy wooden drawbridge leading to the South gate—one of four great gates placed at each point of the compass by the builders of the ancient city.

Signs of a terrific battle were evident everywhere. Trenches were dug around the city gates, and within the city there seemed at first glance nothing but badly shattered houses which had been smashed by Red bombs and shells. It was near the West gate, Father Munday told us, that the attackers had concentrated their most determined efforts. They had loaded dynamite in several coffins and exploded these bizarre devices in tunnels which they had painstakingly scraped out under the walls. Fortunately, the ancient Chinese were such skillful builders that even this tactic was unable to undermine the defenses.

We soon found more indications of the ferocity of the Red assault in the many bullet-holes that scarred the buildings of the Catholic Mission itself. And what an impressive mission it was! It was actually a city within a city, occupying four square blocks. Here were buildings to house the native sisters (*Kukus,* as they were called), the young seminarians, two orphanages—one for boys and one for girls—and homes for the teachers at the mission school. Most impressive, however, were the quarters for some four hundred refugees—poor souls who had been living at the mission ever since they fled there at the time of the siege.

At this point we were interrupted by a sudden war-whoop that made me think for a moment we were facing another Communist attack. I spun around and found the source of the commotion was none other than Father Freddie McGuire, bearing down on us at the head of a troop of familiar, grinning faces. Here were Father Stauble and Father McGillicuddy and Father Gately, too—all old friends of seminary days. They swarmed around us shaking hands and thumping us on the back in the best old college-reunion style.

The head of the Vicariate was Bishop O'Shea. "Just wait until you meet him," Father Freddie said. "Gosh, but he's a likable fellow! He makes you feel right at home the minute you meet him."

Father Melvin and I were still talking to our old confreres when we were summoned to meet the Bishop. He was frail and white-haired, but his blue eyes were lively and his movements were even quicker. Before we had time to open our mouths, the Bishop had skipped spryly across the room and pumped our hands with a grip that was surprisingly firm.

"Well, Frank and Fred, welcome to Kanchow. We're glad to have you with us."

For the next two hours, over several cups of good Chinese tea, Father Melvin and I listened, spellbound, to this kindly and charming old priest as he talked about his beloved Vicariate. Here was a man who had spent the better part of his life surrounded by the all-too-grim reality of China, but he had nevertheless preserved a vision that was much deeper and more beautiful than my own.

"Although we come as missionaries," he said, "there is much that we can learn from these poor children of the soil—the lesson of uncomplaining patience and endurance. The souls we deal with are the sturdy mountain folk who know nothing of the pleasures that we know back home, nor of the niceties of life. Sadly, most of them must bear their burdens without hope, for of God and his goodness they know still less. Ancestor-worship is the only religion that has been handed down to them. For centuries they have been taught to pay homage to the devil himself, to coax and flatter the evil spirit with joss sticks. In this way, they hope to win his good graces and protect themselves from harm."

With obvious pride, Bishop O'Shea talked of the gains that had already been made in leading thousands of pagans from the age-old ignorance that surrounded them. Kiangsi was not a small parish by any means. Throughout the district there were scattered some twenty-four small mission outposts, covering an area larger than Long Island. At these various out-missions there were Chinese catechists stationed to keep watch over the handful of Christians in each tribe and bring them together at evening for prayer and catechism class, preparing them for the day when the shen-fu would arrive to pay his mission visit.

"At the present time," the Bishop said, smiling ruefully, "I'm afraid that the only way we can reach them is by mule or horseback, or sometimes by bicycle. To make a conscientious tour takes six solid weeks in the saddle—a trying ordeal for anyone, yet the missionary must plod on, regardless of all the obstacles he has to face."

Our first year in Kanchow was to be a training year, more or less similar to our Seminary days, the Bishop explained. We were scheduled to receive a year of language study mingled with the companionship of older missionaries who would teach us the ways of China and initiate us into the mysteries of oriental life. Then we would be considered ready to start out on our own for some outlying mission.

"You will have many surprises, many satisfactions, and probably many mishaps," the Bishop said. "A few hard knocks must be the lot of every new missionary in China, but I have confidence in you."

In Kanchow I soon found that practically every Chinese I met greeted me as "Li Shen Fu" or "Father Li." After many futile inquiries, I finally sought an explanation from Professor Tsai, the mission instructor who conducted our daily Chinese language lessons.

"Take off your hat," demanded the Professor. I hastily complied, thinking that possibly my failure to remove the somewhat battered chapeau in the presence of such a distinguished scholar constituted some grave offense against Chinese courtesy. I was about to mumble an apology when a long yellow finger pointed to the place on the sweat-stained hatband where the hatmaker's trademark, Lee, had been stamped.

"There, you see," Professor Tsai said with obvious

satisfaction. "Your name must be Lee—or Li as we write it in Mandarin—because it is written in your hat."

I began to protest, but the Professor raised his hand to silence me. "Please don't insist on using the name Gehring," he said. "Gehring means nothing in Chinese. It is hard for me to pronounce. On the other hand, the name Li is an ancient and honorable one in my country, so I have taken the liberty of telling everyone to call you by that name."

Under the guidance of Professor Tsai, and under the name of Father Li, I began my gradual adjustment to Chinese life. I became accustomed to my small mission room with its Chinese-made furniture: a bed of boards covered with a mat and surrounded by mosquito netting; a kerosene lamp, washstand, and bucket of water. The room opened out upon a porch that encircled the second floor of the mission house. There was plenty of sunlight and an occasional welcome breeze.

Day began at five A.M. for my fellow priests and myself. First, there was an hour of meditation with morning prayers, then Mass, and breakfast at seven. By eight o'clock we were in the classroom with Professor Tsai. We soon discovered that to speak Chinese is one thing; to speak it correctly is another; to pronounce it in its singsong way is still another—and when all this is achieved, only one dialect has been learned. We found there were so many variations of dialects that every little village and section of the vicariate had language peculiarities of its own. Then came the task of reading Chinese characters, not to mention writing them!

We never went to class in the afternoon. Despite our

eagerness to master Chinese, study—or almost any other activity—was out of the question in the brutal heat of midday. Often the temperature, as registered on the thermometer in the mission yard, soared to 112 degrees! After lunch, we would take an enforced Chinese siesta, lying under our mosquito netting with the windows flung wide open to catch the slightest breeze. Sometimes there would be a rattle of rifle shots from the sharp-shooters who maintained their never-ending vigil on the ancient walls nearby. The bandits did not dare to approach Kanchow during the day, but the guards practiced their marksmanship constantly, just to keep it that way. At first the sound of the guns disturbed me, and after each volley I would toss nervously beneath the mosquito netting. But after a month or so I learned to ignore both the rifle shots and the sweltering heat; at least, I was able to sleep.

At three o'clock I would be awakened to rinse away the sweat of perspired sleep in a make-shift shower on the porch. This was a closet-like affair with a big five-gallon can suspended above it from a piece of wash line. The can was perforated and had a trick stopper—you first filled it with water, then hoisted it up, and finally yanked on the line to give yourself a good drenching. By repeating this procedure twice, you could take a warm shower and follow it with a cooling rinse.

Refreshed, I would put on a clean white Chinese cassock called an "esan," and settle down to read Scriptures, study my Chinese letters, and catch up with my correspondence back home. Sometimes, before nightfall, I would have time to explore the teeming streets of

Kanchow. Bicycles had been recently introduced in the town, and work was under way to widen the city gates so that eventually buses would be able to come through.

Everywhere, crumbling old buildings were being torn down. In their place, astonishing modern stores complete with plate glass windows were springing up. Where before there had been narrow, dirty alleys, on every side workmen were busy creating wide city streets with sidewalks in the best Western style—things undreamed of beyond such cities as Hong Kong or Canton only a few years earlier. This was exciting evidence of a New China in the making, a transformation being wrought by the network of roads which was rapidly being extended over the country to link city with city and bring commerce from the seacoast to the inland of China.

On every street I saw men in the blue uniforms of the Nationalist army, and next to some of the modern stores were the broken shells of buildings that had been wrecked by artillery during the Communist siege. Signs of struggle were even more painful, somehow, when I returned to the mission. There, among the hundreds of refugees, were many pitiful children. Some of them were orphans of war. Others came from starving families who had been driven from their lands by the Red onslaught.

There was a slot in the gate of the mission just big enough to allow a basket to be pushed through, and many times poverty-stricken parents would send their children to us by this unconventional route. Even the pagan Chinese knew that the Vincentians had a tradition of helping the poor and the orphaned. Our foreign sisters, the *Kukus,* made heroic efforts to care for these pathetic arrivals and to find space for them in the crowded mission orphanage.

In the evenings, in our own section of the mission, everybody from the Bishop on down would cluster around on the porch outside the priests' house after the evening meal, smoking pipes in the moonlight and listening to scratchy renditions of "Who's Sorry Now?" or "Will You Remember California in September?" It was music, anyway, no matter how old—and there were even a few John McCormack records and a set of the Hungarian Rhapsodies, just to give an occasional concert effect.

So passed a typical evening within the Kanchow walls, while the shadowy forms of the Communist bandits prowled outside, kept at bay by an occasional rifle-shot from the city guards. I suppose that occasionally the Communists must have come close enough to hear the music of our phonograph. It must have sounded very strange to them.

I had only been in China a few months when the military pot began to boil. We were informed that General Chiang Kai-shek was mustering all his forces to exterminate the Reds. The plan called for a large Nationalist army to press down from the North, while loyal troops from Canton simultaneously attacked from the South.

Along the narrow rice paths, long columns of soldiers marched toward the city—mere youngsters, tense with excitement, with bullets and bullet-belts slung in readiness for the attack. There were hundreds of soldiers within the city; the fortified gates and parapets were strengthened, and the bridge leading to the main gate was surrounded by barbed wire and mines.

Observing all these preparations, many of the priests at the mission felt sure that the offensive would succeed. But Bishop O'Shea had spent too many years in China to indulge in such wishful thinking. "If the Reds are completely wiped out," he said, "then we will have much to be thankful for. But I fear that the Communists will do a little housecleaning on their own before they are destroyed. As they are driven through the countryside, they'll wreak their vengeance on our outlying missions and leave an awful mess behind!"

As far as I was concerned, the threat of large-scale fighting couldn't have come at a worse time. It almost seemed like a plot to deprive me of my first real missionary assignment!

Several weeks before the military situation became critical, Father Melvin and I had been called from our studies and ordered to ride to the mission at Tangkiang, where the regular priest had suddenly fallen ill. Naturally, we expressed great sorrow when we were told that the Tangkiang priest would have to return to Kanchow for a long convalescence—but in truth we were delighted at the chance to exchange our musty schoolbooks for the life of a missionary in the field.

No sooner had we assisted the ailing priest to board a sedan chair for his journey back to Kanchow than we two new arrivals began to inspect the Tangkiang mission with a proprietary air. There was a quaint little mission house with stone walls, a schoolhouse with a complement of almost one hundred young scholars, and a lovely, tree-shaded mission yard.

"Fred," Father Melvin said one evening as we sipped our tea in the cool yard, "I'm really getting very fond of this place. Sometimes I find myself wishing that we didn't ever have to leave."

I nodded. "Maybe we won't have to leave," I said. "The Bishop may decide to assign us here permanently, if he thinks we're doing a good job. It's something to hope for, anyway."

But my hope was short-lived. The very next day, I heard a commotion in the mission yard and glanced out of the window to see a man gallop up on the back of a sweat-streaked horse.

"Li Shen Fu!" he cried, struggling to dismount. "The honorable Bishop has sent me double-quick. He say all young'un priests must hurry back to Kanchow chop-chop!"

As our messenger rested from his strenuous ride, we pieced together the story of the rapidly developing military situation. Chiang Kai-shek's great drive was on! Already, Nationalist troops were pressing down from the North to catch the Red forces in a trap between Chiang's men and the loyal Cantonese troops to the South. We were in the direct line of the two opposing armies, with the main body of Reds—some fifty thousand men—moving a little more than thirty miles north of us! What's more, they appeared to be hurrying in our direction.

With Chiang's forces closing in, the desperate Reds had begun plundering and burning, just as Bishop O'Shea had predicted. If this was their last stand, it promised to be a bloody one. We learned that all missionaries had been recalled to the relative safety of Kanchow with the exception of Father Erbe and one other veteran priest, who were to remain at their posts until the very last moment.

It was midafternoon before the last of our little charges had left the mission yard with instructions to stay at home and out of harm's way until the Red wave had passed. We told the youngsters to leave their books behind at the school so that if the Communists searched their homes, they would not find any evidence linking them with the "foreign devils," as we were called by the Reds. Then Father Melvin took all the school's papers and the registration lists and stuffed them into his cassock as a further security precaution. "Besides," he said, "these lists will be needed when the school reopens—and it surely will. You can bet on that!"

Normally, the trip from Tangkiang to Kanchow takes four hours by horseback, riding in the relative cool of the early morning. But on this occasion we reached the city in less than three hours, galloping through the worst heat of the afternoon. At the Kanchow gate our horses were checked up, our identification cards presented to the captain of the guard, and after a thorough search we were finally permitted to enter through the massive walls. None too soon, either! Shortly afterward, the setting sun touched the rim of the mountains and the captain gave the order to close the gate.

As we trudged wearily into the mission, we found eighteen other priests who had, like ourselves, been hastily recalled from their outposts. We also found Bishop O'Shea hurrying about like a small, bright-eyed mother hen. He sighed with relief to see the last of his chicks come home to roost.

So many missionaries had been recalled to Kanchow that Maison Mère was distinctly overcrowded. Kiangsi's entire contingent of foreign legion priests had been assembled, with the single exception of Father Erbe, who was assumed to have taken refuge in some safe spot behind the battle lines. Day after day, we listened to the muted sound of fire in the surrounding hills. Then early one morning one of the servants rushed into my room to announce that Father Erbe had returned. I dressed as quickly as I could and followed the messenger to the main gate. There was Father Erbe, in the early morning light, walking slowly and painfully up the narrow, steeply inclined street with the aid of a long staff, surrounded by what looked like an army of children—some of them so young it seemed they could barely toddle, even while clutching at the missionary's tattered cassock for support!

"Well, good morning," Father Erbe said. "This must be the welcoming delegation! I'm glad everyone at Maison Mère isn't asleep, because I could use a little help."

The older priest swayed on his feet and seemed ready to fall, but I was so dumbfounded that it took me a few seconds to give him support.

"I suppose you're wondering about my young friends," he said, turning his head slowly and pausing, as if counting the noses of the children who stood silently around him. "Hmm, twenty-two," he said. "That's good. I haven't lost a single one!"

"George, for Heaven's sake! Who are these children?"

"Don't you recognize them?" he asked. "You should recognize some, at least. You were in Taoli, weren't you? Don't you recognize them from there?"

Then it dawned on me that Father Erbe must have made his way from his outlying mission while guiding practically the entire Taoli population under ten years of age! What was even more astonishing, this strange latter-day Pied Piper blandly informed me that he had shepherded his entire troop right through the battle lines!

As we made our way slowly toward the mission, Father Erbe told how the Communists had seized his village suddenly and set about transforming it into a key strongpoint which they intended to hold against the advancing Nationalist forces. For two days, one of the Christian families had hidden him in their home, risking certain death if caught.

One night, taking advantage of the dark of the moon, Father Erbe had crept from his hiding place and taken charge of all the young children the villagers could assemble without arousing the suspicions of the Communists. Then he led his little band through the darkness, miraculously dodging the Red sentries and making his way into the hills.

"I decided that the safest thing to do would be to

head for the mission," he said, simply. "There should be plenty of food and plenty of people to care for the youngsters here."

For the next few days, the mission was abuzz with stories about Father Erbe and his brood. Even the older priests said that his feat had been incredible, and that probably not another man in China could have succeeded in dodging past thousands of Communists by himself, much less leading a column of children, some of them barely able to walk!

We were all so busy marveling over Father Erbe's accomplishment, and helping the native sisters take care of their new charges, that we barely noticed that this heroic priest had not recovered from the strain of his incredible journey. He was still very thin, and had developed a persistent, hacking cough. The Bishop insisted that his temperature be taken, and the thermometer rose to a shocking 104 degrees. "You fellows must think I'm getting old," grumbled Father Erbe as he was put to bed. "There's nothing the matter with me but a little cold. Something I caught in the mountain air. I'll be all right in a couple of days."

After some days it became apparent that nothing could save the tormented man who lay in the little bedroom next to mine. We summoned the Bishop, as he had instructed us to do, and Father Erbe was anointed and prepared for death. Then, with the Bishop and all his fellow priests kneeling about the bed, we waited for the end. It came at 4 A.M., the hour of rising in all Vincentian mission houses.

The next morning, there was a small group of Chinese standing at the door of the mission house. They were members of the Taoli congregation who had heard that Father Erbe was sick, and had walked all the way to Kanchow to visit their pastor. When we told them of his death, they knelt down in the dust of the mission yard and cried bitterly. It was only after they had been in the mission for almost an hour that someone realized there was more than ordinary significance in their visit. They had *walked* from Taoli, they said. Did that mean that the roads were now safe to travel? And what of the village itself? Had it been abandoned by the Communists?

It was ironic that even as we were pondering such questions, newspapers half a world away were already carrying headlines that reported Chiang's "big victory" over the Communists. During the long battle that reached a climax shortly before Father Erbe's death, the Red forces had suffered what appeared to be a fatal blow. Driven back with heavy casualties, they had been pushed almost to the borders of Kiangsi. According to jubilant dispatches from Nanking, it would require only a final mopping-up operation to rid China of the Red menace forever!

Father Erbe's parishoners told us that Taoli had miraculously escaped heavy damage when the disheartened Communists gave up their plans to defend the village and suddenly withdrew to new positions further south. Now, just as the villagers were preparing to welcome the return of their pastor with a festival, the news of his death came as a bitter blow.

The funeral procession that followed his coffin seemed

to stretch the entire length of the road from Kanchow to Taoli. A Chinese band with bugles and drums played its traditional eerie music for the dead—a chantlike wail ending with a clash of cymbals.

This was the country that Father Erbe had loved. As we approached Taoli, we saw signs of the recent fighting —an occasional hut with gaping roof, a jagged shell hole, a trench that had collapsed, barely covering the remains of the soldiers who had died there.

Father Erbe was buried in the cemetery near the tiny mission church where he had served for so many years. After giving his final blessing, the Bishop said, "China distinguishes between a life spent for her people and a life spent merely living among her people. She knows of the heroism of this man, who came to plant the Cross of Christ in her midst."

A
Mission
of
My
Own

5

In the days that followed Father Erbe's death, a blessed peace seemed to settle over the ravaged countryside. Instead of soldiers, we saw long columns of peasants traveling along the roads—refugees who had left their homes to seek safety in the city, now happily returning to their villages and their farms. It was a time for hope, and a time for rebuilding. The farmers reclaimed their abandoned plows in the rice paddies; the shattered houses were mended with new-mixed clay and straw; and within the Kanchow walls, the streets were once more busy with their teeming crowds.

As for myself and my young fellow priests, we found ourselves back in the mission classroom listening to our old friend Professor Tsai expound on the complexities of Chinese grammar. After our brief assignment to Tangkiang and the excitement of the Red attack, Father Melvin and I found it difficult to go back to schoolroom ways. We fidgeted with our books or gazed absently out of the window, our minds busy with speculation on the future. Would our schooling never stop? Wouldn't we ever be sent to a mission of our own?

But despite our inattention in the classroom we found that Professor Tsai's lessons were having an effect. Whether by osmosis, or by some even more mysterious process, our ability to converse with the Chinese we met in our rambles rapidly improved. We would haggle like natives with the peddlers who squatted in the crowded market, propping their merchandise against the musty gray wall near the old East gate.

Although Bishop O'Shea was anxious to send his missionaries back to their far-flung congregations, the death of Father Erbe had given grim emphasis to the perils to which his priests might be exposed by Communist warfare. As long as there was a possibility of renewed fighting, he was reluctant to jeopardize the lives of his subordinates. But he was also painfully aware that many Chinese Christians were in need of priestly ministrations—a need that grew more urgent with the passage of each day.

Encouraged by reports that the main body of Communist troops had been swept far to the south and virtually driven from the entire province, the Bishop began to authorize the departure of his missionaries.

Father Jack McLaughlin was one of the first to go, bound for Sinfeng on his sway-backed old mare, with a mournful-looking new-foaled colt lagging behind at the end of a rope. The exodus from Kanchow was accelerated when Bishop O'Shea learned that Father Jack had reached Sinfeng without encountering any difficulty from Communist bandits on the road. Another priest was sent to keep Father McLaughlin company in Sinfeng.

Wherever possible, two priests were to be stationed in all outposts. This new policy delighted the younger priests, because it increased the number of missionaries in the field, and consequently improved their chances for an assignment. In fact, it was only two weeks after Father McLaughlin had departed that Father Melvin burst into my room with good news.

"You'll never guess where I'm going," he gasped. "*Tangkiang!* The very place I was hoping for! Isn't it just swell? Remember, Fred, how much we loved the place? Gee, I hope you'll be sent there too!"

But Tangkiang, that picturesque little mission, wasn't in the cards for me. A few days later I learned that my assignment would be far to the west, in Lungnan, an ancient walled city in the rugged mountains of the interior, the deepest Vincentian outpost in all China!

"You'll *enjoy* Lungnan, Fred. It'll be peace and quiet from now on—no worry about the Reds, just an old hillbilly life for you and me. I tell you, you're a lucky boy!"

Father Frank Moehringer puffed heartily on his pipe, blew a great gust of blue smoke at the ceiling, and beamed at me with obvious satisfaction. Father Moehringer was one of the "old China hands"—a veteran missionary who had spent nearly as many years in China as Father Erbe or Bishop O'Shea himself. Despite my misgivings about the Lungnan assignment, I felt proud that I had been picked to accompany such a distinguished old campaigner. But I did wish Father Moehringer would stop grinning and congratulating me. Could it be that he was pulling my leg?

It seemed that a regular expedition would be required to get us the one hundred miles to Lungnan. Before our departure, we loaded most of our possessions into six huge *lunzas*, which are large baskets designed to be carried by porters. One porter can carry two *lunzas* suspended on a bamboo pole—a load that generally weighs well over a hundred pounds.

Father Moehringer and I went down to the city gate with the porters. Before the luggage was permitted to pass through the gate, every *lunza* had to be opened and inspected by the city guard. This was supposed to be a safeguard against the smuggling of salt and other contraband—but it also gave the Chinese an opportunity to indulge in one characteristic they share with cats: curiosity. Pop-eyed Chinese crowded around as each *lunza* was opened. A simple article like a toothbrush provoked gasps of amazement and demands for an explanation of how the wonderful instrument worked. Then, as I protested helplessly, half a dozen self-appointed inspectors insisted on testing the toothbrush by popping it into their own mouths!

Three days later, Father Moehringer and I began the first stage of the journey to Lungnan by bus—a rickety, high-sprung vehicle which looked like something that might have done yeoman service on the Flatbush Avenue Line about 1911.

After a nightmarish trip which lasted three days, we arrived in Lungnan late on a Saturday afternoon, at the hour when the Angelus was tolling. Although there had been no priest in the city for many months, the sweet-sounding bell still pealed from its mud-brick tower in the little mission, where the gatekeeper, a faithful old Chinese Christian, tugged gravely at the rope. He was determined to preserve the beautiful custom of the Angelus, which was rung wherever Christianity had spread in China. And at the sound of the bell, the chatter of the marketplace would stop and the convert peasants in the fields would bow their heads and sing "The Angel of the Lord Declared Unto Mary."

My weariness fell away as I left the bus and surveyed the mission. There was a modest but carefully built church, a two-room schoolhouse, and even a rectory with a little garden planted with chrysanthemums, shrubs, and a few palm trees. So this was to be my new home.

As I stood in the garden musing, I heard the sound of bugles and the merry pop of firecrackers. The faithful Christians of Lungnan had learned of our arrival and were gathering to welcome their new priests.

Until late into the night, we ministered to a growing crowd of Christians—simple farmers and townsfolk who were anxious to make their long-delayed confessions. I gazed at their faces with elation. Here was evidence that a deeply rooted faith was spreading in China, the fruit of the labors of missionaries who had come long before me.

Early the next morning, I knelt in the candle-lit church as Father Moehringer said Mass. The building was crowded from wall to wall with hundreds of Chinese, some of whom had spent the night huddled in the mission yard so they would be sure of finding a place in church.

Surely, I thought, Christ will bless all of us here—and surely He will not forsake His missionaries, or the long-suffering people of China.

Life was hard in Lungnan. With only two priests in a mountain district which covered more territory than Long Island, Father Moehringer and I were soon occupied from dawn to long past dusk with a seemingly endless succession of tasks. Besides ministering to the religious needs of our scattered parishoners and running a dispensary, we found that it would be necessary to enlarge several buildings at the mission itself.

Our school had been reopened, but the demand for admission far exceeded the modest capacity of our classrooms. With about sixty students jammed shoulder to shoulder, each trying to balance a schoolbook on his knee, Father Moehringer decided that drastic measures were called for. A Chinese contractor was summoned and instructed to start work on an annex, so that before long the mission yard was a busy beehive of carpenters and masons and women carrying loads of sand, lumber, and limestone.

As the younger and junior member of our mission team, I was to handle the traveling assignments that would take me on trips throughout the hundreds of miles that encompassed our mission district. We maintained native catechists at various outposts, but it was necessary for the priest himself to make regular visits to conduct religious worship, perform baptisms, listen to confessions, resolve family problems and neighborly feuds, and play doctor as best he could. But while Father Moehringer occupied himself with getting the annex finished and the whole mission operation back in working order, I took over for him temporarily in the school. Thus, I did not make my first outside trip until I had been in Lungnan for over a month. And this trip resulted from an emergency call.

One morning, I came into the rectory and found Father Moehringer listening to an old peasant farmer. The old man was crying, and tears ran down his long white whiskers. He spoke rapidly, in an urgent, high-pitched voice.

"This man belongs to the Lin tribe, which has a village about three or four miles south of here," Father Moehringer explained. "He says that he is a Christian, and his wife is very sick. Would you go with him? I'll take care of the school today."

It took only a moment to collect the essentials for my journey—the Holy Viaticum, a vial of Holy Oil, and my first-aid kit. I had no idea how long I might have to stay away from the mission. Perhaps, I thought, it would be wise to take along a fresh change of clothes. But I dismissed the idea almost instantly. No time for such luxuries! And besides, I reflected ruefully, I probably didn't have any fresh clothes. Our wardrobes were limited to the few items we had been able to carry with us from Kanchow on the bus. The porters who were to carry most of our belongings seemed long overdue. Since we had reached our isolated outpost, we hadn't even received delivery of our regular mail.

One of our fastest horses from the mission stable was brought to me. I let the old man explain the route to his village and tell me how to find his house. Then, leaving him to follow as quickly as he could on his own sure-footed little donkey, I galloped out of the mission compound and headed south along the winding mountain trail.

Two hours later, I reached the village and made my way to the farmer's humble, mud-walled house. I breathed a prayer of thanksgiving when I entered and found the old woman still alive. She lay on a wooden board that served as a bed in that windowless hut. By the light of a single tallow candle, I could see that her body had been eaten up with cancer. A small group of kinsmen had gathered around the bed. Silently, they drew back and allowed me to approach. The woman had been moaning in pain but now she gazed at me with enormous, dilated eyes. She seemed to recognize my cassock and know that I was a priest. Her eyes flickered and she made an effort to raise her hand, but she was too weak to speak. I immediately gave her an injection of pain-killing morphine.

My vigil lasted until late that night, and I was able to administer the Sacrament before the woman closed her eyes for the last time. The old farmer, whose donkey had almost managed to keep pace with my speedy mount on the long road from Lungnan, was kneeling near the bed. We bowed our heads together in prayer.

Later, one of the farmer's kinsmen guided me to his house, where I was offered a bed on which to sleep. It was a crude wooden affair, little more than a bare and narrow plank which had been elevated from the floor on rough wooden legs. I lay down on the hard surface, too weary to be concerned about the uncomfortable arrangement. Besides, I thought, even a miserable bench must be a prized possession in such a poor village. There wasn't anything better available for that old woman in her dying hour . . . I learned later that the owner of the bed had slept on a cold floor. Like the farmer, he had little to give—but he had given all he could.

The next day, I said a Mass for the old woman's soul and saw that she had a proper Christian funeral. Then I made ready for my return to Lungnan. Just before I left, I was summoned to help in the delivery of a baby, and to baptize it. A life had been called away from the Lin tribe, but a new one had been brought into it.

My emotions had been stirred by this first outside experience. As I rode back to Lungnan, I tried to organize my scattered thoughts. Had my experience really been so extraordinary? Somehow, I felt that it had, although I couldn't explain why.

Father Moehringer was waiting as I rode up to the mission. The corners of his mouth were drawn and his lips were compressed in a thin, straight line. "You'd better come inside right away," he said. "Something very peculiar has happened."

Without another word, he led me into the rectory, where I saw two Chinese men sitting together, jabbering excitedly and wringing their hands. Where had I seen those faces before? They weren't merchants, obviously—their clothes were much too shabby. No, these were lean, hard-muscled peasants. Farmers, probably, or porters. Yes, that was it! These were two of the long-overdue porters I had last seen carrying our baggage through the main gate at Kanchow.

"Tell me, Fred," Father Moehringer said, "do these fellows look like honest men, or are they two of the cleverest lying scoundrels you ever saw?"

I was astonished by the question. "They just look like ordinary porters to me," I said. "The sort you might see carrying *lunzas* anywhere."

"Yes, *lunzas*," Father Moehringer mused. "But that's just it, you see. This morning they found these rascals wandering around outside of town without any *lunzas* at all. I've been trying to decide whether this is a case for the town constable or the Lungnan booby-hatch. They've probably stolen our baggage and sold it to some merchant for money to buy rice wine."

"We'll be in a fine mess if our baggage has been stolen," I groaned.

"We'll be in a worse mess if it hasn't," he replied

grimly. "That would mean their fantastic story may be true."

Before I had a chance to ask the obvious question—what fantastic story?—Father Moehringer demanded to know if I had noticed anything unusual on my ride back to Lungnan.

"Unusual?" I asked. "No, not a thing. As a matter of fact, it was a very peaceful ride. I didn't meet a soul."

Father Moehringer knitted his brow. "Listen, Fred," he said. "If what these fellows have been telling me contains a grain of truth, you may have just ridden through the middle of the entire Communist army!"

My mouth fell open in amazement as I listened to the porters' tale. Eight days ago, they said, they were approaching Lungnan after a hard but uneventful journey when they were suddenly halted by a band of armed men on the trail and forced to march several miles back into the hills. Here they came upon a carefully organized camp, well camouflaged against observation from the air. The man who seemed to be in charge of the camp wore the uniform of a captain in the Communist army. For a week, the men were forced to dig emplacements for their captors. From the conversations of the soldiers, they managed to learn the reason for the secrecy that surrounded the camp. A small body of the Communist army, hard-pressed by Chiang's troops, had decided on a desperate scheme to break out of the trap. Hemmed in by Nationalist forces to the North and blocked by Cantonese troops in the South, they would try to escape inland over the mountainous terrain to the west. In order to prevent the Nationalists from blocking their only escape route, the Communist commanders had been secretly moving many bands of troops into the area surrounding Lungnan. The Reds were ordered to lie hidden in small camps until the breakout began. Then, they were to rise up and devastate the countryside, blocking the road to Chiang's soldiers and keeping it open for their own men.

Fearing that they would be executed when the time for the breakout came, the porters made up their minds to escape. One evening, when they were sent to the stream accompanied by only a single, careless soldier, they knocked him senseless by smashing a water bucket over his head and fled. Shots from the enraged Communists cut the air around them, but luckily they were concealed by the rapidly falling darkness which enabled them to lose their pursuers. They wandered all night through the mountains and at daybreak they made their way to Lungnan, where they were discovered by our city guard.

The porters' rambling, incoherent story did not satisfy the suspicious guardsmen. It seemed incredible that such a number of Communists could be camped nearby, for Lungnan had been a relatively peaceful town, spared by its remoteness from the worst excesses of the civil war. Besides, these ragged men were strangers; therefore not to be trusted.

Because the men kept insisting that the American shen-fus had hired them to carry baggage, however, they were finally brought to the mission. Father Moehringer gave them a chance to sleep for a few hours. When they awoke they repeated their story in detail.

Early next morning, Father Moehringer sent a message to the *Tze-che,* the Mandarin who was the highest-ranking Chinese official in Lungnan, asking him to come to the mission for an important meeting. At the same time, I dispatched a similar message to the various *Tai-piao,* or village elders, who governed the nearby communities. We still weren't wholly convinced that the porters had been telling us the truth, but we felt it was our duty to warn the Chinese that there might be big trouble afoot.

Our visitors exchanged worried glances as Father Moehringer spoke. When he had finished, there was a long silence. Then several elders told us that they, too, had noticed odd things in the last few days: livestock and food had been stolen, strangers had been seen near the villages, a few farmers had even disappeared. Taken separately, any one of these incidents could have been dismissed. But pieced together, a terrifying picture began to appear. The Communists were obviously lurking nearby. All of us, including the government officials, the government press, and Bishop O'Shea, had been overoptimistic in believing that the Reds were virtually finished.

"Lungnan has good, strong walls," the Mandarin said. "But this is a small comfort because the force of home guards is very small. They have only a few guns and not much ammunition. I fear the Communist devils could make short work of our city!"

"If that's the situation, the first thing we should do is close the school," Father Moehringer said. "The children must scatter to their homes. They'll be in less danger that way."

The children were the first to leave Lungnan that day, but as word of the meeting spread through the city many adults, too, began making preparations to depart. The exodus began none too soon. One night there was a frantic pounding on our door and we stumbled out of bed to find a young catechist standing in the dark mission yard. He was from the little village of Anyuan, some thirty miles to the north. There had been a sudden, devastating Red attack, he said, and he had barely managed to escape with his life. All Anyuan was a mass of flames.

By the first light of dawn, we saw the long column of refugees moving along the dirt road that passed Lungnan. They walked slowly, wearily, some with bowed heads and others staring straight ahead with glazed, hopeless eyes. Behind them on the pale horizon we saw a thick smudge of smoke—Anyuan's funeral pyre.

To the North, beyond Anyuan, a second black column rose lazily in the direction of Koupi, a village some forty miles away.

"It looks as if those Reds mean to do a thorough job," Father Moehringer said. "We've got a lot to do, and not much time to do it. I've got an unpleasant feeling it will be our turn next."

All through the morning a steady stream of refugees plodded along the road. They moved like sleepwalkers, so numb with fatigue and hunger that they scarcely seemed to notice their surroundings.

Many of the refugees had burns or other injuries. Some even had bullet wounds. Some were simply suffering from exhaustion, or from minor injuries that could be treated by first aid. These cases we laid in the shelter of the city wall, where they could rest protected from the wind and the afternoon sun. Those with serious wounds we carried to the mission, where a makeshift hospital had been set up in the school. Medicine was in short supply, but we did what we could with the few drugs and antiseptics that we had.

It began to seem that the number of refugees with bullet wounds was steadily increasing—an observation that puzzled me at first, especially when I noted that many of the wounds were so fresh that they still bled. Then, surprisingly close, I heard a dry, rolling, metallic noise, and realized that I was listening to the sound of massed rifle fire. It could mean only one thing: the Communists were close at hand!

We could no longer delay joining the exodus of refugees out of the city, and had to leave the seriously wounded in the schoolhouse under the dubious protection of a few troopers from the city guard. We permitted the walking wounded to join us, but brought along improvised stretchers to carry them if they collapsed.

"We've got to find someplace to rest," Father Moehringer said finally. "I don't care how close the Communists are. It's only a matter of time before we all collapse. We can't just keep walking like this!"

Leaving the road, we began to grope our way through the darkness, hoping to find some peasant hut where there might be shelter and warmth. The ground became rough and cluttered with small, shrublike bushes and dead branches, already shed from the winter-deadened trees.

We stumbled on until we came to a small tribal village. Because it was not far from the roadway, we found that there was even a small Chinese inn. It had been built as a hostelry for the mule drivers who carried wood from the mountainside, although it stood empty now because of the warfare that was ravaging the land. But at the empty inn, we learned that there was no room for "foreign devils."

Pagan and Christian alike, the villagers feared to give us shelter because they knew this might expose them to terrible vengeance from the Communist bands. One woman, whom I had seen receiving gruel at the mission, turned us away with tears in her eyes.

"I would like to help you," she said. "But I am a mother and I must think of my children." But then, just as she was closing the door, the woman lowered her voice and spoke to us in urgent, hurried tones:

"There is an old building nearby that was built by the Christians many years ago, when the French shen-fus were here," she said. "Perhaps you can hide there!"

Following the woman's directions, we made our way along a little overgrown path until the last buildings of the village had fallen behind. We groped through the darkness for what seemed like miles (although I later learned to my amazement that we had progressed from the village only about a thousand yards). Then, miraculously, we found ourselves standing in front of a little chapel with mud-brick walls and a tile roof. Despite long disuse, the oratory was still in good condition—almost as trim as it must have been when the last priest visited it decades ago!

Exhausted, we lay down on the hard-packed clay floor and fell asleep almost immediately—not, however, before offering a prayer of heartfelt thanks to that unknown missionary whose almost-forgotten labor had unexpectedly become our salvation!

We remained for two days and two nights in the little chapel. Sometimes we distinctly heard explosions, shots, and other sounds of fighting close at hand. But it seemed as if nothing could disturb the peace of our refuge. We prayed, not for ourselves, but for God's work in China.

Each day, the kind woman who had told us the way to the chapel came to us from the village. She brought food and rumors of the battle. At last we learned that the fighting had stopped. One afternoon, one of our men set out on a reconnaissance mission to Lungnan. He returned the next day, breathless with excitement. There had been a great victory and the Communists had been driven out. We could return immediately to Lungnan.

Machine guns lined the porch of our mission. Two Nationalist soldiers drew smartly to attention as we picked our way across the rubble-strewn courtyard and began to climb the stairs to the priest-house.

The once-familiar building was one of the few struc-
tures that had escaped major damage in this devastated
area of Lungnan, but even so the casual trappings of
war had transformed it almost beyond recognition.
Bulky wooden ammunition boxes were stacked right
up to the whitewashed ceiling, and cartridges were
strewn over the stone floor. Almost all of our furniture
seemed to have disappeared, except for my writing
desk, which now stood in the center of the barren study
room.

A moon-faced young man wearing the uniform of a
captain in the Nationalist army was seated at the desk,
poring busily over a large map. He rose and bowed po-
litely as we entered the room. "Allow me to introduce
myself. Captain Chung of the 4th Cantonese Regiment
at your service, gentlemen."

Captain Chung quickly lost some of his poise, however, when he noted the stony disapproval with which
Father Moehringer surveyed our despoiled quarters. It
was, he conceded, "most regrettable" that his men had
been obliged to make uninvited guests of themselves,
turning the home of the foreign shen-fus into a bar-
racks, jamming themselves into every available room,
and unhinging all the doors to use them as makeshift
beds.

The captain bombarded us with apologies, but we
soon saw that while he was quite willing to apologize for
the situation it would require a major effort in persua-
sion to get him to do anything about it.

For almost three hours, to the accompaniment of
much bowing, scraping, and flowery phrase-making, a

peculiar Oriental argument raged. Finally, by dint of sheer Yankee dauntlessness and persistence, Father Moehringer succeeded in wresting almost total victory from the captain. It was agreed that the former occupants—and rightful owners—of the priest-house should be permitted the use of two rooms, while Captain Chung and his officers crowded into the dining room and kitchen. As for the soldiers, they would vacate the church (in which they were now cooking and sleeping!) and set up camp in the shelter of the mission porch.

Despite all the bickering, we were genuinely glad to have Captain Chung and his men as our guests. The main body of the Communist army had been pretty well scattered in the fierce fighting around Lungnan, but small groups of Red soldiers were still holding out in the hills near the city. Each day, Nationalist patrols would fan out through the countryside hunting for the enemy—frequently finding them and fighting short but fierce battles, with no quarter asked and none given. But for the presence of troops in the city, these same Reds would probably have occupied themselves raiding Lungnan.

We learned later that Bishop O'Shea at Kanchow was safe and so was Father McGuire at Sinfeng. While the fighting raged close to Sinfeng, an amazing thing happened. A bedraggled, bearded spectre of a man stumbled into the mission compound to confront Father McGuire.

The man was emaciated, his clothing was in rags, and his swollen feet were bound with tattered strips of cloth. He was so covered with grime that Father McGuire failed at first to recognize him as a Westerner. Only after the stranger had been washed and given a chance to rest did Father McGuire learn that he was none other than Father Bravo, a young Dominican priest from the Province east of Kiangsi who had been captured by the Reds thirteen months before.

When Father Bravo had partially regained his health, he submitted a lengthy report to the Bishop in which he described the nightmare he had endured as a prisoner of the Communists.

Sometimes with his hands bound tightly behind him, and sometimes carried in a bamboo cage, Father Bravo had been paraded through Red-occupied cities and goaded with a pointed stick. Wherever he went, he was surrounded by a group of Communist guards who jeered at him and howled such slogans as: "Down with the foreign imperialists!"

The crowds that witnessed the priest's degradation were expected to join in tormenting him. Christians who refused to spit at the priest were often tortured and executed right before his eyes.

When Bishop O'Shea learned that Father Bravo had managed to escape during the confusion of the fighting, he ordered a special Mass of thanksgiving said in Kanchow. He also ordered a Mass for the soul of Father Anselmo, another Dominican who had been captured by the Reds. Father Bravo told us that this priest, after suffering torments similar to those he endured himself, had been murdered by the Communists shortly before the start of Chiang's offensive.

One morning, Captain Chung received a report that

a band of more than one hundred Communist guerillas was lurking in a wooded mountain area only a few miles from Lungnan. He invited me to accompany the Red-hunting expedition.

"This time I think we are going to give these fellows a surprise," he said.

In less than an hour, we were passing through the gates of the city at the head of a long column of gray-coated troops. Before the wooded area came in sight, Captain Chung halted the column and gave a series of instructions to his junior officers.

While the main body of troops waited on the road, a smaller column detached itself and set off in an oblique direction. Their object, the captain said, was to come round behind the Communist camp and attack it from the rear.

"As soon as we hear their guns firing, we ourselves will attack," he said. "If we are lucky, the enemy will think our main force is behind them. Then the main assault will catch them unawares."

The soldiers were now strung out on either side of the roadway, squatting on the soft carpet of fallen pine needles that covered the wooded ground. Next to them, four machine guns were set up, and the crew of the field gun stood by their weapon, its barrel pointed at the crest of the hill. Captain Chung glanced at his watch, then took out his revolver. "We should have only a few moments to wait now," he said.

The staccato firing of the first machine gun rolled up over the crest of the hill, followed by the sound of the second gun and the rapid cracking of rifle shots. Captain

Chung waved his arm, and the soldiers rose and slowly began our advance to the hill crest. They had been instructed not to start firing until we reached the top of the hill, from which we could see the Communist position in a thickly wooded area on the reverse slope.

The mountain howitzer boomed and sent its first round plummeting down into the woods, where it exploded in a bright blossom of fire. At the same time, our machine guns opened up, their bullets lacing through the trees. The troops, crouched down now over their rifles, began to run forward through the waist-high grass.

A ragged volley of shots from the Red camp whizzed over our heads. Then a Communist machine-gun began to fire. The sighting was too low, and the bullets zipped harmlessly through the grass, thudding into the ground some fifty yards ahead of our troops. Then two clouds of acrid gray smoke—one from the hillside and one from the crest—rolled slowly forward and met, and I saw a darker cloud rise in a plume from the woods. At the base of the cloud there was a bright patch of flame, marking a point where a howitzer shell must have exploded, setting fire to the winter-dry undergrowth.

The flames spread with magical rapidity, now shooting along the ground, now rising in bright orange tongues among the pine trees. Until now, we had not seen the enemy, but suddenly I could distinguish several tiny figures scrambling from the woods.

"What wonderful luck!" exclaimed Captain Chung. "We've got them trapped in a perfect furnace down there!" We could hear the screams of men in agony above the rattle of gunfire.

Finally, Captain Chung raised his arm in a signal to stop the slaughter. Moving down the hill, the troops rounded up a handful of dazed survivors. The burned and wounded were loaded onto bamboo stretchers and carried back to Lungnan, where they were imprisoned in the courtyard of the *Yamen,* or city hall.

We had taken a total of fifty Communist prisoners. More than seventy, we learned, had been burned to death in the wooded inferno. Almost as many had been shot down as they fled.

I looked at the pale, anguished faces of the prisoners. Many of them seemed quite young, some still in their teens. Were these the faces of the hated Communist enemy? Perhaps so, but I could not see evil in them any more.

With the Red blockade broken and with Father Moehringer's mission operation now purring smoothly, my traveling began in earnest. For close to two years, I spent much of my time on horseback, bringing the faith to all our outposts, and using my limited medical skills to help heal the ailing and the feeble. My experiences formed a kaleidoscope of life and death, sickness and recovery, happiness and sadness. The most inspiring thing about my work was the large number of Chinese I was able to help wean away from pagan practices. The most disturbing thing was the discovery that I was susceptible to a form of Asian flu. One attack was so bad that Father Moehringer decided to retire me from my traveling role and put me in full charge of the school.

I found teaching to be a heartwarming adventure. The youngsters were pathetically eager to learn, even though their parents usually had no background or interest in education. Since they could get no help from home as American children do, their progress was necessarily slow. Yet each forward step they took brought such a glow of accomplishment to their faces that the same glow was reflected almost at once in the feelings of their inexperienced teacher.

Hours of pure scholarship were hardly typical of normal school routine. Our school and catechumenate were filled to overflowing, and the overcrowded mission buzzed like a beehive. The children, chanting their lessons in what was supposed to be unison, made a first-class racket most of the day.

For all their mischief-making, the peasant youngsters endured great hardship in order to attend our school. Many of these children came from far-off villages scattered throughout the Lungnan district. Although they lived at the mission, they thought nothing of walking thirty miles in a day to visit their homes.

The Lungnan school operated under a regular system organized by the Nationalist government, which frequently sent inspectors to make sure we were living up to standards. The government had ordered that under no condition could we teach religion during school hours. However, we were allowed to say Mass for our Christian youngsters and to give them their catechism and scriptural instructions in the church building.

It seemed that all Chinese, pagan and Christian alike, were anxious to benefit from the missionary schools. Free education was enough to stir up village folk to a high pitch of enthusiasm. The farmers also sent their children, but when planting and harvest seasons arrived we had to let the peasant youngsters go home to help with the plowing or the husking.

The steady influx of new arrivals put a great strain on our limited facilities. Captain Chung's soldiers had already helped to repair our devastated schoolhouse, but it was soon clear that more additions would be needed. To clear the ground for the new construction, the soldiers carried away some of the rubble from the bombing and set about demolishing what remained of the most badly damaged buildings. I was so excited at the prospect of enlarging the school that I devoted as much time as I could to supervising the work of the soldiers.

Our free labor force vanished abruptly one morning, however. Captain Chung announced that our period of "military occupation" was over. He had received orders to march with his men to Kanchow.

A few hours later, the soldiers buckled on their steel helmets and marched through the mission gate. I was really sorry to see Captain Chung go. I found that I had grown quite fond of the little Nationalist officer, and the departure of the troops left the problem of how to complete the work on the school unsolved.

But I had to shelve all my dreams of enlarging the mission a few days later, when Father Moehringer returned from a special meeting with Bishop O'Shea in Kanchow. The depression had hit America, and hard times at home were drying up the stream of contributions on which the overseas missions depended. The Bishop had been forced to cancel all construction projects. We would have to make our present facilities do for at least another year.

Even worse, we would have to cut down on our day-to-day expenditures by firing some of the Chinese teachers and reducing the number of catechists. Most heart-breaking, we would be able to give the youngsters only two bowls of rice a day instead of three, converting the evening bowl of rice into gruel—a mighty poor substitute.

I tried to have faith in the future and console myself with Father Moehringer's words, but the news he brought left me very depressed. I was brooding over the situation when my confrere handed me a dog-eared letter.

"I brought this up personally from Kanchow," he said. "Seems to be from your mother. Open it up. There's nothing quite so cheering as a few words from home."

My eyes raced over the familiar handwriting, but before I finished reading the first page of the letter I felt a shock. My old friend Jolly Charlie Wong was gone, Mother wrote. He had had a heart attack quite unexpectedly one morning, and had died behind the counter of his little laundry. Poor Charlie! He had never returned to his beloved China!

I remembered how I had listened in fascination to Charlie's colorful stories and dreamed of becoming a latter-day Marco Polo. My eyes filled with tears as I thought of the old days in Brooklyn, and my visions of the exotic Orient. Now Charlie was gone, and the visions were gone, too. I was no Marco Polo; I was just a weary priest struggling with poverty and a host of misfortunes that suddenly seemed too much for him.

I went to bed that night with a splitting headache and woke up the next morning feeling even worse. I struggled into my cassock and walked to the church with the intention of saying a Mass, but before I had donned the vestments a wave of nausea swept over me. I stumbled back to my room.

The nightmares of tropical flu plagued me for days and weeks, then one morning they left me as suddenly as they had come, and I learned that I had been ill for six weeks.

My spirits improved markedly when I was able to walk around, but they were dampened again when I learned that Bishop O'Shea had ordered a change in my missionary assignment. My second critical attack of fever had convinced the Bishop that a new priest, presumably immune to tropical flu bugs, should be sent to assist Father Moehringer. I was to be transferred to the Sinfeng mission.

"Sinfeng is a much larger city than Lungnan," Father Moehringer explained. "There are several priests, so that someone will always be around to help you if your fever recurs. It's too dangerous for you to stay alone very long in this isolated mission."

I had to admit that the Bishop's decision seemed reasonable enough, but I still grumbled over the prospect of leaving Lungnan, until Father Moehringer told me that my transfer also involved a change of assignment. There had long been a cry for the Vincentians to publish a news magazine that would bring the doings of the China missionaries to their benefactors and friends back home. Since the depression had made it more difficult than ever to obtain support for our work, this venture had acquired an urgent priority. Frequent reports from China seemed the best way to stimulate lagging contributions from America. It would be my job to write these reports and serve as the magazine editor.

Moving from Lungnan to Sinfeng was like going from a little mission church on Long Island to a big Brooklyn parish. A minimum of three priests were stationed at Sinfeng at all times, and there was a whole contingent of Chinese sisters of the Order of St. Anne. The pastor was Father John McLoughlin, a burly giant of a man whose heart was as big as his body. He was an almost legendary figure among missionaries, one of the original American Vincentians who had come to China in 1921. Many of the old Chinese remembered how he had first traveled through the interior, bringing the charity of St. Vincent de Paul to areas where no white man had ever gone before. In Sinfeng, he had taken over a French mission building and then added several more buildings over the years. There was a splendid church, a mission house with a spacious veranda, a dispensary, quarters for Chinese nuns, catechists, and students—and a school that had a reputation for turning out some of the finest young scholars in all China.

Sinfeng was also an important military post, lying halfway between Kanchow and Lungnan astride a line that divided Chiang Kai-shek's Nationalist army in the North from the Kwangtung forces of the South, led by the celebrated General Yip Chow, who was the commander of the First Cantonese Army. Although allied in opposition to the Communists, there was such chronic rivalry between these two factions that we frequently feared it would erupt into an Oriental version of the Civil War.

The Reds knew how to take advantage of this disunity, and during the recent widespread fighting they had managed to capture Sinfeng, storming in through the East gate so suddenly that Father McLoughlin barely had time to hide his church paraphernalia and slip out through the North gate. The dauntless old priest led his parishioners, pets, and confreres across the war-torn countryside to the relative safety of Kanchow, where he bided his time impatiently until the anti-Communists had mustered their forces and driven the Reds from his beloved city.

But when he returned to his "liberated" mission, Father McLoughlin was confronted with a new problem. General Yip Chow had chosen the impressive stone building as his headquarters.

A quick inspection of the huge veranda and spacious rooms had convinced the general that the mission was made to order for a high military dignitary such as himself. He promptly retreated behind the lofty wall and stationed a twenty-four-hour guard outside the gate to make sure he would not be disturbed.

Using Oriental psychology, Father McLoughlin would present himself at the gate of his own mission and humbly request an opportunity to speak with the Honorable General. But each day the guard's answer was the same: "The General cannot see you now!"

After patiently bearing such rebuffs for two weeks, Father McLoughlin was invited to attend a dinner at the City Hall, accepted on a hunch, and found himself sitting at the head table next to the guest of honor for the evening—General Yip Chow.

The General was quickly impressed with Father McLoughlin's knowledge of the Chinese language, his familiarity with local customs, and especially his ability to make himself at home with his Oriental hosts. Father McLoughlin's head remained clear as a bell, for with cunning worthy of an Oriental he had gorged himself on lichee nuts, an antidote to potent rice wine because the pulpy meat acts like a sponge.

When he judged that the right moment had arrived, Father McLoughlin leaned forward and eloquently described his discomfiture at being barred from his own mission. A tear trickled down the drunken General's cheek as he listened to the piteous tale. "Of course, General," Father McLoughlin said with a comforting smile, "my small discomfort is of little consequence. And I would have had no fear for the property if I had realized that it was in the hands of a gentleman as worthy as yourself. But unfortunately I was unable to gain an audience with you because your guard refused to let me in. Doubtless there was some misunderstanding."

The General was nonplussed. Sensing that he had lost face by being outdone in courtesy, he stammered: "This could not have happened! I never gave orders for the honorable Shen Fu to be sent away!"

Turning around with such violence that he almost toppled out of his seat, the General shouted for an aide and ordered the Captain of the Guard sent for immediately. When the frightened Captain appeared, the General demanded to know why the distinguished Shen Fu had not been presented when he had so humbly appealed for an appointment. The Captain of the Guard was speechless.

"Kneel down!" bellowed the General. He reached for his revolver as the unhappy officer bowed his head. Father McLoughlin realized that he must act quickly to prevent the General from making amends for the discourtesy in a very unchristian manner.

"Stop!" he said. "It is not necessary for you to shoot this miserable fellow. I would prefer a more unusual punishment."

The General paused. "Of course," he said. "Anything the honorable Shen Fu desires."

"I would like you to punish this culprit by sending him to some location far away from my mission."

The General wrinkled his brow and squinted. "I can transfer the wretch quite easily," he said. "But, Shen Fu, it follows that I must then leave the mission myself. Otherwise, the General's guard will be without a General! Clearly, that would be a most unsatisfactory situation."

"Oh, dear," said Father McLoughlin, wringing his

hands. "It would be terrible if my humble mission should lose its illustrious tenant! Still, since we have agreed on the punishment, I suppose we shall have to enforce it, no matter how disagreeable it is to both of us!"

"I suppose so," said the General doubtfully. Then, as a light of understanding dawned, he broke into a sheepish smile. "May all those assembled here bear witness that General Yip Chow knows how to live up to his word!" he said, to the accompaniment of laughter and loud applause.

And he did. A few days later, General Yip Chow moved his entire staff to humbler quarters in another section of the town, not far from the home of the faithful Christian who had housed Father McLoughlin during his banishment.

I arrived in Sinfeng in time to help Father McLoughlin refurbish the mission, which was somewhat dilapidated after its capture by the Reds and service as an officers' quarters.

Since most of his days were spent traveling about the countryside, Father McLoughlin had given me charge of the mission house and school. I was also kept pretty busy writing the Bishop's newsletter, which, while it still didn't rival *Life's* circulation, was being received with a great deal of interest back home.

I acquired a private student in the person of General Wong, commander of the Nationalist Army 3rd Division. He came to me one day to ask for lessons in German. I couldn't imagine why General Wong should want to learn the language. But he had good reason.

"I have applied to my government for permission to visit Germany for a year," he explained. "I have heard a great deal about how the Germans are developing tanks for use in modern warfare, and I would like to go abroad to study them. The Japanese also have many tanks. I fear there may soon be a need for someone who knows about tanks in this country."

There had long been a threat of further Japanese attack against China. Ever since the invasion of Manchuria in 1931 and the Shanghai Incident of 1932, Japan's warlords had been casting hungry eyes at the rich northern provinces of her neighbor. It seemed to them that China—weakened and divided by civil war— would prove an easy victim to Japan's growing might. Wiser men in the Japanese government were attempting to curb the militarists, but the warlords were boldly talking of new attacks.

The General spent many long off-duty hours struggling to master German. It was pretty grueling for me as well, for every word that I wanted to teach him had first to be translated into Chinese. But the General refused to admit defeat. I decided that if my pupil could fight as doggedly as he could study, China had nothing to fear from the Japanese.

Just as the burden of this extra-curricular teaching seemed to be growing insupportable, however, permission for General Wong to leave for Germany came through from the government.

It was only a few months after General Wong's departure that his worst fears about Japanese designs on his country were realized. After a skirmish between a small, supposedly friendly Japanese military detachment and a Chinese patrol on a bridge outside Peking in the summer of 1937, Japanese troops suddenly poured out of Manchuria to attack and capture Peking. They followed this with air raids and then a seaborne invasion of Shanghai. After months of bloody fighting, and a wild orgy of looting and raping, the invaders took complete control of Shanghai and Nanking.

The war news was grim, but there was no indication that we in Kiangsi Province had anything directly to fear. The Japanese gave no indication that they wanted control of the heart of China. In December, they put forward peace proposals which would give them economic and military privileges in China's major cities. Presumably, this was all they were after. While the proposals were being considered, there was a respite in hostilities. In Sinfeng, we prayed for peace and prepared for Christmas.

This turned out to be a Christmas to remember. It was December 25, 1937—the day the Japanese brought war to our part of China. At the conclusion of the morning Mass, I started for my quarters. Then I became aware of an unusual yet somehow familiar sound. I stopped and looked up. Planes were coming. I counted the planes as they came closer: four . . . five . . . seven. . . .

The wings of the first plane rocked rhythmically and the formation split up, the leader continuing southward on a course that would take him directly over the city. His companions, in formations of three planes each, circled and began to gain altitude. It was a neat maneuver, I thought, probably staged by some of Chiang Kaishek's pilots showing off for General Yip. But then the drone of the engines changed to a shrill whine. The planes were pivoting on their wings, flipping over. One of them was plummeting straight down at us and spitting fire. I heard the thud of machine-gun bullets as they slammed into the crowd coming from Mass. A peasant woman with a baby strapped to her back spun violently and toppled forward. A bearded man screamed, clutched his stomach, and fell over the woman's body. The others stood rooted to the road in terror. Then the bomb struck.

There was a dazzling flash and a concussion that sent me sprawling. The bomb hit just outside the mission gate and a mound of debris shot up in the air. Then there were two more sickening explosions that came from the direction of the school and the nurses' quarters.

"Pick up the wounded and follow me!"

It was the voice of Father McLoughlin, who had disentangled himself from the mass of Chinese and taken charge. His towering figure was silhouetted against the flames of the explosion. I ran to join him.

"We've got to get these people to some sort of shelter quick!" he said. "I think the mission house is the safest place—in the basement. Fred, I'm sending you to the nuns' quarters. See that they round up the children and bring them there, too. And don't waste any time!"

I reached the shelter of the nuns' door and looked back to see bullets lacing across the courtyard. To my immense relief, I found that the children were already with the nuns, and that none of them had been hurt. The wide, flat expanse that separated us from the mission house measured almost eighty yards. It was fine for the children to romp on in peacetime, but it was another matter for them to have to cross it under machine-gun fire.

"It's no use," I whispered to the Sisters. "I think we'd better stay right here and hope the machine-gun fire spares us. At least, we can pray together."

And we did pray, the Sisters calmly repeating the words in their low voices as the deadly bullets shrieked their own litany around us. All of us lay close to the floor as bullets shattered the windows, spraying us with broken glass. The sturdy mud-brick walls could not be pierced, but as the firing continued we became aware of a new danger. Bullet after bullet plowed into the roof, and I began to fear that they would start a fire in the heavy timbers and bring the roof down.

The planes seemed to be turning now, and I saw my chance. Head down, I raced across the open space, and leaped over the rubble that blocked the entrance to the schoolhouse. Inside the first classroom, I saw the American flag hanging in its place of honor above the blackboard. It took only a few seconds to unfasten it. Then I ran into the yard, holding the flag above me with both hands so it streamed back into the wind.

The planes were not visible for a moment, and I breathed a sigh of relief. But suddenly they returned. I quickly spread the flag before me on the ground and began pointing to it in the hope that the pilots would see it.

The first plane banked slightly, dipped its nose, and seemed to bear directly down on me. It kept coming, getting larger and larger; then, with an ear-splitting roar, the plane zoomed by, raising its nose and climbing in a steep parabola. At an altitude of about a thousand feet the pilot banked and joined the rest of his formation. Then the planes turned east, shrinking to small spots that rapidly disappeared in the distance.

"Fred," said Father McLoughlin a few hours later, "everybody's been telling me about that stunt you pulled with the Japanese pilot. In times like these we need every priest we can get. We can't afford to have them go around committing suicide! You seem to be taking a lot for granted when you assume those pilots flew away just because you waved a flag at them. I don't suppose you attach much importance to the fact that those Japs stopped their attack on a lot of other targets —including the headquarters of General Yip's Division."

"What do you mean?"

"Just this, Fred. I think you're the luckiest man I know. If my theory is correct—and I'm afraid it probably is—there's only one reason why those Japs didn't shoot you dead. They just happened to have used up all their ammunition!"

The conduct of the Japanese pilots in the raids that followed seemed to bear out Father McLoughlin's point that the flag of a neutral nation was not much of a deterrent. All our missions were given strict orders to display the flag prominently, but all too many American missions, churches, hospitals, and schools in China were bombed anyway. When it happened, our government would protest, and the Japanese would offer profuse apologies for the "accident." But it happened too often for any intelligent person to accept the "accident" explanation.

Why did they keep staging such "incidents"? My own thought is that the Japanese militarists didn't just want to beat China in a war. They wanted to enslave her permanently. To do that, they realized that they would have to drive American teachers and missionaries out of China. They weren't quite ready to attack America herself yet—although that plan was probably already on the drawing boards—so they just made the campaign of terror "accidental" and "unofficial."

The men I knew in China used to quip that it was just as inconvenient to be dead "unofficially" as any other way, but the Japanese made a big mistake when they thought their tactics would scare the missionaries away.

Father McLoughlin was a fine example. Instead of closing down our school, he had us pile up sandbags around it. We soon had an air-raid siren in Sinfeng, and the children got so used to Japanese planes that when the alarm sounded they would calmly file into the shelter, wait until the bombing was over, and then return to class without ever missing the place in their textbooks.

Japan had followed up its air attacks on China with a land invasion, and the first report we had on Generals Wong and Yip was that they were involved in the heavy land fighting in the coastal areas. The Japanese won impressive victories in those areas, and captured Shanghai, Canton, and other big cities. But the Nationalist troops retreated to the interior and continued a defensive battle.

The bombings frequently disrupted our water supply, so the problem of sanitation forever plagued us in the dispensary. It became impossible to sterilize our few medical instruments properly, and even to insure that bandaging was sterile. Infections proved very difficult to control, and killed many with only minor wounds. My own susceptibility to infection laid me low once again with fever. This happened late in 1938.

Though my illness was not as severe as it had been in Lungnan, I was left with an aftereffect—conjunctivitis. I thought of this at first as only a mild discomfort, and went back to work in the dispensary and the school. But the condition got steadily worse, and in time I couldn't see with my right eye at all. Bishop O'Shea, on a visit to Sinfeng, decided I should go for professional treatment in Shanghai. He was afraid I might permanently lose my sight in both eyes. If they couldn't do much for me in Shanghai, he would have no alternative but to order my return to the United States.

"Things are hard in China now, and we just can't care for you here properly," he said. "Your eye condition and your recurring illnesses make it plain that you're in no condition to do a full-time job. It wouldn't be fair to you, and it wouldn't be fair to us, if I listened to your pleading and let you remain if they fail to help you in Shanghai."

When I arrived in Shanghai, I was jolted by my first

sight of Japanese troops in their field-gray, sharply cut uniforms. Recalling the atrocities that were reported to have taken place when they first captured the city, and aware of their deep hatred for American missionaries, I wondered how they would treat me. It turned out that I had nothing to fear. On the surface, the official face they presented to America and Americans was ceremonially polite. The customs officer who came aboard our riverboat was coolly correct toward me. Another unsmiling, but circumspect, officer took my passport, fingered it gingerly, and then handed it back with a slight bow.

I remained for several weeks at the French Catholic Mission which was inside the International Settlement at Shanghai. The settlement and the various foreign concessions were still being respected as neutral area by the Japanese armies. I was given a series of treatments for my eyes, but the improvement was slight and the doctor told me finally that I had better return to the States for specialized care.

It was already hard for me to visualize the world I had just left. The gaiety and insouciance that characterized the foreign concessions in Shanghai was a kind of shade drawn by the residents to keep desolation and destruction out of their range of focus.

This world came vividly back to me, however, in a letter I received the afternoon of my departure, and which I read that night on the deck of the liner *President Taylor*. It was from Father McLoughlin: "Forty-one planes hit Namyung the other day," he wrote. "We had four raids recently in Sinfeng. Tayu was bombed last week. They had many killed and wounded. The situation is as bad as ever in Kanchow. The bombing raids have been so heavy they are evacuating the local population. But we've all got our chins up here and we keep doing our jobs. . . ."

As I gazed up at the crescent moon, I wondered whether I had done *my* job. Certainly, I had fallen far short of realizing all the dreams I had spun for myself when I first set out for the East. I had hoped to be a knight in missionary garb, slaying all the dragons of paganism, want, ignorance, and disease that ran rampant in this historic land. Instead, I had been felled by disease so often that I was being shipped off while my more energetic colleagues stayed on to continue the good fight.

Still, I reflected, I would never have to apologize for having been part of a team that was so gloriously translating the ideals of self-sacrifice and love of man into day-to-day reality. Though the militarists were on the march, and although my team—and indeed all of China —was in retreat, I felt certain that the agents of destruction would eventually be defeated. Down through the centuries, China has survived untold disasters. It would surely survive this one, and even other ones that might follow.

6

When I finished my saga, I found that my companions of the Guadalcanal foxholes had become a
bunch of Sinophiles. During the nights of foxhole-
sitting and the lulls between combat operations in the
daytime, they needed something to take their minds off
the misery of the present, and they seized on the Orient
as a good escapist subject. They plied me with dozens
of questions about China's history and about phases of
Chinese life I'd omitted telling them about.

Gene Markey took a somewhat jaded view of all this.
"The boys prefer to dwell on the colorful part of life in

China, but I'll bet when you were on that boat going home, you spent your time thanking your lucky stars that you finally got out of there," he commented.

"Well, I'll admit it was a relief to get away from Communist attacks and Japanese bombs, but truthfully, Gene, I had come to love the country and the people so much that after I was home for a short while I found myself fidgety to get back. But my eye needed treatment for a long time, and my superiors felt I should spend a year or so in the States helping to raise money for the missions. After that, there was the attack on Pearl Harbor, and I felt I had a responsibility to volunteer at once to serve as a chaplain.

"After graduating from the Chaplain's School at the Naval Base in Norfolk, I did have qualms when the orders came to board the transport that was to take us out to these islands. I knew what to do with little Chinese orphans all right, but I'd never worked with American boys before. Then there were the Seabees— older men who had left good jobs as carpenters, steel-fitters, and engineers to join up. They'd be looking to me for guidance and spiritual help, too, and I didn't know if I could do right by them. I remembered though that I'd often played little games with my Chinese tykes to get their affection, so I organized some recreation for the men on shipboard and started a little mimeographed newspaper for them, and this seemed to warm them up to me."

"Well, so we see the Chinese influence is still clinging to your career," Gene observed. "And there must be meaning in the fact that the founder of your Vincentian order took care of orphans, that you did the same in China, and that here in the middle of a miserable jungle war, thousands of miles from good old Kiangsi Province, the good Lord sends you three natives with another Chinese orphan."

I nodded agreement. "I'm sure that it wasn't just coincidence that led those three first to Patsy's body and then to my tent."

"What do you intend doing now with Patsy?" Gene wanted to know. "I suppose you can't keep her here much longer."

"No, though I'm frank to admit I've become so attached to the child I hate to lose her. But, of course, she's got to be moved to a peaceful, normal environment where she can receive maternal love and care again, go to school, and put the terror of the past behind her. I've decided that the best place for me to take her would be Espiritu Santo, that island in the New Hebrides where we stopped off on our way out here. I guess you know the Navy is using the island as a supply base, but there's no active combat going on around there."

"Who would take care of Patsy there?" Gene asked.

"Well, there's a little mission on the island and a mission hospital. I met the priest in charge when I was there—a jolly Frenchman named Père Jean. I'm quite sure they have a mission school and maybe an orphanage where Patsy could grow up, or perhaps stay for a while till they can find a nice family to adopt her. I've been meaning to contact Espiritu Santo by radio, but with the Japanese still controlling the sea lanes and with our planes needed here so desperately, there's just no safe way of getting the tyke out of here."

"Padre, if things keep going the way they have been, none of us will be able to get off this island, except in a box."

"Now, now, Gene, remember, in your movies, the sun always bursts through the black clouds just when everything seems gloomiest. I'm going to make a wild, happy-ending prediction. Starting tonight, the Japanese will decide they've taken too many casualties and will start running the other way."

But my glib prediction proved agonizingly inaccurate. In the evening, only an hour after Tokyo Rose finished trumpeting the news that more Japanese were coming our way, they put a huge troop convoy ashore. Their landing point was close enough for us to see what was happening. At midnight, they launched a sea and land assault which for sheer, naked fury surpassed even their most frenzied attacks of September and early October. Our outnumbered Marines could not possibly hold the line, and had to fall back. From my trench, I saw shell after shell thunder into our positions and explode with such shuddering impact it seemed impossible that any of us would survive.

All that day and throughout the next day, the Japanese kept up the assault. Another shelling session at night was almost more than I could bear. When it was over, I was so bone-weary I barely managed to get back to my tent with my terrified little waif in my arms.

There was an officer waiting for me—Commander Raymond Cliffords, the executive officer of the Navy

Cub I Unit. Cliffords was overage for combat service but he drove himself mercilessly. This latest bombardment had left him so unsteady that he had wandered into the chaplain's tent hoping I could relax him. I tucked Patsy in and got out my checkerboard. But as we dozed over our game the Japanese unexpectedly opened up again. I shook the Commander awake. "They're shelling us again," I yelled over the fearsome noise of the attack. Then I grabbed Patsy and rushed to the big foxhole outside my tent. Shells were coming from both directions, indicating that Japanese land artillery was in operation, too. While the attack lasted, the ground around us heaved convulsively, and the flash of explosions lit up the sky with weird crimson and yellow streaks.

The next day, Japanese dive bombers swarmed over Henderson Field and destroyed some of our planes that had landed after dogfights. Japanese artillery pockmarked the runways with so many craters that the whole field was temporarily put out of commission. Working feverishly, the Seabees were able to fashion a makeshift field nearby so that we could still get some planes up, but in the meantime a banzai ground attack enabled the Japanese to get close enough to the precious field to virtually encircle it. Our situation was fast going from grim to desperate.

At this point in our ordeal on Guadalcanal, Admiral William "Bull" Halsey unexpectedly flew into the island on a C-47. Halsey had been named to relieve his Annapolis classmate and friend, Admiral Robert Ghormley, as commander of all South Pacific forces.

With audacious unconcern for Japanese Zeroes, he had decided to come to Guadalcanal and see our situation for himself. He first closeted himself with General Vandegrift, then hopped into a jeep to look at our forward positions in the jungle. Halfway along, the vehicle bogged down in mud. I chanced along in my own jeep a few minutes later, and a Marine officer, who had been detailed to drive Halsey, flagged me down. He explained the situation. I said I was on the way to a Marine unit up front myself and would be glad to play chauffeur. He brought Halsey and the Admiral's aide over, introduced me, and had them climb aboard.

I looked at Halsey closely. He was wearing an open-collar shirt and was barely distinguishable from an enlisted man. His beetle-browed eyes, his manner, even the iron gray in his hair, exuded vigor, determination, and self-confidence. "This is the kind of man who won't stand for defeat," I thought to myself.

Meanwhile, the Admiral was eyeing me just as closely. "What's the morale situation, Padre? You're a man who ought to know. Let's have it straight—no soft soap."

"I'm glad to give it to you straight, sir," I said. "These boys have shown a courage and spirit that's almost unbelievable. But they're not superhuman. They know we've been running low on ammunition, guns, everything. Our food is down to Spam and Japanese rice. We've still got enough Atabrine and quinine, but there are plenty of malaria cases anyway. What hurts most of all is that we keep watching the Japs land more troops and more supplies, while we see almost nothing coming for us. Tokyo Rose says Admiral Yamamoto is all ready to come here and accept our surrender, and although we laugh at her when we're in a group, some of the boys privately believe her. Their big fear is that what happened on Bataan will be repeated here."

"This won't be another Bataan, dammit," Halsey shot at me. "It won't be another Singapore either. It'll be more like Thermopylae. Maybe that's the wrong comparison too. The Greeks held at Thermopylae, but they didn't win. We're going to win, and you and I will both see Yamamoto in hell!"

He was silent the rest of the way to the front, but when I let him out, he swung his hand in an arc around the island and the water beyond. "You're not going to be sitting ducks much longer," he said. Then, by way of good-by, he added, "I didn't just come here for a two-dollar tour of your jungle!"

On November 8, Halsey began making good his promise of action. With his small fleet augmented by new warships that we later learned had been diverted to him by Washington, he sent us transports loaded with Marine and Army reinforcements, ammunition, and supplies.

Crack P-38 planes from the Army Air Corps, manned by eager and able young pilots, flew into Henderson Field. For Joe Foss and his dog-tired Marine vets, they were the greatest sight since Christmas. On the night of November 13—a night so black I felt as if the whole Pacific had been suddenly shunted into a subway tunnel —Halsey got word that a great Japanese armada of fourteen warships was steaming toward the narrow waters of the "Slot." The armada included two battlewagons and was shepherding Japanese troopships and supply ships for their "final" offensive on the Canal. Two cruiser forces, headed by Rear Admirals Callaghan and Scott, rushed forward to block the enemy armada. They sailed right into the middle of the Japanese fleet between Guadalcanal and Savo Island.

At 1:40 A.M., thunder and lightning erupted across the moonless sky. Salvo followed salvo, flash followed flash, and ship fires began to rage out of control. From our ringside seat on shore, it almost seemed as if we were watching a dazzling fireworks show at Coney Island or Jones Beach.

As the broadsides continued across the water, debris from exploding and sinking ships began floating in. In the flickering light, we made out scores of corpses piled on the drifting wreckage. We also saw men frantically swimming toward shore and others clinging to flotsam and small craft. We rushed to the beach and began hauling in the burned and wounded. We learned that the daring maneuver of our cruisers had unnerved the Japanese fleet commander, and that a giant Japanese battleship and three other ships had gone down, while the others scattered. Japanese naval guns, however, had sunk two of our cruisers and killed Admirals Callaghan and Scott.

The naval battle continued for three more days as the Japanese armada re-formed and the new U. S. battleships, *Washington* and *South Dakota,* as well as the carrier *Enterprise,* steamed into the action. On shore, we worked feverishly, fishing more injured and burned out of the sea and giving them first-aid treatment in our tents till the doctors could tend to them. No one worked harder at this than Commander Cliffords, but this final strain broke him down completely. He had to be hospitalized for physical and nervous exhaustion and was later sent to a Stateside hospital.

The Navy battle ended on the night of the 16th with a tremendous victory for Halsey. Eight Japanese warships had gone down, and their troopships and supply transports had been either sunk or forced to turn back. Most important of all, Japanese command of the sea lanes and the supply lines feeding Guadalcanal had been completely broken. The tide of battle had made an about-face in our favor. Coupled with our victory at sea, our reinforced air fleet shot thirty-one Zeroes out of the skies. Admiral Yamamoto, the man who was coming to the Solomons to accept our surrender, never lived to reach us. His plane was shot out of the sky by a P-38 pilot, Army Lieutenant Thomas G. Lanphier, Jr.

Our ground forces also switched from the defensive to the offensive. Backed by new artillery weapons, our Marines and Army men broke out of the tight circle around Henderson Field and pushed across the Matanikau River. My friend Barney Ross proved one of the heroes in this fighting. He volunteered to join a patrol to scout the strength of the Japanese ahead of our positions. His patrol was cut off at night by an enemy company, and he helped four wounded buddies into a shellhole. All through the night, he kept firing his buddies' guns and throwing grenades to fool the Japanese into thinking they were opposed by a sizable unit. Meanwhile, mortar shells and machine-gun bullets rained

around him. In the morning, the 2nd Marines came up
and rescued him. He'd been shot up and was half out
of his head with shellshock, but he had killed twenty-
two Japanese.

With the dramatic change in our fortunes on Guadalcanal, and the lifting of the siege of Henderson Field,
I could now take Patsy Li to a new life in the New
Hebrides: Through radio contact with Père Jean on
Espiritu Santo, I learned that French Sisters ran both
a little school and a little orphanage on the nearby
island of Efate. Père Jean would make the necessary arrangements to bring the little girl to the orphanage as
soon as I placed her in his care.

Patsy's farewell to the Solomons will always remain
one of the most touching scenes in my memory. As Al
and I drove her slowly toward the airfield from my tent,
crowds of Marines and sailors swarmed around to wave
good-by to the little waif who had come to us in a
manner that still strained belief, and who had lived with
us through so many days and nights of fear, disease, and
death. The boys pelted her with flowers and forced
chocolate bars on her. Some, like Jim O'Leary, insisted
on stopping the jeep so they could hug and kiss the
little belle of Guadalcanal. Though ordinarily Patsy
never smiled or laughed, this time her face glowed. She
sensed that she was Queen of the May being cheered by
an admiring court as she left for an exciting adventure.
She had, of course, no idea yet that her court was saying
good-by to her forever.

As we drove past the hospital tent, I had Al stop the
jeep while I dashed in for a moment to see Barney. He

looked gaunt and hollow-eyed. He became nostalgic when I told him where I was taking Patsy.

"Orphanages aren't so bad, Padre," he said. "An orphanage helped make me champion of the world." He explained that his father, a poor Chicago grocer, had been murdered by holdup men. His mother had suffered a breakdown as a result, and his brothers and sister had been put in an orphan asylum. "I thought orphanages were the most horrible places, and that the most important thing for me to do was make enough money to set up a home and get them out," he said. "I had never intended to be a fighter, but that was the quickest way to make money, so I went into the ring and became a champ. When I brought the kids out, they were grateful, but they also said, 'You know, the orphanage wasn't so bad!'

"You can tell Patsy that, when she finds out where she's going," Barney said with a weak smile. Then he added, "Hey, tell her something else, too. Tell her that after the war, we'll find her again and have a big reunion party up at Grossinger's. That's the resort in the Catskills where I used to train for my big bouts. Jennie Grossinger, who runs the place, used to feed me so much I almost couldn't fight. She'll put some flesh on skin-and-bones Patsy if anybody can."

"I'll try to tell her all that, Barney—if I can only get her to understand it in sign language!" I laughed. Then I gave Barney a Catholic medal to wear next to his Hebrew mezuzah, wished him a speedy recovery and hurried back to the jeep. Patsy was still being fêted by her admirers and we had to shoo them off to get her to the field. When we reached the plane, Al kissed and hugged her, then drove off in a hurry before the tears welling up in his eyes could trickle down.

I led Patsy into the plane, and then we were off amid good-by shouts and a volley of shots fired by Marines who felt Patsy deserved a noisy sendoff.

It took us over three hours to fly the six hundred miles to Espiritu Santo. Patsy sat very close to me through the whole journey and kept staring down at the sea. Approaching the New Hebrides, the pilot—a Navy flier based on Espiritu Santo—pointed to the wreckage of a great ship. "That transport had a load of big guns and supplies it was supposed to deliver to you at the Canal, but it never got there," he said. "It hit a mine and took all the equipment down with it."

"What was the name of the ship?"

"It was a luxury liner that was converted into a war transport. It was one of those President ships—the *President Coolidge*."

"Oh no, not the *Coolidge*!" I cried. The pilot turned and looked at me strangely, and I explained that I had fond memories of that ship. He flew low over the wreckage, but I could hardly bear to look at it. As I thought of my good friends of the "Coolidge Family" and those happy times we'd had on the ship that took me to the Orient, I felt torn with self-pity. Saying good-by to both Patsy and the *Coolidge* on the same day was going to be too much!

Père Jean was waiting for me as we landed. There were also some Navy personnel and a Navy photographer. My thought was to make my parting from Patsy as quick and clean as possible. I thought that any lingering good-bys would only add to the deep hurt she would most certainly suffer when she realized she had been abandoned by the person who, over the past weeks, had been the focal figure in her life. Père Jean had promised that he and the others at the mission would make a great fuss over her while they had her, and that, when he arranged the boat trip over to Efate, the Sisters would also take pains to ease her through this difficult transition period.

The quick parting was not so easily arranged, however. The minute I handed Patsy into Père Jean's arms, she seemed to sense that this was not the same kind of "hide and seek" game we had played on Guadalcanal. She became hysterical and fought desperately to get out of the missioner's arms and back into mine. Père Jean tried all his charm on her, but it didn't work. I tried to soothe her, too, but when I avoided taking her back in my arms, she in turn refused to stop screaming. I felt ashamed of my complete inadequacy, and I was at a loss whether to stay or run. If only I could talk to this child, I thought!

At long last, and probably out of sheer exhaustion, Patsy's sobs died down. I bent quickly to kiss her, shook hands with Père Jean, and walked away. I heard her screaming for me again, and the tears welled up in my eyes. I gritted my teeth and told myself I must not go back. But I could not stop myself from turning around and giving a final wave. "Let me know how she gets along," I called to Père Jean. Then to Patsy I shouted suddenly, "If you ever need my help again, my child, you shall have it." I knew immediately that this was a silly, sentimental thing to say to a sobbing child who couldn't understand me, but somehow I had to say it to silence the little inner voice that kept chiding me as a cruel child-deserter.

My plan was to return to Guadalcanal the same day, but the weather clouded up and the pilot said I would have to remain overnight. That afternoon, I sought out Captain Joel White, a Navy doctor who had just been transferred from Guadalcanal to run a base hospital at Espiritu Santo. I found he had a visitor in his office, an urbane and soft-spoken gentleman whom he introduced as Foster Hailey, foreign correspondent for *The New York Times*. Hailey became intensely interested when he heard me describing to Dr. White my tearful parting from Patsy. He asked me to recount to him the details of how Patsy came to me in the first place. When I finished, the correspondent said, "You may have lost your child, chaplain, but I've found a very good feature story for my paper!"

7

Memories of Patsy remained sentimentally green with us on Guadalcanal even after she had gone. We talked about her frequently and reminisced about her habits and mannerisms. We wondered what would happen to her, whether she would remember us, and whether she would be able to overcome the handicap of having lost her family so early in life and in so savage a manner.

The three Melanese who had originally brought Patsy to me always asked after the child when they came for supplies for their missionaries in hiding. They felt very proud when I was able to tell them that the waif had been removed from the war zone, and that because of their heroism she would not have to live in danger again. They left me in a buoyant mood, but, a few nights later, returned with lines of deep sorrow on their faces. Once again, they had something for me—only this time their cargo was beyond all medical help.

The Melanese were carrying a leaf-woven basket covered with palm shreds. As they began uncovering the leaves, I found myself staring in horror at arms that had been severed from human bodies.

"Two missionaries murdered by Japanese," the natives told me in their pidgin English. "Two Sisters also murdered."

It was all I could do to keep from being sick right in front of the brave Melanese. After a great deal of effort, I got my stomach under control and asked them to tell me what had happened. They said they had received these human remains and their information from two native boys. The boys had been seized by the Japanese at the same time as the missionary priests and the nuns, but had managed to escape execution.

The missionaries were Father Arthur Duhamel, who was an American serving with the French Marists, and Father Henry Oude Engberink. They had decided to remain at the Ruavatu Mission on the western tip of the island and take their chances, although they'd been warned to join the others in hiding. The Japanese let them alone for a while, but the crucial shift in the island battle picture in our favor put them in a mood of wild desperation. One morning, they appeared at the mission and dragged the two priests, along with three Sisters who had remained at the mission, to the headquarters of their commanding officer.

The Japanese commander ordered them to go through our lines, seek out our commander, and induce him to withdraw all our troops from Guadalcanal. They were to warn the Americans that huge new Japanese convoys were coming, that many thousands of fresh Japanese soldiers would land on the island, and that it would be suicide for our men to remain. The missionaries refused to do this. They said their work was religious and they would not interfere in military matters. After a bitter argument, the Japanese officer allowed the priests and the nuns to go back to their mission.

A few days later, however, the Japanese returned to the little mission, sacked and pillaged it, and dragged the two missionaries back to their general. Sister Mary Salome, who had helped found the Ruavatu Mission twenty-two years earlier, and Sister Mary Odelia were taken away with them. The two native boys were also seized at this time. The third nun, Sister Mary Edmee, was on a mission call to sick natives and was not taken. She had not turned up, however, and nobody seemed to know what had happened to her.

The two priests were again ordered by the Japanese commander to contact our American commander and get him to withdraw from the island. Again, they refused. This time, they were tied up in a hut and starved for over two weeks. The two native boys were not as closely guarded and managed to escape. Meanwhile, the Japanese set up machine-gun and antiaircraft emplacements in the bush surrounding the mission and used them to fire on American planes returning to Henderson Field. The planes raided the mission area in turn and bombed out the gun emplacements. In the attack, however, the mission house itself was razed.

The Japanese then left the Ruavatu area, and the natives quickly launched a search for the missionaries and the Sisters. They found the Japanese had taken the four prisoners from the hut to a point along the beach above Lunga Point. There, they were ordered for the last time to take a white flag through American lines and sound the warning that our forces quit the island. When they persisted in their refusal, they were all stabbed to death with bayonets. The bodies of the Sisters were found near the beach by the natives and were buried on the scene. The bodies of the priests had been hacked to pieces. The natives kept the limbs in their palm-covered basket until they met my three Melanese friends, who agreed to take the remains to me.

I informed Captain Compton, who commanded the Navy Cub I Unit at Lunga, of the tragedy, and he quickly notified General Vandegrift. Meanwhile, I had the remains of the missionaries encased in wax and buried right behind the altar outside my tent. The Seabees built a beautiful shrine as a memorial to the two martyred men.

A few days later, the General called me in to tell me he had decided to rescue the thirty-odd missionaries and Sisters who were still in hiding on Guadalcanal. Major Richard Clements, an Australian officer who was acting as our intelligence liaison with the Christian natives, had come into camp to report that the missionaries were in a desperate way. The Japanese were out to exterminate them. They were now scouring the native settlements and the bush areas for them.

The Vicar of the South Solomons area, Bishop Jean Aubin, had narrowly escaped capture himself. Ill with malaria and dysentery, he had been carried for many miles over the mountainous part of Guadalcanal, and then taken by outrigger canoe to Malaita Island which was still free of enemy troops. A Japanese raiding unit had missed the Bishop and a party of faithful followers by a matter of minutes. A native who had purposely misdirected the Japanese on their trail of the Bishop had his head blown off when they realized what he'd done.

The General told me he had made contact with Bishop Aubin on Malaita and received authorization to get the Guadalcanal missionaries out. The Bishop was afraid, however, that the priests and Sisters would not want to leave, no matter what their peril, because they would construe this as a desertion of their duty.

"I know you were a missionary in China before the war," General Vandegrift told me. "I wonder if you would be willing to volunteer to go along with a party to evacuate the missionaries? As a former missionary, I think you're the one man who could convince them that their religious superior feels it is their duty to leave and save themselves."

"I'd be most happy and eager to go," I answered.

Preparations went forward rapidly during the next

few days. Major Clements called in his native scouts, and through an ingenious communications system of jungle tom-toms they signaled coded messages from village to village that the missionary priests and Sisters were to be evacuated. Trusted natives who would act as our guides were instructed to go to designated points along the coastline of Guadalcanal and wait for our arrival.

General Vandegrift explained that we were going to go around and behind the Japanese lines by boat to effect the rescue. He could not send a party of Marines along, because if they were spotted the Japanese would promptly open fire. The Navy had a PT squadron operating in the waters around the Solomons, and consideration was given the idea of using a PT boat for the rescue. However, it was decided that this was also too risky. The Japanese were accustomed to seeing native craft in the waters and might not be suspicious if they spotted one on a leisurely trip around the island. The General decided we were to use one of these boats, and Major Clements arranged for a native launch to be brought to a cove just above Lunga. He then told me to be ready to leave after nightfall.

I made arrangements for two officers, Captain Jack Leonard, a career Marine, and Captain Ed McGuinness, a former basketball star for Manhattan College, to fill in for me at the chapel tent. Both had served my Mass before. Leonard commanded a gun unit at Lunga Beach. He had a knack for scenic design and had improvised rows upon rows of brambles to look like guns

from the air. His artistry duped the Japanese reconnaissance planes into thinking we were much better
armed than was actually the case.

I had met Ed McGuinness under fateful conditions
on one of my first days up at the front lines. He was
commanding a unit at a key ridge in our defense line,
and I had just finished giving absolution to a group of
his young Marines when the Japanese staged a sudden
attack. They were beaten back but they left six of the
boys whom I had just blessed with their blood draining
away in the sands. They were the first American boys
I had seen killed in combat, and the sight left me
stunned and heartsick. Sensing my feelings, Captain Ed
was kind enough to play chaplain to *me* for a moment
and said, "Isn't it comforting to know these boys saw a
priest just before they died?"

When darkness came, I said my good-bys to McGuinness and Leonard and quipped to Leonard that if I
failed to come back, he could have the chaplain's job
permanently. "You've got to come back," he insisted.
"I've got a girl back home in Philadelphia I want to
marry after the war, and I'm giving you the assignment
here and now to perform the ceremony!"

Following Major Clements' instructions, I removed
all my insignia and went forward to meet the Major
and the native scouts who would escort us. I noticed
that our bushy-haired guides were heavily armed with
machetes, knives, and Marine tommy guns. Just as we
were about to leave, a Marine sergeant named Hennessey ran up to me and asked me if I would try to locate

his brother, a priest from Boston who was with one of the missions in the Solomons. I told him I would do whatever I could.

Our group then crept out of camp and went about half a mile to reach the cove where the launch had been moored. We climbed aboard and the Major waved for me to keep down and out of sight. The natives paddled us slowly and quietly out to deep water. We then sailed about twenty-five miles around the coast until we reached an inland waterway. Dawn was breaking, and we beached our launch and went ashore. Then, while most of us set to work camouflaging the boat with foliage, two of our scouts went ahead to contact other natives. They carried hollow bamboo sticks to tap code messages to fellow natives and also to contact Major Clements. They also had a prearranged signal tap which would warn us if they spotted enemy patrols.

After an hour's wait, we got the signal to follow our advance men, and we walked stealthily for about ten miles along old native trails. The heat was unbearable, and the sweat cascaded down my face. I began to sprout blisters on my feet like so many quarters. We talked only in hushed whispers for fear that undue noise would arouse the enemy. Twice, we got the ominous signal tap that warned that the Japanese were close by and dived into the jungle growth to wait until the danger had passed. Huddled in the dense, steaming foliage, I felt so weak I nearly fainted. The crouch position was awkward and uncomfortable, and once I felt I just had to stand up and straighten my legs. As I did so, I caught a glimpse of a Japanese soldier passing by at the tail end of his patrol. I dropped down to my awkward position so fast I was afraid the soldier would hear the twigs and leaves cracking. The Major did not have to remind me that capture by the Japanese would almost certainly result in our execution as spies.

We finally came to a village that seemed abandoned. Major Clements told me that although the residents of the village had left it after it had been raided by the Japanese, Christian natives had later brought a group of missionary priests and Sisters here and secretly installed them in the native huts. In a few minutes, our Scouts appeared, shepherding ten priests and Sisters and a group of half-naked native girls. The missionaries' clothes were torn, they were hardly able to walk, and their bones stood out so prominently from their flesh that it was obvious they were half-starved. Despite their condition, the good Sisters were still aware of the proprieties. When they saw that two white men were in the company greeting them, they swiftly found a batch of muumuus (native-type chemises which the native girls wore only with reluctance) and draped them over the protesting girls!

When we told the missionaries we had come to take them out of the jungle to safety, they balked at going just as General Vandegrift had predicted. They'd rather die than desert their obligations and their people, they said. Some had been on the island for over thirty-five years and had forgotten any other life.

It was then that I introduced myself as an American priest and told them I was carrying instructions from their Bishop ordering them out. The Sisters looked at me with suspicion. "You're not a priest," one of them said flatly. "You're not dressed like a priest, and you don't look like one."

I said that I was also an officer in the American Navy and explained that because our mission was a secret one, I carried no identifying papers and wore no insignia. Neither the priests nor the Sisters were satisfied with this. They continued to regard me with suspicion and to insist they would not go back with me. Major Clements pleaded with them, but to no avail. Finally, he had an idea. "How about reciting some prayers for them, Padre?" he said to me. "Maybe that way you can prove you're not a phony."

I promptly recited the Confiteor and some other prayers of the Mass, and a light came into the eyes of the missionaries. They seemed satisfied, but to make sure I hadn't memorized a few special prayers for their benefit, they demanded more prayers from me. I obliged them and apparently gave a good account of myself, for when I finished, they shook my hand and agreed I was the real McCoy. They also agreed that I must be carrying an authentic message from their Bishop, and that they were therefore obliged to leave with our party.

We supplied the priests and Sisters with K rations, which they devoured ravenously. Major Clements then told us to go to the native huts and rest until his scouts made contact with the other missionaries we wanted to rescue. While chatting with Father Donatum Coicand, one of the missionary priests, I found that his group already knew the grisly details of the murder of their compatriots from the Ruavatu Mission.

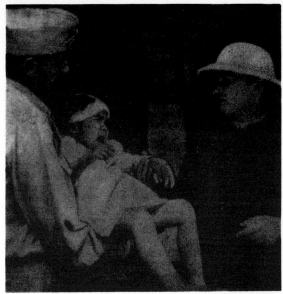

(*Above*) Father Gehring hands over a sobbing Patsy to Père Jean on the island of Espiritu Santo, a few months after she was found by U.S. Marines on Guadalcanal.

(*Below*) A Sister of the French Mission on Efate comforts Patsy in the Mission's orphanage, where Patsy was brought from Espiritu Santo in 1943 through the help of Père Jean.

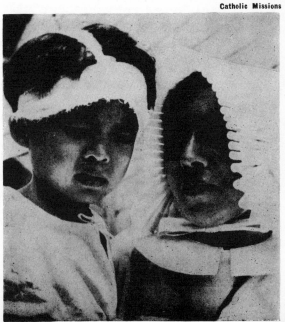

Reunited in 1946, Patsy and her mother spend nine months in Sydney, Australia, so that Patsy can adjust to her new life and learn English.

Eleanor Bumgardner welcomes Patsy at the Los Angeles Airport on her
arrival from Singapore on Christmas Day, 1950. "Lady" Eleanor became Patsy's legal guardian.

William Eccles

William Eccles

Santa is also on hand to
greet Patsy Li.

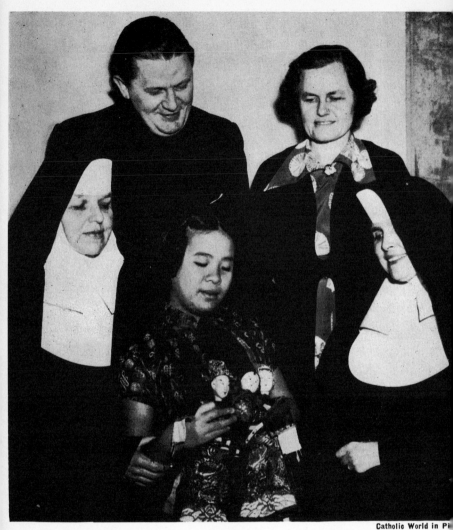

Patsy shows the China dolls she brought Miss Bumgardner to Mother Bernard and Mother Patricia of the Sisters of Mercy, founders of Walsingham Academy in Williamsburg, Virginia. It was Mother Bernard who gave Father Gehring the scholarship for Patsy.

Furthermore, Christian natives who had fled Bougainville and other parts of the Northern Solomons had relayed even more tragic news to them. The missions there had been ransacked and destroyed. Most of the Christian natives had been put to work as slave laborers. Churches had been turned into munition dumps. The Americans had bombed these dumps heavily, and the shock of relentless, low-level bombardments had killed some of the older and more feeble missionaries. Many other missionaries who had fled from the Japanese to live deep in the jungle had found themselves cut off from quinine and had died of tropical fever. About twenty-five of the younger missionaries, including a few Americans, had been taken away by the Japanese, and it was feared that some of them had been put to death.

"Do you know anything about an American Marist missionary named Father James Hennessey?" I asked. "His brother is one of our Marines."

"I'm sorry to say Father Hennessey was one of those arrested by the Japanese," Father Coicand said. "They were particularly rough on him because he was an American. We have no idea of what has happened to him." (I learned later that Father Hennessey had been placed aboard a crowded prison ship which struck a mine and sank, leaving no survivors.)

The tradition of bravery and self-sacrifice was a longtime thing among the Marists of the Solomon Islands, Father Coicand told me. The first Marists came to the Solomons in 1845. They were the first missionaries to be seen on any of the Pacific islands, and the wild natives regarded them as deadly enemies. They killed them with tomahawks and then devoured their flesh. "The Solomons were known as the 'Savage Solomons' in those days, and for good reason," Father Coicand commented dryly.

Other Marist missionaries doggedly followed the early martyrs. Despite jungle diseases, malnutrition, and the perils they faced from both man-eating natives and man-eating sharks and crocodiles, they eventually managed to pacify the backward islands and build twelve flourishing missions. Because cannibal tribes traditionally treated their women as subhuman and unfit to leave the native compounds, the Marists were joined by missionary sisters from the Society of St. Mary. They worked to improve the status of the native women, taught them sanitation, and brought them and their children out to the missions and the mission schools. The work of the missionaries had gone unnoticed by the world at large, which knew the Solomons only as a vague and primitive outpost. When the islands were first discovered by Spanish explorers, the Spaniards decided that they formed the Biblical land of Ophir to which King Solomon sent his fleet to obtain gold. Hence, they named them for King Solomon. But the islands disgorged no gold after all—only coconuts and some rubber—and so their importance faded quickly in the public mind.

"The only contact we used to have with the outside world was an old steamer which came every six weeks with supplies and mail for the planters and for the missions," Father Coicand said. "Now, because of the war, the Solomons have exploded into world prominence and the most modern ships and airplanes have found their way out here. But the tragedy is that they have come only to destroy, and we are heartsick over the ruination of everything we have worked so hard and long to build up. The crocodiles and the wild man-eaters are still a problem in some parts of these islands, but compared to the weapons of war, they represent an insignificant menace indeed."

The searing heat of the jungle day was now beginning to have its effect on us, and at my urging Father Coicand and his confreres settled down in the huts for a siesta. The huts, which were built on stilts, looked very rickety to me, and I decided to do my napping in a sleeping bag beside a shade tree. I fell asleep amid dreams of those man-eaters Father Coicand talked about, and when my slumber was interrupted late in the day by a scratching sensation on my face, I awoke in a fright. I saw several pairs of baleful black eyes staring at me, and with a half-scream I leaped out of the sleeping bag. The crocodiles had come to get me!

Once on my feet, however, and in full command of my senses, I saw that the enemies who had invaded my sleep were not crocodiles or sharks but a horde of land crabs. They were ugly little creatures, but they were scarcely capable of ingesting a full-grown Navy chaplain, and I had to laugh at my own fit of panic. When two of the Sisters looked out of their hut to ask what had happened, I pointed to my pesky visitors. "I've had an education," I said. "Now I know why the natives build their homes on stilts!"

Major Clements and his scouts returned at night to

tell us they had not been able to make contact with the other missionaries. We would have to return for them another day. We then started on our arduous hike back to the place where we had moored our launch. The natives made stretchers out of blankets and bamboo sticks to carry some of the Sisters who were too weak to walk. We stopped three times to hide out in bushes when the rattling of the sticks by our advance scouts warned us that the Japanese were near. But we reached our boat and then got back to our camp at Lunga Point without incident.

Major Clements and his scouts began a new series of tom-tom messages, and in the next three days I made two more trips with them in the launch behind enemy lines. We brought out twenty more missionaries. Most were Catholic, but there were also a few Anglicans. The last one our scouts took us to was a tattered, emaciated nun who had been hiding in a mountain cave with two wild-haired native women. The cave was called "Cave of Gold" because it was once mistakenly believed to be the source of the mineral. The women had subsisted on scraps of food they had taken with them and on pieces of fruit they had managed to forage. Their shockingly gaunt appearance and the difficulty they had in moving around made it evident that they could not have remained in their hideout much longer without starving to death.

The nun told me her name was Sister Mary Edmee. She was the Mary Edmee from the Ruavatu Mission who had been out on a sick call when her confreres were dragged off to their doom. "Thank God, you're alive," I told her. "The natives from your mission had no idea what happened to you. They were afraid the Japanese had found you."

Like the other missionaries, Sister Mary Edmee took a bit of convincing before she deigned to accept my credentials as a priest. Despite her agonizing ordeal, she too was reluctant to leave because she said she had hopes of resuming her work at the mission.

"There's no possible chance of that until the fighting is over," I told her. I then recalled to her my own missionary experiences in China and stressed what Bishop O'Shea had told me in Kiangsi: "A dead missionary may be a martyr, but a live missionary can always come back to carry on his work another day." "Too many missionaries have become martyrs already, Sister," I told her. "We want you to live, to come back another day."

When we returned to Lunga with the last crop of missionaries and native girls, we found that a Navy transport had come into our harbor and could take the rescued group to New Caledonia. From there, they would make arrangements to return to their families. A large crowd of sailors and Marines rushed to the beach to gape at the native girls. They had been told that these girls wore no clothing, but they found to their chagrin that they had been chastely draped with muumuus. Bob Brumby, a former sports writer turned war correspondent for the United Press, was watching the scene with amusement. He turned to me and said with a wink, "Padre, this could have been a wonderful show—but those darned muumuus crabbed the act!"

The Sisters and priests were raised up the sides of the ship in basketlike rigs. Then they were helped into the ship's sick bay for treatment. Just as the rigs were going to be lowered again to pick up the native girls, the skipper got a report that Japanese planes were believed to be heading our way. Fearful of being caught in the harbor by the planes, he ordered huge cargo nets thrown over the sides for the girls. Squealing and screaming, the girls were hauled up en masse like a giant bunch of bananas. The minute they were dumped on deck, the ship lifted anchor and steamed out to sea. When the planes arrived, they came from the opposite direction and concentrated on pounding us on shore.

The rescue of the missionaries and the arrival of Army troops to help drive the Japanese back across the jungle made my Christmas on Guadalcanal a holiday of thanksgiving. I supervised the Seabees as they put up a new chapel tent; the old one had been ripped by so much shrapnel that it was in tatters. The furnishings in the new tent were what a decorator might describe as modern Japanese—the altar was made of Japanese wood and we used captured shells for candlesticks and flower vases.

On Christmas Eve, Marines and sailors headed in droves toward the tent for Midnight Mass. Barney Ross was feeling a little better, so he came limping over from the aid station to wish me a Merry Christmas. I showed Barney a new portable organ the Navy boys had brought over from Tulagi. "Who plays?" he wanted to know.

"That's the trouble," I explained. "We've got an organ, but no organist."

"Well, I'm available for the job," he said.

He explained that he could play a little, but was too weak as yet to push the pedals, so I assigned a sailor to that chore. Just before Mass, as Barney played Christmas carols and the boys sang, Washing Machine Charlie clattered overhead and even dropped a few bombs. We didn't take the usual precaution of running for the foxholes this time, though. To a man, we all decided that Charlie's aim would have to be bad on Christmas Eve—and it was!

After the Mass, I thanked Barney for his performance on the organ, and was surprised to see how moved he was. In a choked voice, he said he'd been thinking of his mother, and that he'd like to sing and play a song in her honor—"My Yiddishe Mama." "I know the tune," I told him, "and I'd like to accompany you."

I fished into my gear and found my violin. Seven hundred muddy, sweat-stained Marines and soldiers and a good number of Christian natives sat in silence—it seemed that the war itself stood still—as the Yiddish words of the old, familiar song sounded in that eerie jungle night. Then Barney sang it again, in English, as "My Wonderful Mama," and dedicated it to the mothers of all the boys who could not observe this Christmas Eve at home. When he finished, there were many tear-stained faces in the front rows, and no doubt many more hidden in the darkness beyond.

By New Year's Day the Japanese were well on the run, and Admiral Halsey sent orders that all of us who had been on the island for several months should leave and go to rest islands. I asked for and got permission to remain, however. I felt I ought to stay at my job until the fighting was all over. I was hopeful, too, that by remaining on the Canal, I might get a chance to see my little Patsy again.

On January 9, 1943, we captured the Japanese headquarters at Kokumbora. On February 9, six months after the 1st Marines landed on the island, Army General Patch, who had taken over from General Vandegrift, announced that organized enemy resistance had ended. Whatever remnants of Japanese troops had been left alive were taken off the island at night by their own ships.

Two days later, a young Navy lieutenant named Martin Merson, who had succeeded Cliffords as our Executive Officer, was assigned to go on a "junk" expedition at Point Esperance. He was to scour the debris the Japanese had left behind in their final, hasty exodus and see if he could pluck some valuable maps or plans from the rubbish that would help in our next invasion. I joined his party. We beached our craft at the Point, then went rummaging through a litter of smashed equipment that was strewn all over the beach. When we stopped for a break, we heard a rustling movement in the bush nearby. To our surprise, four Japanese soldiers —four more than were supposed to be still afoot on the island—popped into view. Our men reached for their rifles, but lowered them at Merson's command. The Japanese were staggering toward us; they were emaciated, exhausted, tattered, and unarmed.

With hands raised, the first three stumbled blindly into our boat as prisoners. The fourth man, their leader, collapsed at my feet. He was half-dead from starvation and covered with vermin. As I looked down on this last Japanese soldier to fight on Guadalcanal, one of the sailors called out, "Let him die there, Padre. Who needs him?"

I shook my head, bent over and picked him up. Then I carried him gingerly to the boat. Lieutenant Merson smiled thoughtfully at me. "For six months, the Japs have soaked this island in blood," he said. "Not only did they kill so many of your boys, but they massacred missionaries, women, and harmless natives, and nearly massacred your little Patsy Li. Yet when one of their poor devils falls on his face in front of you, you pick him up —lice and all—and tote him like a baby. I salute you, Padre. You really do love your enemies!"

The next day, I was given firm orders to leave the island for a rest period in New Caledonia. At the same time, I was notified that President Roosevelt had awarded me the Legion of Merit for my part in the rescue of the missionaries, and Admiral Halsey had awarded me a citation for helping to save lives under enemy shellfire and air attacks. I would also receive a Presidential Unit citation which was being presented to all men of the 1st Marine Division and its supporting echelons.

This unexpected sprinkling of kudos left me dizzier than the effects of a malarial attack. When I saw some of the newspaper correspondents approach my tent, I threw up my hands and said, "All right, boys, you don't have to say it. You want to know what sort of pantywaist war we're running when we start handing out medals to a sky pilot who probably doesn't even know which end of a gun the bullets come from!"

Bob Brumby, the leader of the contingent, laughed and said, "Well, we'll give you that speech another time. Right now, we've got an award of our own to make to the Padre of Guadalcanal." Then he handed me a scroll which read as follows:

Award of the D.F.C. (Distinguished Friendship Cross)

It has come to our attention since the early days of the Battle of Guadalcanal until the present that Father Gehring is the swellest guy on the island. The Padre was continually doing something for us—in fact so generously that often we suffered embarrassment in so frequently accepting his kindnesses. More important, his good cheer and his companionship were an inspiration and a joy to all the correspondents. And we know what his presence on this island battlefield has meant to all the men with whom he has come in contact.

Therefore, on this day, upon his leave-taking, we hereby award to Father Frederic P. Gehring the D.F.C., and wish him the heartiest good luck, good health, and God-speed.

It was signed by the members of the Guadalcanal Press Club, including Brumby, Bill Hipple of the Associated Press, Boo Miller of United Press, Winston Triont of the *Sydney Sun,* Douglas Gardner of the *Sydney Morning Herald,* Robert Cromie of the *Chicago Tribune,* John G. Dowling of the *Chicago Sun,* Henry Keys of the *London Express,* Allan Jackson of International News Photos, Ralph Morse of *Life,* and "Bocky" Bockhurst of "News of the Day" Newsreels.

I was so moved by the spirit behind this award that I stammered like a schoolboy in trying to express my thanks. As the correspondents crowded around to shake hands and say good-by, I managed to smile weakly and say, "To get something like this from a supposedly hard-bitten group of cynics is equivalent to climbing Everest. I feel like bawling—but lucky for you, I bawled so much when I had to give my little Patsy away that I'm all cried out!"

My two gallant Hollywood favorites, Gene Markey and Robert Montgomery, left with me on the plane for New Caledonia. When we reached our rest hostel, the insidious aftereffects of life in a jungle hell-hole struck us down like a row of ninepins. I was felled by dengue fever germs I apparently had been carrying around with me, Gene was toppled by backwater fever contracted on a dangerous spying mission to islands adjoining the Solomons, and Bob was laid low with malaria.

There would be more islands for me before Japan would be ready to throw in the sponge—islands like Woodlark, Buna, and New Guinea, where I would witness more courage, more tragedy, more disease, and more death. But after Guadalcanal, it was in a sense anticlimax, because it was on Guadalcanal that our Pacific war was won. On that brooding, ninety-mile stretch of jungle, mountains, and volcanic ash, we bought precious time with blood; we tasted bitter defeat and yet came back from the lip of disaster to push the Japanese into the sea. Here, under the most noxious conditions of terrain and climate, American boys who had been scorned as soft, luxury-loving whimperers gave the lie to all the disparaging things that had been said about them, and showed they had the spark of valor and determination that would save the free world.

Letters
from
a
Mother

8

After the war ended, I found myself on a Navy transport assigned to ferry troops back from the Pacific to California, and also to bring out supplies to occupation units that would remain in Japan, and on the Pacific islands. I now had a good deal of time to catch up on my letters, most of which came from and went to my fellow Guadalcanal survivors. We had formed—as men who have gone through great travail together frequently do—a kind of alumni society. I found myself acting as the core of the alumni group, with many of my boys relying on me to supply them with news about other comrades who did not keep in touch with them directly.

One thread ran continually through all our letters: Patsy Li. The little girl who had unexpectedly fallen into our circle in the middle of a war remained a vivid memory to us three and a half years later.

I had no real answers, however, when the boys kept writing: "What do you hear about Patsy?" I had been able to get only one communication from Père Jean in regard to the child. All I learned from this was that she had been taken to the orphanage on the island of Efate, as per the original plan, and that she was "all right." Just what "all right" meant, I didn't know.

From Anne Kafka Lemanski, an Army nurse who had been stationed in the New Hebrides and who had visited the Efate orphanage, I learned that Patsy had experienced many nightmares during her first weeks with the Sisters. She was frightened by every passing airplane, for they awoke memories of the bombardments she had lived through on Guadalcanal. When an Army unit was stationed on Efate, she at first lived in fear of the soldiers. This, of course, was similar to what she had gone through when she first saw the armed Marines who visited my tent. She had learned to accept the Marines as friends, but since our soldiers wore different uniforms, she apparently associated them with the Japanese soldiers who had attacked her. Indeed, when she saw soldiers with bayonets passing one day, she cried hysterically, and via gestures and pantomime showed how terrible things had been done to her and those around her by men with bayonets.

The nurse told me, however, that the Sisters had been giving Patsy special attention, as promised, and that after the first few weeks, the child's emotional condition began to show improvement. A little orphan boy who had attached himself to Patsy proved helpful in soothing her during her outbreaks of hysteria. She seemed to enjoy his company and that of other children. There were about twenty youngsters in the orphanage huts, and each day they were taken by truck to the mission school a mile away. Patsy was going with the others. Her teachers noticed that she had a keen mind, but also showed a streak of obstinacy and a tendency toward tantrums.

Mrs. Lemanski's report was necessarily sketchy since she hadn't spent much time at the orphanage. Besides, her visit was made in 1943, and I had no idea how Patsy had developed since then. It was difficult to get detailed information from the Sisters. They were overwhelmed with work and responsibility at the orphanage and school (many other youngsters besides the orphans attended the school), and had no time to send long letters to a far-off Navy chaplain, whose interest in one of their children was a sentimental one, not a legal one.

I had thought of trying to correspond directly with the youngster. But then I realized that the Sisters were French, and that the language the child was learning in school was obviously French. I could write to her in English, German, or Mandarin, and I had some command of Latin, but the language of La Belle France was beyond my capabilities.

The absence of detailed information about Patsy was

particularly frustrating to me because I could not down a queasy sense of guilt that I had abandoned her.

I knew, of course, that I had done the right thing in commending her to the care of Père Jean and the Sisters. I knew that it was important to get her out of a combat zone, and that it would have been utterly impossible for me to take her along on my different assignments after I left Guadalcanal. The Navy would never have permitted such a thing even if I had been foolish enough to entertain the thought. But knowing something intellectually and convincing oneself of the same thing emotionally are two different things. I could not black out the memory of that tear-streaked, terrified little face, or the sound of Patsy's shrieks as she was being taken bodily away from me.

The promise I had made Patsy that day—"If you ever need my help, you will have it"—had been made impulsively, but it was a promise I faithfully intended to keep. I regarded it as sacred, even if Patsy had not understood a syllable of what I was saying. I was also determined that I would see Patsy again some day, probably when I returned to mission work and could arrange another assignment to the Far East. I even had grandiose thoughts that I might somehow arrange for the child to come for a visit to America someday, and be a guest of honor at a meeting of our Guadalcanal "Alumni Society."

On the afternoon in the spring of 1946 when my ship docked at San Francisco, I checked in at the offices of the 12th Naval District and was told that there was an urgent message for me to get in touch with Cardinal

Spellman in New York City. The Cardinal was then head of the Military Ordinariate, in charge of Catholic chaplains.

When my call was put through, I got a surprising message. A woman in far-off Singapore named Mrs. Ruth Li had, after all this time, come upon Foster Hailey's story in *The New York Times* about my discovery of Patsy Li. She had had a child with the same name —Patsy Li—who had been lost in the waters off Singapore at the beginning of the war. When she saw the Navy picture which had been published with Hailey's story, she had studied it carefully and decided there was a resemblance to her own Patsy. Admittedly, it was hard to tell, for the *Times* picture had shown a child's face contorted by sobs and partially covered with bandages. Mrs. Li had written to the Red Cross asking if I could tell her whether the war waif I had cared for could possibly be her child. The Red Cross had in turn directed the letter to the Military Ordinariate and asked them to check my whereabouts.

"The child can't possibly be hers, because the name I gave my 'Pao-Pei' on Guadalcanal was made up out of my head," I told New York. I took down Mrs. Li's address in Singapore and immediately wrote her a letter which explained how Patsy came to us and how I had invented a fictitious name for the little girl.

"I was very sorry to learn of the tragic loss of your youngster," I wrote Mrs. Li, "but of course, this could not be the same child. It's simply a matter of coincidence that I gave her the same name as your child."

Not long afterward, I went back to sea again and put

the incident out of my mind. But it was not to die so easily. When our transport docked in Hawaii, there was a shipment of mail waiting for us. Included in it was another letter from Mrs. Li.

"Perhaps," she suggested, "the child who was brought to you on Guadalcanal mumbled the name Patsy Li in her delirium. Perhaps that name stuck in your mind and came to you when you were in the foxhole with your Marines and decided to give the child a regular name."

I wrote, saying gently but firmly for the second time that Mrs. Li was undoubtedly mistaken. The child, I pointed out, had mumbled nothing whatever when she was brought to me, for she was unconscious. She had never, I added, given me any indication of what her real name might be, for she had been in a traumatic state and had not talked at all.

The child, I agreed, was Chinese rather than Melanese, but a number of Chinese families had lived on Guadalcanal before the war. They had worked on copra plantations and no doubt moved into the little native villages after the Japanese took over the island and arrested their overseers. The child must have come from one of those families.

On my next trip back to San Francisco, there was still another letter from Mrs. Li. This one was an amazingly long and detailed personal history, as gripping and heartbreaking a human story as I had ever read. For Mrs. Li, despite what I had written her, still refused to accept the idea that my little Patsy could not be *her* little Patsy. In fact, she was becoming increasingly convinced that the two were one and the same—a matter of mother's intuition, she explained. She wanted me to know everything about her child, including the child's upbringing and family background, and everything that had led up to her loss. In this way, Mrs. Li hoped that I might recall something in the face, the personality, and the behavior of the girl we had saved on Guadalcanal that could identify her with the girl last seen off Singapore.

Ruth Li was (from her picture) a petite and attractive woman. She was the oldest of six children and came from a well-to-do, highly cultured Chinese family. Her father had been one of China's most distinguished eye doctors. He had received his college education in the United States at the University of Pennsylvania, and his medical training and internship at St. John's Medical College in Shanghai. He had subsequently set up practice in Canton, where Ruth was born, then moved his family to Peking, where for ten years he served as ophthalmologist at a medical college financed by the Rockefeller Foundation. Later, he moved to Shanghai. He had wanted all his children to be physicians, and only Ruth disappointed him. Three of her sisters and her only brother had become doctors. Her brother and one of her sisters, Katherine, had also married doctors.

Ruth went to the University of Shanghai, where she studied economics. In her senior year, she began keeping company with Dah Chiao Li, her classmate. Her father opposed the relationship because he felt Li did not measure up to Ruth's proud family heritage. When

Ruth graduated, her father tried to send her away for advanced study in the United States, but instead she married Li and took a job teaching at the Shanghai Municipal Council Primary School. (This was in 1933, and I suddenly remembered that I had been taken on a brief visit to a primary school in Shanghai that year. Could I have passed Ruth Li in the corridor? Could I even have exchanged a greeting with her?)

Ruth gave up teaching when Patsy was born. The child was a pretty youngster, she said, though somewhat different in appearance from her petite mother. She was also very bright and personable, and made friends easily. Patsy was still a toddler when the Lis moved to the British Crown Colony of Singapore. D. C. Li—as he was usually called—had gone into the insurance business in Shanghai, and his firm wanted him to head a Singapore branch office. When Patsy was four, the couple had another child, whom they named Lottie. Both Ruth and her husband spoke English fluently. They frequently spoke English, as well as their native Cantonese, at home.

In November, 1941, D. C. Li had to go to Shanghai on business. Ruth was anxious to visit her father, who had suffered a stroke, so she and the children accompanied her husband on the two-thousand-mile trip. By the time they were ready to leave for home, new war clouds were gathering over Asia. Businessmen leaving Shanghai were jamming the passenger lists of all outgoing ships, and D. C. Li found it difficult to book passage for his family.

"The children and I will stay here in Shanghai for

the time being, since the situation is becoming dangerous and since passage for us is so difficult," Ruth Li told
her husband. "We'll join you in Singapore later on."

He insisted, however, that the family sail together.
"If worst comes to worst and we are attacked at sea, then
let us all go down together," he said.

He finally was able to make arrangements for Ruth
and the children to leave Shanghai with him on a British vessel. They sailed on December 4, 1941. On December 7 they were off Saigon, and there the captain
heard the report on the ship's radio that Pearl Harbor
had been attacked and that the Japanese were at war
with America and the British Empire.

"Ordinarily, it takes one day from Saigon to Singapore, but this time it took us three days and nights,"
Ruth Li recalled to me. "We went very slowly and traveled a zigzag course. At night, we were completely
blacked out. I was terrified by all this. I had always had
a great fear of the water. I had never learned to swim.
As a girl, growing up, I had never gone rowboating or
canoeing because I was afraid of small boats. The
thought that our ship might be bombed and that I
might have to get into a small lifeboat with my children
filled me with horror. I could not wait to get my feet
on solid ground again. And I vowed that if I did get
back safely on land, I would never venture out to sea
again as long as there was any possible danger of attack."

When the Lis docked in Singapore harbor, they
found a city overwhelmed by terror and panic. The two
giant British warships, the *Prince of Wales* and the
Repulse, which were the chief naval weapons of the sea-

port fortress, had just been sunk by Japanese bombers. The Japanese also had begun a land attack down the Malay peninsula, aimed at Singapore. Their planes had ripped up the principal British airfields on the peninsula, and they had heavily bombed Singapore's airport.

"I found that our beautiful home was crowded with people—friends of ours who lived near the airport where the heavy bombardments had taken place," Mrs. Li remembered. "They had to get out of their houses, and since our home was a large one and was some distance from the airport, they thought they could be safe there."

As the Japanese air attacks increased, and as the Japanese infantry continued to move down the Malay peninsula, British families began to leave Singapore and many of the Lis' friends left also. D. C. Li now began insisting that his family evacuate the city, too, before the invaders came. But Ruth refused to budge.

"If I must die, let me die on land," she told him. "I told you I would never go out on the water again, as long as there is danger. I fear the sea more than anything else. If I were to die at sea, I would come back and haunt you for the rest of your days."

He argued that the evacuation ships that were going out were going as part of a convoy and that they would be afforded some protection by warships. "What good will these warships be against the Japanese planes?" Ruth asked him. She pointed out that the biggest British warships of all—the *Prince of Wales* and the *Repulse* —had not been able to save themselves, let alone protect unarmed merchant and passenger ships.

Japanese air raids on Singapore began to mount in intensity. The Lis had built an air-raid shelter underneath their garden, and when the warning sirens sounded, they would race to the shelter and stay there until the all-clear sounded. One bomb dug a crater in their backyard not very far from where their shelter was located. The impact of other bombs crashing down into neighborhood streets nearby would smash windows in their home and send dishes and glasses flying across their kitchen and dining room. During night attacks, they would have to rouse the children out of their beds, run frantically to the shelter and huddle with them in the damp, cold subterranean chamber, sometimes for hours.

The air attacks sent both Patsy and baby Lottie into hysterics. "I had to preserve an icy control of myself in order to calm the children," Ruth Li told me. "Believe me, I was a mass of raw nerves, and I can't tell you how many times I came close to breaking down completely. But I knew that if *I* showed signs of hysteria, the children would have no strength whatever to lean on. I had to appear composed for their sakes. I was able to do it because I have always been a strong, determined person, with an unusual amount of self-discipline and a firm dedication to certain standards. I inherited this from my father. In appearance I resemble my mother, but in personal characteristics I have always been closer to my father than to any other member of my family."

One day in January 1942, while Patsy was visiting a friend's house, the Japanese made the most devastating of all their raids on Singapore. The downtown section

was literally torn apart by blockbuster after blockbuster, and the explosions sent giant columns of smoke
billowing up over the city and across the Straits of
Johore. The moment the air raid ended, Ruth dashed
out of her shelter and went to the friend's house looking for her child. The house was empty, and Mrs. Li
noticed with alarm that bombs had struck close by, de-
stroying several homes. She ran up and down the street
shouting for Patsy, fearing the worst. Just then, the
youngster popped out of a nearby shelter with a group
of friends. None of them had been hurt.

The British had always expected that the dense jun-
gles on Malay would swallow up any invader who tried
to reach Singapore by the land route, but this turned
out to be a serious mistake. The Japanese, commanded
by General Tomoyuki Yamashita, had extensive training in jungle warfare. They wore very light uniforms,
carried light equipment, and knew how to slip through
the heavy brush swiftly and quietly. They would steal
around the back of fixed British positions, then suddenly surround the defenders and throw them into
chaos. The British were not trained for night fighting
and the Japanese were. This had a decisive effect on the
outcome of the fighting. While the British were resting
at night, the Japs would infiltrate their lines and would
have their guns at the defenders' throats before they
realized what was happening to them.

The Japanese Twenty-fifth Army, which carried the
main brunt of the attack through Malay, also outnumbered the defenders and had a tremendous amount
of aerial support. Japanese air bases had been set up

just north of the Malay border and their planes flew just ahead of their infantry columns to blow up British ammunition dumps and cause devastation along the entire British front line.

The day-in, day-out nightmare grew worse when the British and Australian troops were thrown out of Kuala Lumpur and began to retreat toward Singapore itself. On January 31, they retreated across the Straits of Johore and blew up the causeway linking Singapore island with the mainland. The Japanese closed in on the Straits and began to shell Singapore across the narrow stretch of water. So now the residents found themselves menaced by ground artillery as well as by attacks from the air.

Strangely enough, D. C. Li, as well as the other businessmen of the city—or at least those who hadn't been evacuated—kept going to their offices in the usual manner each day. They would, of course, seek shelter during raids, but otherwise they would pursue their regular business duties as though the enemy were far off in the hinterlands instead of knocking at their front doors. In this British Crown City, the leaders of commerce still clung to the old British attitude of "Chins up, everybody, let's not get too disturbed about what's going on." Despite all the evidence at hand that irresistible Japanese power was about to engulf them, they were still deluding themselves with the old bromide that Singapore was impregnable to any attacker.

D. C. Li himself, however, had no illusions that Singapore could be saved. He had again begun to insist that Ruth and the children join him in getting passage on some ship leaving the city. Ruth continued to refuse. "Another characteristic that I inherited from my father is stubbornness," she told me. "As a matter of fact, my Patsy has that quality, too."

The arguments between Mrs. Li and her husband became more and more heated as more of their friends took to the escape route by sea, and as the defenses of their city kept getting steadily weaker.

On February 7, the first contingent of Japanese invaders swarmed across the Straits of Johore. Ruth Li was a member of the Singapore YWCA Committee, which decided after a hasty meeting that as many families as possible should take refuge in a French convent. The Lis brought over a few possessions and as much food as they could carry. Other families did the same. The YWCA Committee felt that if many families lived together in a group at the convent it would provide some kind of security against enemy atrocities.

They were extremely fearful of what the Japanese invaders would do to the women of the community, particularly members of the upper-class Chinese families whom the Japanese hated with special venom. The "Rape of Nanking" was very much on the mind of these Singapore women. In that infamous episode, the Japanese sacked and looted the city after capturing it; then they battered down homes and doors to criminally attack women of all ages.

On the afternoon of February 13, 1942, D. C. Li came to the convent from his office and waved some papers at his wife. "I just bought passage for us to leave with the children on an Australian ship," he said. "Hurry and pack whatever you can. The ship will sail in a few hours. I think it'll be the last evacuation ship out of the city."

Ruth Li looked at him in disbelief and dismay. "I couldn't believe that after all the arguments we had had about evacuation, and after I had told him so many times that I would rather submit to the worst dangers on land than risk the horror of a bombing at sea, that he would still go ahead and arrange for us to evacuate," she recalled. She protested this plan, as she had done before, but this time her husband refused to listen to her arguments. He insisted that their ship would be safe and would have protection, whereas if they remained in Singapore the Japanese would surely kill them all.

"I decided finally, and with heavy heart, that we would go," Mrs. Li told me. "If I still refused to leave and made him stay with us in Singapore, I would hold myself accountable for his life. If the Japanese were indeed to kill us after capturing the city, his blood would be on my hands. By the same token, when I decided I would sail with my husband, I told him very plainly that I would hold *him* responsible if anything happened to us at sea. He agreed to this, and we began to gather our things together."

The Lis packed two suitcases with the help of their servants, who, incidentally, refused to go along with them. Then they hired a car to drive them to the pier where the S.S. *Kuala,* a ship of Australian registry, was getting ready to sail. A second ship was going to leave at the same time. These were to be the last Allied ships to sail from Singapore harbor until after the war ended.

Just as the Lis approached the pier, the air-raid siren

began to screech, and enemy planes appeared overhead. Bombs fell thick and fast near the *Kuala*. People scattered from the pier in all directions. One bomb landed on the pier, blowing part of it sky-high. While running from the dock to take cover with their sobbing children, the Lis dropped the suitcases, which contained all their essential belongings. When the air raid ended, they searched frantically, but the pier was in such chaos that they could not find them.

When the Lis prepared to board the *Kuala*, they were told that except for a few officials, only women and children were to be taken aboard this ship. The men, including D. C. Li, were separated from their wives and put aboard a smaller ship, the *Tien Kwang*. Like the *Kuala*, the *Tien Kwang* was an auxiliary merchant ship which the British government had taken over in the emergency from a petroleum company.

Once on board her evacuation ship, Ruth Li found swarms of British women and a smaller number of Chinese women and children milling about. The British women were wives of British Army and Air Force officers, and nurses from the Singapore General Hospital. One nurse had been killed in the air raid, and funeral services were held on deck for her before sailing. It was a grim way to start a sea voyage—particularly a voyage that Ruth Li was undertaking only with the gravest of doubts and trepidations.

Because the vessel was so overcrowded, there was no room for many of the evacuees in the passenger section of the ship. The ship's captain didn't want any of them sitting on deck where they would attract the attention of

Japanese planes, so Ruth Li and a number of fellow passengers were ordered to go down into the hold near the furnace. Before she went down, she took one last look at her city. Dense smoke from rubber-processing plants that were being sabotaged to keep them from falling intact to the enemy billowed so high in the air they blacked out the sun. Intermingled with the smoke were the flames leaping from buildings that had been struck by Japanese artillery shells. Ruth Li shuddered. Then she led her children quickly down the steps.

There were only a few chairs in the hold, so Mrs. Li and her children had to sit on the floor. It was beastly hot. There were no vents to allow fresh air to come in, and no water or food was available. There was only a small washroom, and because of the crowds that were using it, the place soon became filthy. After a while, something went wrong with the plumbing and the toilet facilities would not work.

The stench in the hold became unbearable. Children began to throw up on the floor. Others cried pitifully for food or bottles of milk. When one person left a chair for a moment, four or five others would squabble angrily over it. The ship did not leave port until 6:30 P.M., and then some sailors came down and distributed biscuits. A woman walked away from a canvas chair, and Mrs. Li took it temporarily so she could keep baby Lottie on her lap and feed her. When the woman came back, she pushed Mrs. Li off the chair and upbraided her for having sat there. When she found crumbs from the biscuit on the chair, she shook a fist at Patsy and Lottie and called them foul names.

"I would not descend to her level in turn," Mrs. Li told me. "I simply said to her that at a time like this one would expect understanding on the part of people. After all, there was a good chance none of us would live to see the morning."

9

After a sleepless, tortured night, two members of the ship's crew came down to the hold and told the women they could go up on deck to wash and get a drink of water. Glad to escape the sweltering, fetid chamber, Ruth Li hurried up the stairs with her children. "They were covered with grime," she recalled. "They needed to be fumigated, rather than just washed. Looking at them made me feel ill. I had always prided myself on my cleanliness, and our servants had kept our home in Singapore so spick-and-span that people would say it was dustproof and germproof. I knew that these were emergency conditions and that I would have to adapt myself to things I would never tolerate under ordinary peacetime circumstances. But still I could not put aside my deep feelings of vexation, even disgust, at conditions on the ship."

On deck, Mrs. Li was astonished to find that her ship had dropped anchor. It had sailed only about seventy miles during the night, because the mines strewn in Singapore harbor and along the sea approaches leading to the harbor had made it necessary for the ship to move at a snail's pace. It had gone through the Singapore Straits, then south and along the Riouw Archipelago. It was then supposed to continue down to the Java Sea and head eastward toward Australia.

Nearby, Mrs. Li could see a network of small islands which apparently were uninhabited. The *Tien Kwang*, carrying her husband and the various British and Chinese officials and business leaders, had anchored about a half-mile behind the *Kuala*. To the left of the *Kuala* she could see a third ship. She saw with horror that this ship was partially wrecked and seemed to have been abandoned. Obviously, it had been bombed by enemy aircraft a day or two before, which meant that an umbrella of Japanese planes was covering the sea lanes leading out of Singapore. They had no intention of letting evacuation ships enjoy a free passage to other countries, even if they carried no war supplies and were not armed.

Ruth Li threaded her way through the crowd on deck to seek out a ship's officer. When she found one, she immediately demanded information about the

Father Gehring introduces Patsy to her new schoolmates at Walsingham in the spring term of 1951.

Patsy and Father Gehring admire the many Christmas gifts which awaited her in New York, where she was a guest of the Vanderbilt Hotel.

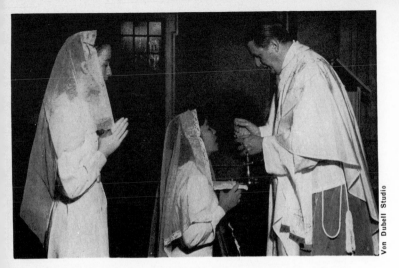

(*Above*) At Walsingham, on the Feast of Corpus Christi, Father Gehring administers to Patsy her First Holy Communion. She was baptized on the same day.

(*Below*) Patsy Li and her Japanese roommate at Gwenyd Mercy Junior College, to which Patsy was awarded a scholarship, ask permission to go out.

Patsy and her bridegroom, Joe Lee, leave St. Thomas the Apostle Church in Washington, D.C., after their wedding, which was performed by Father Gehring on May 12, 1962.

Patsy, photographed in Miss Bumgardner's Washington home.

wrecked ship, and he admitted that it had been bombed by the Japanese. "All the fears which had impelled me to say I would never leave Singapore by sea, no matter what the crisis on land, had now been confirmed to me," she said. "I was sure that the absolute worst was going to happen to Lottie, Patsy, and myself, and I felt a surge of bitterness toward my husband for having forced me to leave our city when I wanted above all else to stay where we were."

While Ruth was washing the children, she heard the ominous drone of airplane motors. A few moments later, planes flew high over the ship. Ruth froze, waiting for the bombs to fall, but the planes kept on going until they were out of sight.

"Although these planes went by us, I was sure it was only a question of time before they or other planes came back and did their worst," she said. "I felt it was of crucial importance that the women and children be taken off the boat immediately and rowed to one of the small islands. This would save us from the attack that was bound to come."

Sailors began to lower some of the *Kuala's* small boats. However, instead of calling women and children to be helped into the boats, a contingent of the sailors got in instead. Two officers of the ship were directing the operation, and Mrs. Li and another woman went up to them and demanded to know why they weren't putting women and children aboard and rowing them to a safe haven. One of the officers—who they were told was the captain—said he had not been able to make out whether the planes that passed were Japanese, British,

American, or Dutch. He said they were probably reconnaissance planes. As a precautionary measure, he was sending the sailors to a nearby island to cut branches. They were to bring the branches back and use them to camouflage the ship.

Mrs. Li said it would be far better to get the passengers off the ship than send sailors out for camouflage materials that had questionable value. The captain told her, however, that there was a bad current in the Straits and that it would be too risky to try to get passengers ashore. Mrs. Li felt this explanation was ridiculous.

"If the sailors can row ashore to get branches, despite the current, why can't the women and children be rowed ashore on the same boats?" she wanted to know. She got no satisfactory answer, she said. She felt, too, that if the ship was not going to unload its passengers, it should sail on, instead of waiting like a sitting duck for the enemy to strike from above. She also believed that it was naïve for the ship's officers to think that the reconnaissance planes might have been friendly, and that they might not be in any danger.

As she pointed out to me, "We had the appalling example of the wrecked ship staring us in the face and warning us that the Japanese controlled the air in these parts and were determined to destroy us. How could any sea captain delude himself into thinking that he was not facing the most extreme emergency and that he shouldn't bother to get us off his ship?

"Our position was already known to the reconnaissance planes, so what was the point of wasting time on camouflage? Besides, a covering of branches would hardly fool an airplane into thinking we were just part of the forest. Since we were anchored in the water, it would be perfectly obvious to even the most inexperienced pilot that what was down below was a ship and nothing else. The men in charge of the ship were playing God with our lives, and I felt they were offering us up as a human sacrifice."

When the sailors came back with the branches, the decks were ordered cleared. Ruth Li returned with her children to the torrid hold. Again, there was nothing to eat but some hard biscuits. Baby Lottie began to cry, and her mother rocked her in her arms to soothe her. Patsy complained bitterly of the stifling atmosphere, and said her stomach was so empty she felt as if she had a "hole" there. Ruth Li prayed to herself that the ship's officers would be proved right in their judgment, even though she still felt convinced that they were making the most tragic kind of blunder.

At eleven o'clock, Ruth Li again heard the growl of motors overhead. More planes were coming! This time, the noise was so loud she instinctively clapped her hands over her ears to shut it out—and realized at once that these planes were flying at a much lower altitude than the earlier flight.

Suddenly, there was a catastrophic burst of thunder and the whole ship seemed to heave wildly up out of the water. Mrs. Li and her children were flung across the floor. Stunned, she looked up to see the engine room explode in a sheet of orange flame that devoured all the women who had been sitting close to that section of the hold. The *Kuala* was being bombed by Japanese planes, and one of the first bombs to fall had scored a direct hit on the ship's engine room.

For a few minutes, Ruth lay prostrate. She opened her mouth to cry and no words came out. She couldn't move her arms or legs. Her whole body felt numb. The impact of the explosion had paralyzed her temporarily.

Over the screams of the wounded and the dying and the clamor of survivors pushing their way up the stairs, Ruth heard the sobs of her own two children. Their cries acted as a powerful stimulant to bring her out of her state of terror and shock, and prod her into doing something to save her family. Slowly, she forced herself up off the floor. Her nerves were tingling again and her sensations were returning, bringing with them a feeling of grinding pain.

She picked up baby Lottie and held her tight in her arms. Then she extended a hand to the hysterical Patsy and said, "Stop crying now, Patsy. We're going to get off this ship and go back to land. We're going to be all right."

Her face smeared and her hair wildly disheveled, Ruth Li hurried to the stairs. The ghastly sight of women lying on the floor cruelly burned or rolling over and over in agony made her feel so faint she nearly keeled over again. She bit her lip hard, turned her face away from the horror around her, and edged her way up the stairs.

On deck, she saw a mass of flame and smoke. People were shouting and running in wild confusion. There were more bodies strewn about, some of them badly mutilated. She circled around the bodies and picked her way over mounds of debris toward the railing of the ship. She walked very carefully lest she trip and drop her baby.

Some of the British nurses were at the railing. They began to take off their shoes and dive into the water. Apparently, they meant to fight the current and try to swim to shore. One of the nurses who was getting ready to dive overboard noticed her and called out, "Can you swim?" Ruth Li shook her head. She also pointed to her children, to indicate that she couldn't possibly take them into the water with her even if she could swim.

"Go to the other end of the deck," the nurse told her. "They're putting a rope ladder down, and they're trying to lower a few boats, too."

Mrs. Li began walking to the other end of the deck, holding baby Lottie in her left arm while clutching Patsy's hand and leading her with her right hand. Suddenly, she heard airplane motors again, and she cowered against a post, holding her children tight against her. The Japanese dive-bombers had come back and were swooping low over the burning ship. Their machine-guns chattered angrily, and bullets spattered up and down the deck. She saw a sailor throw his hands up and topple over and heard others cry out in pain. The machine-gun fire was also spraying the water around the boat. Some of the swimmers who were desperately trying to reach shore were struck by bullets and drowned.

"Animals! Savages!" Ruth Li cried at the planes overhead. "Of course, nobody could hear me," she told me, "yet I had to scream. I had to give voice to my feelings. My screams were my hopeless way of protesting against this despicable murder of innocent people. Why, according to the rules of warfare, you are not even supposed to kill enemy soldiers when you find them unarmed and defenseless, yet here these airplanes were cold-bloodedly massacring not soldiers, but women and children.

"It was hard for me to accept the fact that what was happening in front of my eyes was real. I come from a cultured, very intelligent, and highly proper family. I had never known violence of any kind throughout my entire life. Because of my father's profession and the interest of our family in medicine, I had been conditioned to think of human life as precious, something that one does everything possible to preserve and protect against harm and illness. Yet I had been thrown into a situation where human life seemed meaningless and worthless; where violence was breaking out all around me, and where I was witnessing acts of barbarism that seemed utterly inconceivable for anyone calling himself a human being to commit. I felt that even gorillas and hyenas would not act this way. Hatred of other people has never been part of my makeup, but when I saw those swimmers being killed in the water, I felt such loathing for the men in those planes I wanted their planes and their own bodies to be blown apart into a thousand pieces. I felt they did not belong in civilization."

When the dive bombers had gone, Mrs. Li continued on to the section of the deck where the rope ladder had been lowered. A sailor helped her and her children to the top of the railing so she could get on the ladder and descend to the water. She told Patsy to start down the ladder first while she followed immediately after her, still holding baby Lottie in her left arm while gripping the rungs of the rope with her right hand.

Other passengers, frantic to get off the doomed ship, came down the ladder after Ruth. Their weight was heavy on the rope and it began to sway dangerously. "Be careful," Ruth shouted.

As Patsy reached the bottom of the rope, just at the level of the water, her mother saw a suitcase floating by. She pushed Patsy toward it, thinking it would keep her safe until she was picked up. "Hold on to the suitcase and do not let it go," she instructed the girl. Patsy grabbed hold of the suitcase and drifted off.

The weight of the other passengers pushing their way down from the top of the ladder made it sway sharply again. Mrs. Li felt the rope slipping out of her hands. Suddenly, it was gone. With a startled cry, she was swept under water. She lost her hold on Lottie as she went down, and the infant was crushed under the impact of other passengers falling off the overloaded ropes on top of her.

"When I found myself under water, I did not struggle at all," Ruth Li told me. "Since I could not swim, I felt I was doomed to perish and that there was nothing to do but accept my fate. But I shot up again, and perhaps because I had not tried to thrash around, I came up close to the lifeline and reached out instinctively to seize it."

Dazed, she clung motionless to the rope for a few moments. Then she remembered the children.

"Lottie! Patsy!" she screamed. Lottie had not come up. Patsy had vanished.

"I lost my children!" Ruth Li shrieked at heads that bobbed around in the water. "Please God, find them! I can't swim!"

Two of the swimmers obediently dived under, but they couldn't find anything. Then the fast current took them away from the ship.

"Find Lottie! Find Patsy!" Ruth Li cried hysterically. But now her shouts were drowned out by the roar of an enemy plane returning for yet another machine-gun pass at the survivors of the bombed ship. Ruth clung desperately to the rope while the heads in the water around her disappeared below the surface to escape the spitting cones of fire. She was still clinging to the rope, and to life, when a wooden shape loomed up out of the water.

It was a lifeboat, one of the few the crew of the *Kuala* had been able to float. A man reached out, grabbed Ruth Li, and pulled her into the boat. "My children are drowning! Jump in and save them!" she cried. He pushed her toward the back of the boat. "We'll pick up everybody who's out in the water," he assured her.

He scoured the water, but reported that there were no children in sight. "Maybe another boat picked them up," he said. Other survivors were climbing into the boat now, and when they heard what had happened to Mrs. Li's children, they tried to soothe the distraught woman. "There are a couple of other lifeboats out, and maybe one of them picked your children up," they said, echoing the crewman in charge of the boat.

"There are some boats and rafts out from the *Tien Kwang*, too," somebody told her. "Maybe one of them could have picked up your youngsters."

"I don't think so," Ruth Li answered. She begged the crewman in charge to row the lifeboat all around the ship so she could look for her children. He shook his head. "We've got to get out of here and get you ashore," he said. "The way the ship is burning it may go down any minute, and if we're too close to it we'll be swept under."

The crew began to row toward the nearest island, which was about a third of a mile away. On the way, it picked up a few swimmers, but the boat was so crowded that the sailors soon had to wave off other swimmers who wanted to be picked up. "You'll make the shore without our help; you're practically there," the crewman in charge called out to encourage them. Some had lifebelts and did manage to make it to shore. Others were carried by the strong current to other islands. And some drifted out past the islands, never to be seen again.

Pieces of wreckage and luggage from their ship floated by them, along with dismembered and mutilated bodies. A raft swerved close to their boat. It was so crowded it tilted dangerously down at one side. Mrs. Li saw a swimmer, who had been unable to find space either on their boat or the raft, swallow water, choke, and drown. The cries of other swimmers who were too weak to fight the current were too much for her to bear, and she clapped her hands over her ears. She learned later that the raft did not reach the shore, but instead was carried out to open sea. All of the twenty-six people on it were lost, save for one man who jumped off the raft and swam to one of the outer islands.

Mrs. Li kept scouring the water, straining to examine every piece of floating luggage, but there was no sign of her child.

Once she had been put ashore, Mrs. Li ran from one survivor to another, frantically searching for information. "Did any of you pick up a child? Did you see someone pick a child up?" she asked. Each one she questioned sadly shook his head. When a few more lifeboats came in, she ran up to every passenger who got off, and asked the same questions. She realized by now that there was no hope whatever for Lottie. The infant had never come up to the surface after being crushed by the weight of the falling bodies. Patsy was a different story, however. She could have hung on to the suitcase for some time and attracted the attention of some craft. The only trouble was that not a single survivor had seen her, and none could provide any information.

When the last survivor had been brought to the beach, Ruth Li buried her head in her hands and sobbed convulsively. "I am a woman who rarely if ever makes a public display of my emotions, and I don't believe in histrionics, but this was one time I could not maintain my self-control," she recalls.

The island to which Ruth Li and the others had been brought was called Pom Pong. It was shaped like a round loaf of bread. It was uninhabited, which meant that the castaways would probably find little or nothing to eat there. It was very steep, and was composed almost entirely of sharp rocks and jungle, save for a sandy stretch of beach where the lifeboats landed.

The sailors who had rowed ashore decided to take one of the small boats back to the *Kuala,* in hopes of getting some supplies off the ship while it was still afloat. They found the ship to be an almost total wreck, but apparently it was not going to sink as they had expected. They took off whatever canned goods they could find—which wasn't much—then scuttled the ship to make sure it would go under. They were afraid that if Japanese bombers returned the next day and saw the hulk still afloat, they might bomb it again, and might bomb or shoot up their island as well.

One of the ship's officers ordered the supplies to be cut up into small rations, to be doled out twice daily to the 300-odd people on shore. "We don't know how long we'll have to be here, and we've got to make whatever we have last," he said. That night Ruth Li was given a ration of a piece of cold bully beef. A British nurse also gave her a biscuit. The biscuit was one of several that were in her handbag, which had washed ashore with some of the wreckage from the ship.

There were three nurses, members of the British Colonial Nursing Service. One of them, named Helen Moore, said they had worked in a hospital on the Malay peninsula, and then were shifted to a hospital in Singapore when the British were driven off the peninsula. Forty-eight of these Colonial Service nurses had shipped out on the *Kuala,* Miss Moore said, and she thought that the threesome represented the only survivors. (Later, she learned that a total of eight had survived from her group.)

Like Ruth Li, Helen Moore had preferred to remain in Singapore and take her chances with the land invaders, rather than risk a bombing at sea. However, she was still shaky from an attack of malaria, and her chief medical officer had ruled that all of the nurses who were ill must be evacuated. Only a tiny skeleton crew of civilian nurses and doctors had remained behind to await the Japanese. All military nurses had shipped out a few days before.

Some of the *Kuala* passengers who had been brought ashore had been burned or badly hurt when the ship's engine room exploded, while others had been wounded by the machine-gun fire from the raiding planes. The nurses treated them as best they could, but they had few medical supplies. Several came down with fever and died only a few hours after they were brought to the island. It was decided to bury them in one of the wooded patches. Makeshift graves were dug, and markers made of tree branches were placed next to the pits. An officer read a brief funeral service while the survivors huddled around him in a mournful knot and bowed their heads.

There was no place to sleep on the island except the rocky ground. Ruth Li was exhausted from her ordeal, but she still could not fall asleep on the ground. She spent the night tossing and thrashing, and crying for her children. In the morning, the hundred-degree temperature parched the throats of the survivors. The island was believed to have no water, but a group of men were sent to scour every inch of the landscape in hopes of finding a hidden spring. "Without water, we can't last here too long," an officer warned. Luckily, a spring was found. After the bully beef ration and an occasional biscuit was handed out at seven each morning and six each evening, the castaways would line up in front of the fount and be handed a tin of water each.

At noon, they heard the dreaded sound of airplanes again. They were ordered to disperse quickly and hide behind trees so the Japanese pilots in the air would not spot them. The planes passed over the site of the sunken *Kuala* and kept on going. Apparently, the band of castaways on Pom Pong had not been seen.

"We were on the island for eight days, and not a day passed that the planes didn't come," Ruth Li recalls. "It seemed as if our nightmare would never end and that the Japanese would not be happy until they found every last one of us and killed us all. Our ship had been destroyed, but they were still not satisfied. They were so bloodthirsty they did not want any survivor to escape."

During the second night of their stay on the island, Mrs. Li's husband made his way to her. He had survived the attack on the *Tien Kwang*—which had been bombed and destroyed at the same time as the *Kuala*—and had been taken ashore at the opposite end of the rocky, thickly forested island. He had just learned where the *Kuala* survivors had made camp. He had an ugly wound on his head, which he said had been caused by a flying object striking him during the raid on his ship.

"When he saw me sitting there, my head in my hands

and no children around, he knew immediately what had happened," Ruth Li reported. "He bowed his head slightly, but he didn't act grieved. I felt bitter toward him; even more than bitter, I felt enraged because he was the one who had forced us to go to sea and now he wasn't even showing remorse over what had been done to us. 'Don't the children mean anything to you?' I asked him. He said that of course they did, but in view of what had happened to our ship, he had felt certain that the children had been killed, and had already resigned himself to their loss. He thought I should be very grateful for the fact that I had survived; since I could not swim, I should count myself very, very lucky that I had not drowned. I said, 'I don't feel lucky about anything, because my children are gone.'

"He would not accept a particle of responsibility for what had happened, though in Singapore he had agreed that if anything happened to us at sea, it would be on his head. Now he said simply, 'It was Fate, that's all there is to it.' I disagreed, but I could have accepted his point of view and forgiven him if he had shown some feeling of sorrow.

"For the first time in our married life, I saw a side to him that my father must have seen and understood from the first. I now felt him to be cold and unfeeling. When I told him I refused to give up all hopes for Patsy and that we should try to find out whether she could have been rescued and taken by someone to an adjoining island, he told me to put the idea out of my head. He insisted that she could not possibly have been saved, and I must learn to accept the act of Fate. Here was coldness all over again, and this antagonized me all the more."

On the third day the survivors spent on Pom Pong, a Chinese junk passed by. The people on the island waved and shouted for it, but it kept on going. "They're probably afraid that if they help us, the Japanese will make them suffer for it," one of the nurses told Ruth Li. Later that day, a sampan sailed close to the island, but just then Japanese planes came roaring overhead. One pilot spotted the sampan, and dropped a few bombs. They missed the boat, but one landed on the island, killing three British officers who had been on the *Tien Kwang*. Meanwhile, the sampan decided it was too risky to stop in these waters and scurried off.

"We had been saved from the hell and fire of a bombing and from being drowned at sea, but now we began to feel it was all for nothing, that we were doomed to starve to death on Pom Pong," Ruth Li told me. The burning heat of the daytime, coupled with the cold, monsoon-like winds that swept the island at night, and the meagre ration of food and water, had weakened all the survivors considerably. They were dirty, ragged, and uncomfortable. They could not wash because the water was too precious to waste on anything but drinking. The Straits were still covered with the oil of the sunken ships and it kept washing up on the beach, and splattering them. Each time planes were sighted, it took all of their strength to rush into the jungle growth and hide behind the bushes and trees. Otherwise, they spent their time simply lying down—or weeping.

They had to form long queues when the rations were

doled out and the tiresome wait aggravated their tensions and worries and caused flare-ups. Many of the survivors vented their bitterness on the ship's officers who had survived. They complained of the mistake in stopping the ship and trying to camouflage it with branches. Some were bitter because the ship had not tried to hide among the clusters of islands during the day, traveling only by night. They also castigated the officers for not having sent out an S.O.S. wireless message when the Japanese bombers attacked.

Tension gave way to despair when two more days passed without help arriving. Then, on their fifth night on the island, one of the lookouts spotted a boat making its way toward them. At first there was fear it might be Japanese, but as it approached the shore, it was identified as an East Indies fishing boat. It had been sent out to pick up as many survivors as it could possibly fit on board. It turned out that a launch which the British kept hidden in the islands along the Riouw Archipelago had seen the air strikes on the *Kuala* and the *Tien Kwang* and had gone to the large island of Sumatra in the Dutch East Indies seeking help. The captain said he would take back as many survivors as he could, and that other boats were also coming out to them from Sumatra.

Because of the rocks along the shore, the fishing boat couldn't come up to the beach. Wounded and sick survivors were put on the lifeboats and rowed out to the bigger boat. Then the women and children were ordered to gather in a group to be rowed to the boat.

The loading process was slow and tedious and took

most of the night. After a few hours, it developed there wasn't enough room for many of the women. Ruth Li was one of those who were told to remain on shore and wait for the next boat. If Fate had been her enemy up to this point, it became her friend now. For this boat never reached safe harbor. No one ever saw it—or any of its passengers—after it left the island to return to Sumatra across the Malacca Straits. It was probably sighted and sunk by a Japanese warship.

Helen Moore and her two friends from the British Colonial Nursing Service were among those selected to leave on the fishing craft. Miss Moore, however, had a premonition this boat was going to meet with disaster and decided she didn't want to go. A few of the wounded survivors had elected to remain behind, too, because they had friends on the island and they preferred to wait with them for the next boat. These wounded needed nursing attention, and as a result, a few nurses had been detailed to remain behind with them. These nurses were agreeable to the idea of going in place of Miss Moore and her friends, and a last-minute switch was made.

The next morning, a motor launch came out from Sumatra and took a second group away. On the eighth day, a barge came for the remainder of the survivors. Mrs. Li, her husband, and Johnny Chin, a friend from Singapore who had been on the *Tien Kwang* with D. C. Li, were part of the final group to leave the island. Several Europeans, including the three British nurses, were included in this group.

The barge heaved and rocked so much during its

trip across the Malacca Straits that Mrs. Li and her fellow passengers became violently seasick. One of them also suffered a case of sunstroke from the exposure in the open boat, but they reached Sumatra without being sighted or stopped by any Japanese ships.

As they touched the shore of the Dutch-owned island, natives came out to wave to them. Some of the natives scampered up trees to bring down a haul of coconuts. They presented these coconuts to the people on the barge with much pomp and ceremony. The passengers were so thirsty they broke open their presents and greedily drank the fresh milk.

The barge continued up a narrow interior river called the Indragiri River and stopped at the first village. The village had a good-sized Chinese settlement, and a Mr. Zia, the head man of the settlement, offered to shelter the Chinese refugees for as long as they wanted to stay there. The British survivors were told they would be taken across the island to the city of Padang. There, the British consul would make arrangements for them to get transportation on ships heading for India and Australia.

The Chinese were told they could accompany the Europeans to Padang if they wanted to, but they elected to accept Mr. Zia's offer and stay in the village instead. In addition to Mrs. Li, her husband, and Johnny Chin, there were about twenty other Chinese who had survived the bombing of the two evacuation ships.

The people of the village not only took these survivors in, but they also gave them clothing and fed them.

Three days passed without incident. Then, on the fourth day, they received ominous news. Japanese forces, which had already landed on the southern tip of Sumatra, were now pushing northward up the island. The Dutch defenders could not seem to hold them off and were retreating steadily. A few days later, the Dutch were completely routed and the Japanese took over control of the island. Meanwhile, the villagers heard that an Allied naval force had been defeated by the Japanese in a battle in the Java Sea and that the Japanese had successfully landed in nearby Java, the largest of the Indies Islands.

"The small hopes we still entertained that the British and the Americans could recover quickly from their early defeats and retake Singapore and the rest of Malaya were now dashed completely," Mrs. Li observed. "It was now frighteningly clear to us that the Japanese would be in control of our part of the world for a long time—and that all we could do was pray that some day in the future, the Allies would become strong enough to free us."

The village where the evacuees had settled was bypassed in the fighting between the Japanese and the Dutch, and Mrs. Li hoped fervently that the Japanese would continue to ignore it. But it was not to be. One morning, a Japanese army patrol drove up. The evacuees were told to quickly hide themselves under beds, while Mr. Zia went out to greet the patrol. The officer in charge said there had been reports that some of the survivors of the Singapore evacuation ships were being sheltered somewhere in the area. If any of these people were in this village, they were to be surrendered at once.

Mr. Zia assured the Japanese officer that no strangers had come to their village in recent weeks, and the patrol went away. "They may be back, however," Mr. Zia told the evacuees. "We'll have to find a good hiding place for you people—some place where the soldiers won't think of looking."

A number of potential hiding places were explored, and rejected as being unsuitable for one reason or another. Finally, Zia hit on the idea of cutting openings in the floorboards of the houses and having the evacuees hide under the boards when the soldiers came. The houses in this village all bordered on the river. The front of the houses were kept elevated by wooden stilts, but the back part was practically ground level. When the evacuees practiced crouching under the boards in the back part of the houses, they found that they were on dry ground when the river was at low tide, but as soon as the tide came up, the water would wash up underneath them and soak their feet.

A week later, another patrol came to the village. This time it was water-borne. It consisted of an officer and four soldiers who came via patrol boat. Mr. Zia now maintained a lookout at all times so that the patrol was sighted in time for the evacuees to scramble into their hiding places. When the boat came alongside the shore, the officer jumped out and immediately sought out Mr. Zia.

"We have information that you are sheltering people from Singapore right in this village," he said angrily. "Unless they are surrendered to us at once, you will suffer serious consequences, and so will the people of your village."

Listening in her stuffy, awkward hiding place, Mrs. Li felt a tremor of fear go through her. Mr. Zia and the people of his village had been very good to the people who had come to them, but would they now expose themselves to terrible personal risks in order to protect a group of strangers?

It turned out her fears were groundless. The natives of this Sumatran village were people of courage—they were not the kind to cooperate or collaborate with conquerors. "We are not sheltering anyone here who does not belong here," Mr. Zia insisted. "On this island, you may hear all kinds of wild rumors and stories, particularly during this war period. But most of the stories you will hear—like this one you are telling me—are so much nonsense."

"Very well, we will look for ourselves and see if you are telling the truth," the officer said. He ordered his men to go through the houses along the river and check the identity of everyone there.

When she felt the step of one of the Japanese soldiers in the room above her hiding place, Mrs. Li began to shiver despite the torrid heat. As the step came closer to the section of floorboard under which she was crouching, she felt sure that the soldier had found out her hiding place. She clenched her fists and began to pray silently. This time, she was sure that all hope was gone. At any moment, she expected the soldier to pick up the loosened board, and drag her up by the hair. Then the Japanese would either shoot her on the spot or lead her to a firing squad. It was all she could do to keep from screaming out in utter despair.

Suddenly, the noise of feet shuffling around in the room above her started to grow fainter. Then it died altogether. The soldier had not been observant enough to locate the loose boards or to go prying under them. He had left—and she was still safe! She sighed deeply in relief; then abruptly covered her mouth with her hand. There was still a chance, she thought, that the soldier had fooled her into thinking he had gone, while all the time he was still waiting above, trying to detect the sound of her breathing.

Even when she heard the patrol boat go away, Ruth Li refused to leave her hiding place. Finally, Mr. Zia began to call her, and one of the villagers pulled up the board and asked her why she was still crouching down there. "Everybody else has come out; it's perfectly safe," he told her.

"I wanted to be one hundred percent sure," she said. "When that soldier came into the room, I nearly died of fright. I'm still shaking so much I can hardly move."

"Well, things will be all right now," the villager assured her. "Now that they've made a thorough search and found nothing, they must be convinced there is nobody hiding here. They won't come back again."

But they did come back—again and again, at regular intervals. Sometimes, they stopped just briefly in their patrol boats to ask whether any strangers had been seen in the village since their last visit, and at other times, they conducted a house-to-house search similar to the first search. Luckily, they never thought to try to pry up the floorboards. One time, however, a soldier bent down in front of one house and noticed what looked to him like someone crouching. "Oh, it's my little youngster," a villager told him. "She likes to play little games and hide herself when visitors come to the village."

The soldier accepted this story and went back to his boat. Mrs. Li and her fellow evacuees, who had been holding their breath again, were able to congratulate themselves on another narrow escape.

"You can imagine the strain we lived under, knowing that the Japanese were determined to keep on searching for us, no matter how long it took," Mrs. Li told me. "I thought to myself, 'What kind of vampires are these to want the blood of a pitiful group of civilians who happened to survive their terrible bombing? We represented no threat to them of any kind. We were not important people; we had no connection with any military organization, or with the government. Why must they hunt us like dogs; why is it so important for them to find and kill us?'" (Later on, she learned that the Japanese had encountered stiffer resistance than they expected when they were fighting at the gates of Singapore. This resistance had enabled the defenders to blow up many important factories and rubber-processing plants. This angered the Japanese, and they were particularly incensed over the fact that the prominent Chinese citizens in Singapore had supported the British administration. As a result, they vowed special vengeance on those Chinese who had escaped the city on British evacuation ships.)

During the time that they were not hiding from

Japanese patrols, the evacuees, including Mrs. Li's husband, took part in many village activities. But Mrs. Li remained alone and apart from the others. She continued to brood over the loss of her children. She could not bear to look at any children in the village, for they reminded her of her own. Her husband was unable to rouse her out of her mood of depression. The strained feelings that had developed between them as a result of the tragedy of the *Kuala* continued and even deepened. D. C. Li felt that brooding would not bring back those who had been lost, while Ruth Li felt bitter over his "unfeeling" attitude. She continued to think of how she might go about searching for Patsy, while he continued to dismiss the idea as hopeless and senseless.

Mrs. Li was anxious to return home as soon as possible. In Singapore, she felt, she might find news of Patsy. And then there was always the faint hope that the child had been picked up by a boat going toward Singapore, instead of away from it. Such a boat, she had to admit to herself, would almost certainly have to be Japanese. After all, who else would try to come into Singapore harbor at a time when the city was ready to fall to the invader? But she reasoned that even the Japanese would not stoop to the deliberate murder of a castaway child, and if they had indeed picked up Patsy, they would likely have brought her into port and turned her over to a hospital.

When she broached the subject of returning to Singapore to Mr. Zia, however, he shook his head firmly. "We have heard that the Japanese maintain a very tight guard around Singapore harbor, and they have sea patrols all through the Straits," he said. "It would be very dangerous for you to try to go there now. In fact, it would be suicide."

After they had been in Sumatra for three months, Zia said he had learned that the vigil around Singapore harbor had relaxed and that her chances of getting back home safely had improved.

"It is still very risky, and you would be safer remaining here with us, but if you feel you must go, I will give you a sampan," he said. Because Mrs. Li was so anxious to go, her husband, Johnny Chin, and a few other evacuees agreed to go with her. Zia told them that the Japanese occupation troops were getting ready to celebrate the birthday of their emperor in a few days. He suggested that they time their arrival in the harbor for the day of the actual celebration. He felt the guards would be in a festive mood for the occasion and might adopt a tolerant attitude toward strange boats that docked in the harbor.

They sailed slowly up the Malacca Straits, hugging the shoreline for as long as possible and until it was time to cross the Straits into Singapore harbor. To avoid the Japanese sea patrols, they sailed their sampan only at night. During the day, they hid out on land. When they entered Singapore harbor, on the day of the celebration for the emperor, they thought they might slip ashore unnoticed, but instead they were hailed by a guard on the dock. Once again, Ruth Li felt herself gripped by icy fingers of fright. When she and her husband explained that they were poor natives from Sumatra who had come to visit relatives in Singapore, the guard expressed disbelief and demanded to see their pass.

"Any boat coming into this harbor must have a pass from the authorities," he said. They pointed to their ragged, borrowed clothes to try to convince him that they were only poor travelers, but he still regarded them with suspicion. Zia, however, had thoughtfully provided them with an armful of tinsel and ornaments from his island. They offered them now to the guard and told him they had brought them along for the emperor's birthday celebration. With a broad smile, he accepted them as presents for himself and stalked off, allowing them to land without incident.

The Lis promptly called Dr. T. K. Hu, a physician friend who lived near their old neighborhood. He was astounded to hear their voices. "Thank God you're still alive," he said. He immediately sent a car down to the dock to pick them up and bring them to his home.

10

Dr. Hu explained that he was one resident of
Singapore who had not suffered since the Japanese occupied the city. Doctors were badly needed, and so the
Japanese allowed him to have privileges denied to the
rest of the occupied city. The Lis' home had been occupied by the Japanese, so they couldn't go back there.
Besides, the Japanese were checking on survivors of
evacuation ships who might have sneaked back into
Singapore, even as their patrols in Sumatra were hunting for the same people. So the Lis not only could not go
back home, but they had to keep themselves in hiding.

Dr. Hu agreed to hide Ruth Li in his home, but he told D. C. Li that he would have to arrange to secrete him in another Chinese home. It was too dangerous, he said, for two evacuees to be kept in the same house. If the Japanese found out about one visitor, he or she could be passed off as a relative who had come to stay with the family. But if they found a couple, they would immediately suspect that these were evacuees, and both the evacuees and Dr. Hu would be shot or thrown into prison.

D. C. Li named a few other friends who might shelter him, but Dr. Hu told him sadly that these men had been seized by the Japanese right after they conquered the city.

Dr. Hu finally located a Chinese friend who had not been harmed by the Japanese and who lived several blocks away. This friend agreed to hide D. C. Li in his house.

Now the days and months passed with interminable slowness for Ruth Li. None of her friends had heard any news about Patsy, and there had been no reports of any child being plucked out of the water near the Riouw Archipelago and brought back to port. This was a bitter blow for the grieving mother, and yet she still refused to "adjust" to the idea that her child was gone forever. Her small circle of friends was hardly the whole world. She wanted to broaden her area of search, to get out and seek information from those who knew more about the comings and goings of ships in and out of Singapore. Yet her movements had to be severely restricted for her own safety. This was galling to her. She felt like a prisoner who had been handed a long sentence and locked in a narrow room with no window to the outside world.

Some of her friends felt that time would heal Ruth's hurt and induce her to forget her "obsession." However, with nothing to keep her busy, her mind was free to dwell interminably on the same subject of the *Kuala's* sinking and Patsy's disappearance. So instead of time acting as a healer, in this case it acted only to accent and emphasize this "obsession." She would lie awake most of the night thinking, thinking, thinking. Only toward morning would she succumb to a restless sleep.

Dr. Hu had children at home, and it was acutely painful for her to hear them laugh or to watch them at play. She could not stand in the street and see little girls scamper about without having the memory of Patsy go through her like a knife. Once, she saw a girl running through the streets and noticed something in her gait that reminded her of her lost child. She impulsively hurried after the youngster. This was dangerous, for Hu had told her she should stay only in the immediate area outside his house when she was not actually in hiding. All of the Chinese women—not only Mrs. Li—had been warned to keep off the streets as much as possible. Japanese soldiers had a habit of coming through this neighborhood and seizing and raping women if they found them outside. Some women from good families had even been dragged off and forced to live as camp followers.

When Ruth caught up with the youngster, she

whirled her around to get a good look at her face. The child was not Patsy. "What do you want?" the child asked.

"Nothing, I'm sorry, I just thought you were somebody else," Mrs. Li explained.

"Why do you look so sad?" the child demanded, noting the anguish in the lady's eyes.

"I lost something very precious," Mrs. Li answered, trying not to cry. Then she ordered the child to go right home and not stay in the streets, and trudged wearily for several blocks back to Dr. Hu's house.

Another time, she was told of a new child who had come to live with a family about a mile away. The child supposedly had been taken from an orphanage, and little was known of her background. Could she possibly be Patsy? Mrs. Li took the risk of going to the home of this family—and returned empty-handed. The story she had been told was all wrong. The child had not come from an orphanage—she was instead the child of a relative who had been badly beaten by Japanese troops on the first day they entered Singapore and had finally died in a hospital.

To help her pass the long, sad hours, Dr. Hu's wife gave her all the books in the house to read. Ruth went through them quickly. Then Dr. Hu told her that a friend in the house opposite theirs had an enormous library, filled primarily with detective books. The friend would permit her to come there every day and read for as long as she wanted. He also had a convenient cellar to hide her whenever Japanese searchers came around.

For the next two years, Ruth Li spent virtually every day in the friend's library with his detective stories. She read an average of one book a day, and many times would go back and reread a story she had already finished. "I never seemed to remember what I read, and many books seemed brand-new to me when I picked them up, even though it turned out I had read them not long before," she told me. "You see, I wasn't reading to entertain myself or because I was interested in what I was reading. I was reading only to forget. Detective stories, I found, had the best quality for keeping my mind occupied and for shutting me away from the world for a little while.

"I would have given anything if I had been able to go out and do some kind of work—any kind. But it was too dangerous for me to try anything like that."

Meanwhile, her husband had been able to occupy his time in a more satisfactory manner. He had always had a working knowledge of Japanese and he used his time in hiding to study the language and improve his grasp of it. The Japanese overlords of the city had demanded that all children be taught in their language. So he helped the children of the family which sheltered him with their Japanese lessons. He was also able to make friends with certain businessmen who were on good terms with the Japanese, apparently because they were doing business with them. They were able to get him a job teaching other children, and he began to travel openly around the city. He felt his friends could protect him if his identity as an evacuee were discovered.

D. C. Li would visit his wife periodically, but the relationship between them did not improve. What's more, they now seemed to be living in different worlds, with different ideas, and it was difficult for them to find any shared interests.

One day, one of Ruth Li's friends, a woman named Biao Luan, suggested that she go to fortune-tellers to see if they could tell her whether her child was really alive and where she might find her. Like any Oriental city, Singapore has always abounded in fortune-tellers and mediums. The ones the friend referred to were Malayan women who had not been disturbed by the Japanese occupation and were allowed to ply their trade as before. The Malayan population of Singapore represented generally the docile lower classes, and since the conquerors felt they had nothing to fear from them, they left them unmolested. The only difference the war had made to the fortune-tellers was to expand the business they did with troubled souls, and also to boost their prices.

At first, Ruth Li recoiled at the very idea of seeking out a fortune-teller. She was not superstitious, and to a person of intelligence and cultural background, these so-called experts in the affairs of the occult were nothing but quacks. "Ordinarily, I would have laughed at the mere suggestion that I go to them," she told me. "But this was not an ordinary time, and I was not in an ordinary mood. I was so frantic for news, and so desperately anxious to have my faith in Patsy's survival confirmed by somebody else—almost anybody else would do—that against all my best judgment, I finally decided to go."

The friend who had suggested a fortune-teller to Ruth Li agreed to drive her to one near the outskirts of the city. Mrs. Luan's husband was an expert auto mechanic who had been drafted by the Japanese overlords of Singapore to repair the motors of their cars. In return, they gave him a special permit which allowed him to have gasoline so he could travel around in his own car. Outside of the Japanese, very few people in the city were allowed to have or buy gasoline.

The fortune-teller was located in a dark room in the back of a gold-domed native temple. When Mrs. Li entered, she saw a plump, swarthy woman wearing long, flowing robes and a headpiece shaped like a turban. She was burning incense, and the odor made Ruth Li feel sick to the stomach. The woman had been murmuring incantations when they came in, and for about five minutes she made the two visitors stand there while she continued her mumbo-jumbo.

At last, she motioned for Ruth to sit down, handed her joss sticks, and greeted her in Malayan. Ruth indicated she couldn't speak the language, and the fortune-teller frowned and indicated that was the only language she spoke. Fortunately, Mrs. Luan was able to speak Malayan, and she volunteered to act as interpreter.

The fortune-teller stared into Mrs. Li's eyes, studied her palms, and burned more incense. Then she asked her visitor to tell her what she had come for. Mrs. Li told the whole story of the *Kuala* disaster and her search for the child who she hoped had not drowned. When she finished, the mystic closed her eyes and held her hands aloft.

"She's gone into a trance," Ruth's friend whispered.

When the mystic came out of her trance and opened her eyes, they gleamed like red-hot coals. "Rejoice, your child lives!" she told Ruth Li, through the interpreter-friend.

"Where is she? What happened to her? How can I get to her?" Ruth Li shot back.

The woman again shut her eyes and raised her hands aloft. After a few minutes of silence, she renewed her incantations. Then she stopped, and stared upward at the ceiling. Ruth Li and Mrs. Luan looked upward with her. The mystic's eyes were fixed on a skylight above, and Ruth Li kept staring, too, as if she were hypnotized. "What do you think she sees?" she murmured finally to Mrs. Luan.

"I don't know," her friend said breathlessly. "But isn't it wonderful? She's sure Patsy's alive, and that's the most important thing."

The mystic finally brought her head down and said something to Ruth Li's friend. "She says she is unable to tell you anything more about your daughter right now," Mrs. Luan translated. "She says the spirits have gone away for the time being and she will have to contact them again another time. But they did give her the information that your child is still alive. She said you should feel very, very happy. And she'd like to be paid now."

"How do I know that anything she says is true?" Mrs. Li demanded angrily.

"Well, Ruth, you'll have to take her word for it right

now. But we'll return in four or five days, when she feels she'll be able to contact the spirits again."

Ruth paid the woman and left the temple with her friend. She felt dispirited and disappointed. She had had a momentary flash of hope when the fortune-teller made the announcement that her child was alive, but the fact that no explanation had been made about what happened to Patsy, and no directions given where to find the child, made the whole business suspect. As a rational person, Ruth Li felt she'd been taken in.

"I appreciate very much your taking me here, but I'm afraid the woman has been making a fool of me," she told her friend. "I think she just wants my money. She'll take a little more each time, and she'll end up telling me nothing that really matters."

"You must not give up on this so easily," Mrs. Luan cautioned her. "I've known women who swear by these fortune-tellers and who insist they can find out things in the spirit world which are mysteries to everyone else. Give her one more chance. In the meantime, try to look on the bright side of life. She has told you that you have been right in thinking that Patsy is still alive. Give her the benefit of the doubt and get a good night's sleep tonight. Lord knows you need it."

Five days later, Ruth Li returned to the temple of the fortune-teller. She had derided, in her own mind, the idea of returning; yet when her friend called for her in the car, she went immediately. The lure of the mystic was for the moment irresistible. Ruth was sure the woman was a charlatan, but a small part of her nourished the faint hope that the charlatan somehow had an acquaintanceship with the supernatural.

Once again, there was the ritual of the incense, the incantations, the palm-reading, and the trance. Once again, the fortune-teller insisted that she had received a positive sign that the missing Patsy Li, daughter of Ruth Li, was alive. And again, she found it difficult to communicate with the spirits after they provided this basic information. But when Ruth Li got to her feet and angrily demanded information on pain of denouncing the mystic as a complete and utter phony, the woman went back into her trance.

The trance lasted several minutes and when she came out of it, she said she had another message to report. "I see a child floating in the water, holding on to wreckage," she intoned. "I see a man in a small boat reaching down and rescuing her just as she is about to go under."

Biao Luan suddenly nudged Ruth. "You see, she has gotten an accurate picture of what happened," she whispered. "Now we're really getting somewhere."

"I see the little child being handed up on a boat," the mystic continued. "Let me see—where is the boat going? It is hard to say—but I will know in a minute."

"Where is it going?" Ruth Li demanded. "I've got to know!"

"Singapore," the mystic said suddenly. "Yes, it came right back here to Singapore. And when it arrived, the mother and father of the child could not be found anywhere. It was thought that the mother and father had perished. So the child was placed in an orphan home."

She named an institution in the northern part of the

city. Then she asked for her fee. Ruth Li paid quickly and hurried out with her friend to the car. She was excited—yet she was besieged with qualms and doubts. Had the fortune-teller made up the story out of whole cloth? The fact that she had learned—in a so-called trance— that Patsy had been picked up by a man in a boat was no evidence of any occult powers. Obviously, if Patsy had been saved, it would be logical for anyone to assume that a man had picked her up in a boat.

That same evening, Ruth Li and Mrs. Luan drove to the orphanage. They asked the head of the orphanage for information about a strange child who had been brought there in recent months, and were told there was no such child. They asked to see every youngster in the home. The head of the home angrily refused and said she couldn't see why the place should be turned inside out to oblige somebody with a silly story. Ruth's friend then explained how Ruth had been tormented by the loss of her child and pleaded that she be allowed to look at the children just to satisfy herself that she had not overlooked an opportunity to find her. "Very well," the woman said, with a shrug. "But you're wasting your time."

Mrs. Li was taken on a tour through every room in the home. She inspected every child. Patsy was not there. She apologized profusely for having caused a disturbance and left quickly. "I'm mortified and crushed," Ruth Li told her friend on the drive home. "I should have known better than to take any stock whatever in what a fortune-teller tells me," she said. "We'll go back to her one more time," Mrs. Luan urged. "Maybe the

child is at some other institution. Maybe the fortune-
teller's information was right, but she got the place
wrong."

On their third trip to the gold-domed temple, the fortune-teller repeated at the end of her trance that the
lost child had indeed been brought to this particular
orphanage. However, she now added the fact that just a
day before Mrs. Li got there, the child had been taken
to the home of a Malayan family. This family intended
to bring up the child as their own. When Mrs. Li demanded to know the name and address of the family,
the mystic went into another trance and then wrote
something on a piece of paper.

"Go quickly and you will find her," she said. "If you
wait too long, this family may move away with her."

When Mrs. Li found the home of this Malayan family, the woman of the house said she knew nothing of
any Chinese child. Her manner seemed furtive and
suspicious, however. Mrs. Li and her friend decided
that she might be hiding information from them. They
questioned other Malayans in the neighborhood and
were told that the woman was indeed sheltering a little
Chinese girl. They said she would make no explana-
tions about where the girl had come from, and kept her
hidden most of the time so that they did not know what
she looked like.

Here at last was exciting news! The woman actually
had a Chinese child—could the child be Patsy Li? Ruth
Li and her friend hurried back to the woman's house
and demanded to see the child. "We know you have a
Chinese girl here and that you lied to us before," they

said. "If the child is the one we are seeking, we will pay you a reward."

"If the child is not yours, will you keep my secret and tell nothing of this to anyone?" the woman asked.

"Of course," Ruth Li assured her. "But for God's sake, hurry and bring out the child."

The woman disappeared into a little back room and came out a moment later, leading a frightened, tight-lipped Chinese girl. Ruth Li's heart sank. The child was not her daughter.

Sadly, Ruth turned to go. Mrs. Luan, however, was still curious about the little girl. "Who does she belong to and why have you been hiding her?" she asked the Malayan woman. The woman explained that she had been a servant in the home of a prominent Chinese family in Malaya. The family had left the youngster with her when they took a vacation trip to India in November, 1941. She had been cut off from all communication with them after the Japanese began their war at Pearl Harbor on December 7th. She had fled to Singapore with the child when the Japanese army came storming down the Malay peninsula. Now she was being as secretive as possible about the child lest the Japanese authorities in the city discover her identity. The Japanese had regarded the child's parents as "British spies."

During their drive home, Ruth Li said bitterly to her friend, "That fortune-teller must have known all the time that the child kept by this Malayan woman was not mine. She has been sending us on wild-goose chases just to keep taking good money from me."

"There are other fortune-tellers," Mrs. Luan said hopefully.

"No, no—no thanks," Ruth told her. "None of them can help me. I'm certain of that."

Despite this feeling, her ears perked up a week later when she heard talk of the so-called magical powers of another fortune-teller. Her emotional need to have her hopes for Patsy's survival continually refueled outweighed her practical estimates of the value of these mystics. She sought out her friend and asked with some embarrassment if she would take her to see this maker of magic. Mrs. Luan was again happy to take her.

The second fortune-teller did not read palms as the first one had, but instead operated with a crystal ball. She spent a long time pondering what the crystal held in store for Ruth Li, then concluded, as the first mystic had, that there was joy ahead and a safe-and-sound child in her future. It took several visits to elicit from the fortune-teller the place to go to find the lost child. When Ruth and her friend were given an address at long last and hurried there, it turned out to be another false alarm.

In the months that followed, Mrs. Li made many other impulsive trips to the gloomy little aeries of the mystics. She sought out mediums, palmists, spiritualists, soothsayers, and sorcerers of all sorts. They went into trances, held seances, consulted ouija boards, conducted telepathic demonstrations, had her read fortune scrolls, hypnotized her, and communed with assorted spirits. Each of them did things a little differently but in each case the results were the same. The mystics—every last one of them—told Ruth Li the thing she wanted to hear, namely that her child was alive. They also dragged out the number of visits, sent her on wild-goose hunts, and took her money. This last was becoming a serious problem, inasmuch as the Lis had lost all their considerable assets to the Japanese, save for the cash they had been able to take with them in their hasty evacuation.

Each time, Ruth Li would tell her obliging friend that there would be no more useless trips to the temples and hideaways of quacks. Then after an interval of a couple of weeks, she would invariably reverse herself and go to see "just one last medium." Though she discounted practically everything these women said, she always went to the places they sent her. She felt driven to check out every last lead, no matter how faint and dubious it appeared to be. Dr. Hu frowned on all this traveling. He kept reminding her how dangerous it was for her to roam away from the house. But Ruth kept going anyway, because by now she needed these excursions as an outlet for her nervous energy and as a means of temporarily escaping from her own prison of despair.

One day, she hit on the idea of putting an ad in the local newspaper asking for information about her missing child. The ad gave a box number, rather than her name, but it immediately attracted the attention of the Japanese security police. They thought the ad was a code message by an underground movement, and they rushed to the newspaper office to demand the identity of the advertiser. Mrs. Li had not given her own name to the newspaper, but she had used the name of Hu and given Dr. Hu's address, so the police swooped down on the doctor's home. Luckily, the newspaper office had called the doctor to tell him what happened. This gave him a few minutes' advance warning. Dr. Hu rushed Mrs. Li into hiding at his neighbor's home, before the police arrived. When they came, he assured them that the message meant what it said, and that there had been no code involved. The ad was placed by a relative of his, he said, who had lost a child and was in a state of almost complete melancholia as a result. The ad, he agreed, had been a foolish thing, but no harm was meant by it.

"Where is this relative of yours?" the police wanted to know. Dr. Hu said she had stayed with him for a while, but was now living with other relatives. Because of the high regard in which he was held as a doctor, the police did not ask any more questions. They searched the house briefly to satisfy themselves that the relative was not there and then left. Ruth Li was beside herself when she learned how close she had come to endangering the Hus.

"I decided I would give up my frantic search for Patsy at least until the war ended," she told me. "I didn't care so much about myself, but I was afraid of doing something that would again place my friends in jeopardy. Next time, they might not be so lucky."

For several months, she stuck by that decision. Then she was tantalized by stories of yet another medium—one who had supposedly located another Singapore resident who had been swept away in the backwash of war. Her trusted friend still had the use of her car and sufficient gasoline in the tank to take her places. This time her destination was an eerie-looking house in back of a native shrine. The medium wore the exotic garb of her trade, and her crystal-ball theatrics did not vary much from the psychical demonstrations Ruth Li had seen so many times before. There seemed little reason to place any more faith in this particular spiritualist than in all the others who had failed her and lied to her before. And yet when the session was over, Ruth told her friend that she had been given a "vital clue" in the hunt for Patsy.

The "clue" that the medium had handed Ruth was that the child was being held south of the city. The medium would not elaborate on just what was happening to her there, and she would not tell her whether Patsy was healthy or deathly ill. "I can only tell you what the crystal ball tells me," she told Mrs. Li. "It has not told me any more, and I will not make up any stories to deceive you."

Because this mystic would not give her the glib and easy assurances about her child's safety she was accustomed to getting from previous mediums, Ruth Li felt she could be trusted more than the others. Furthermore, she knew that Changi Prison was south of Singapore city and felt than Changi could well be the place where Patsy had been taken. This could explain why all of Ruth's other attempts to track down the child had ended in failure and despair.

Also, from the point of view of logic, it seemed more likely that a live Patsy would be in a prison rather than an orphanage or a private home. If she had been picked up by the Japanese, their brutal instincts would undoubtedly have directed them to throw this Chinese child behind bars rather than hand her over to the comparatively tender ministrations of an orphanage director.

Ruth Li knew that Changi Prison was one of the civilian jails that had been converted by the Japanese conquerors into a concentration camp for "enemies of the empire." Changi had no men, only women and children. Almost all the prisoners were British civilians—wives of government officials, Army personnel, and merchants, as well as nurses and Red Cross workers. They had either been unable to get on an evacuation ship out of Singapore and thus were trapped when the city surrendered, or had deliberately stayed behind because they did not want to take the chance of being bombed at sea. Changi normally had room for only about four hundred inmates, but Mrs. Li had heard that the Japanese had jammed it to about three times its normal capacity. The prison was about eighteen miles south of Singapore.

The husbands of the female prisoners were kept in an adjoining jail. The men sent to this jail, and the women and children in Changi, had all been forced to walk the eighteen miles from Singapore in a temperature of over 100 degrees. Some had collapsed and died on the way.

The Japanese had an even fiercer hatred for Chinese civilians in Singapore who had been closely identified with the British government than they did for the British themselves. These Chinese "enemies of the empire" had been driven to a beach just outside the city, and ordered to dig their own graves. Then they were toppled into these graves by a hail of machine-gun bullets.

Many of the widows and members of the families of these Chinese civilians had been arrested by the Japanese. They were sent to different jails, but Mrs. Li learned that some of them and their children were in Changi with the British women. Thus, if Patsy had been picked up by a Japanese ship coming into Singapore and identified as a child of a prominent Chinese family, there was a good chance that she could have been thrown into Changi.

Mrs. Li asked Biao Luan's husband whether he could get a list of the children confined at Changi. He made a few discreet inquiries but got nowhere. Then one day, another friend told Ruth Li that a Shanghai merchant who had been a classmate of hers in school had turned up in Singapore. He was doing business with the Japanese and was in good favor with them. Mrs. Li's first reaction was a feeling of contempt toward an old friend who was actively collaborating with the enemy. But she also realized that he might be the one person she knew who could get the information she was seeking. She got word to him that she was anxious to see him, and he visited her at Dr. Hu's house a few days later.

When Ruth told him what she wanted, he at first shook his head. "I have nothing to do with the administrators of prisons; I have no business with them, and I would have no access to their records," he said.

"But surely you know some important Japanese officials who might find out what you want, or would at least direct you to the proper party," Ruth Li argued.

"No, no, no, they will become suspicious of me if I ask too many strange questions," the merchant said. "They will say, 'These things are none of your business. . . . You are acting like a spy.' "

Mrs. Li continued to plead with him, however, and when he left he gave her a grudging promise that he would "try" to get some information. A week passed and nothing happened. Mrs. Li contacted the merchant again, and he sent back word that he had no news to report yet. She had almost given up hope of getting any help from him when he came to Dr. Hu's house again in a state of high excitement.

"I have found an important Japanese who can help you," he announced to her.

"Who is he? Is he from the prison? When can I see him?"

"He is not from the prison, but don't you worry about that," the merchant told her. "He is a man who can get to the right people and get exactly what you want. He is a diplomat. It took me a while to cultivate him and to get up enough nerve to ask for a favor for an old school friend who I told him is in a terrible state of depression because she has lost her child. He asked many questions about you. I told him you were a very fine, high-type Chinese woman, from one of the best families. He said he is most anxious to meet you. When he meets you, he will discuss the manner in which he can help you."

"Is he going to come here?" Ruth Li wanted to know.

"No, he wants to have dinner with you in a fine restaurant. I am to bring you there tomorrow night. Oh, he is a very distinguished-looking gentleman, a civilized, cultured man, not a military man. You will like him, I am sure."

Mrs. Li sat silently for a moment. She was not at all sure that going out to have dinner with a Japanese diplomat was a safe or a wise thing to do. She did not relish the idea in any way. She wondered whether she could behave in a civil, friendly way toward a Japanese official and whether she could prevent the vitriolic feelings she had for the enemy from pouring out at an inopportune time. She felt a surge of resentment over the whole idea of having to ask a favor of the people who were responsible for all her suffering.

"Well, what do you say, are you still interested in trying to find your child, or aren't you?" her old classmate demanded.

Of course she was still interested, Mrs. Li hastened to say. She simply thought the prospect of having dinner out with the Japanese diplomat would be risky for both of them. There was, after all, the question of appearances.

"Don't worry about appearances and don't worry about risks. He's got enough influence and position to protect both himself and you in case you're seen and reported. I'll be here tomorrow night to take you to the restaurant. You'll enjoy having dinner with him, I assure you."

Promptly at 6:30 the next evening, the merchant returned to Dr. Hu's house and drove Ruth Li to her dinner rendezvous. The Japanese diplomat turned out to be a courtly-looking gentleman, of medium height, and with graying hair. Their dinner was the best meal Ruth Li had had since she returned to her occupied city. The diplomat pumped Mrs. Li for all the details of her personal and family life and insisted on telling her about his own background and personal history. As a diplomat, he said, he had made many friendships in the past among the Chinese, the British, the Australians, and the Americans. As a man of peace, he abhorred fighting and killing, but once the war broke out he naturally had to support the war effort of his country. It would not be too long, he felt, before the Americans and the British were totally defeated. Asia, he said, would come under complete Japanese domination, and then there would be no need for any more wars or bloodshed.

When Mrs. Li tried to turn the conversation to Changi Prison, he ignored her to go into voluminous detail about all the women of different nationalities he had met in his diplomatic career. He began to ask her personal questions again, and wanted to know where her husband was. She told him simply that they had to live apart because of the war conditions, and his eyes glowed at this revelation. Again, she brought up Changi Prison, and this time he said, with obvious irritation, "Can't you forget about that for a while?"

"No, I can't forget it, even for a moment," Ruth Li told him. "I have been living a never-ending nightmare since that moment I told my child to cling to a suitcase in the water and she floated out of my sight. The nightmare will end for me only if and when I find my child again."

"Oh, very well," the diplomat said wearily. "I will check with the people who run the prison and get the names of all the children who are being held there. You will look at the list and see if you can find your daughter. If she is there, I will use my influence to get her out."

Warmed by this positive, if reluctant, assurance, Ruth Li went home that night feeling she was approaching her goal. She thought that the word of a diplomat, even a Japanese diplomat, was a good one. It was true that he had not seemed interested in her child, but she believed that once he had given his promise to do something concrete, he would not go back on it.

Ruth Li and the diplomat met several more times for dinner. Each time, he told her that he had not been able to get the information she wanted because of red tape, but that he would have it very soon. Mrs. Li began to get increasingly edgy over the fact that their meetings had still produced nothing tangible. But when she acted impatient, he put her off by saying, "Rome wasn't built in a day. These things take time."

One night, as she was getting ready to go to bed, there was a knock on the front door. Dr. Hu opened it to admit the diplomat. He had obviously been drinking heavily, because his eyes were bloodshot and his gait was unsteady. He loudly insisted on seeing Ruth Li alone. Dr. Hu was unsure what to do. He didn't like the idea of leaving Ruth alone with a man who was tipsy. Yet he didn't want to antagonize an important Japanese official. "Mrs. Li isn't feeling too well tonight. Why don't you come back another time?" he said.

The diplomat said he had come to see Mrs. Li and that he wasn't leaving until he saw her. Despite his condition, it was possible that he had brought some useful information, so Dr. Hu called Mrs. Li in and left to go to his own room. But he told his wife he didn't like the looks of things and that he might have to intercede if the diplomat became abusive. "If I give him the idea that I am acting as the physician for some of his superiors, I may be able to scare him into leaving," he said.

Mrs. Li was also frightened at the appearance of her visitor, but she pretended not to notice anything out of the ordinary. "I hope you've been able to get the list for me at last," she said.

"No, I didn't get it," the Japanese said sharply.

Mrs. Li was taken aback. "But you have other information for me?" she asked hopefully.

"No, I have no information, and I don't expect to get any," the Japanese railed at her. "I'm not interested in any lost children. You're the one I want—and right now."

He seized her hand, and twisted it as she tried to break free. She reproached herself bitterly for not having realized that the diplomat had never meant to help her and that he was interested in her only as an object of his pleasure. "Please let me go! Please!" she cried. She tried again to break free, but he wouldn't release her. Instead, he tried to draw her closer. She screamed. Dr. Hu came running into the room, and the diplomat, startled, loosened his grip. Mrs. Li broke away. Dr. Hu ordered her to go to her room and lock the door. Then he propelled the diplomat toward the front door.

"I think it best that you do not come back here again," Dr. Hu said.

The Japanese swore angrily and threatened to have both Dr. Hu and Mrs. Li arrested. "I think it would be to your own advantage to put such thoughts out of your mind," Dr. Hu told him. "You will please forget that you were ever here or ever met Mrs. Li, and we will forget that we ever met you. If you make trouble for us, we will have to make trouble for you."

"What do you mean you'll make trouble for me?" the Japanese shouted. "Do you realize who I am? Don't you know that we are the rulers here? I can have you and that woman shot if I want to!"

"I must remind you that I am on very friendly terms with some of your superiors, and have also attended them as a physician," Dr. Hu told him boldly. "If I were to tell them that you have been out a number of times with a Chinese woman, that you have gotten drunk and revealed secrets, and that you have been engaged in a plot with the Chinese woman to have prisoners escape from Changi Prison, I'm afraid you would be in a very difficult situation. I repeat—let us all forget that we have ever met. It will be to your advantage more than mine, I assure you."

The diplomat stormed angrily out the door. The bluff apparently worked, for Mrs. Li never heard from him again.

Despite this near-disastrous incident with the Japanese diplomat, Ruth Li was still determined to find out whether her child was incarcerated in Changi. She turned to other members of the Chinese community who had direct or indirect dealings with the Japanese in quest of information about the prison. She was referred from one to another until she made contact with a tradesman who had given surreptitious aid to inmates of the prison. He and a few fellow tradesmen were thought by the Japanese to be friendly to their cause, but actually they had exposed themselves to great danger by smuggling both food and money to prisoners in Changi. For a brief period, the Japanese commandant of Changi had allowed a few of the imprisoned nurses to go by truck to Singapore and buy supplies in the marketplace. They had very little 'money, but these Chinese friends who saw them in the marketplace devised ways to hand them additional money for purchases and to load their truck with extra supplies. Apparently, the Japanese got wind of what was going on, because the shopping trips were canceled.

"I will try to find out if your child is one of those at Changi, but for your sake, I hope and pray she is not there," he told Mrs. Li.

"It's better if she is in a prison, alive, than dead at the bottom of the sea," Mrs. Li retorted.

The tradesman shook his head sadly. "From what I have learned of Changi, the poor women there are experiencing a living death," he said. "If any of them survive until the war finally ends, it will be because they are made of iron and steel, not flesh and blood."

The Japanese formula for the women and children

of Changi was slow but steady starvation, he explained. All the prisoners were given to eat was watery, tasteless soup. This was their entire menu, served in a cup three times a day. In desperation, the women were feeding the children grasshoppers and other insects that they found around the prison camp. Sometimes they even ate paper and wood. Once in a great while, they were able to catch a bird and cook it. Packages were coming to the prisoners through the International Red Cross, but the Japanese were not delivering them.

Sanitation conditions were vile, and the cells had become filthy because the women prisoners had little strength to clean them and nobody else was going to do it. The crowding was even worse than anyone had imagined. Each cell that had been built for one person was now accommodating three or four. When a prisoner came down with an infection, the Japanese would take their time about removing her to the prison hospital. They preferred to have her infect several other prisoners before she was isolated, and by delaying her hospitalization, they usually accomplished their purpose.

Dysentery, typhoid fever, and malaria were rife in the prison. In their weakened condition, the women who came down with infection had little or no strength to fight it. Inevitably, they died. The tradesman said he had seen some of the bodies of the dead who had been taken out of the camp for burial in Singapore. They were shrunken, starved bags of bones. In death, the faces of the corpses retained a ghastly pallor that made one ill merely to look at them.

The fact that the husbands of many of the women

were imprisoned right nearby in an adjoining concrete enclosure simply added to the torture of the inmates. Their men were so near—and yet so far. The Japanese captors apparently took exquisite delight in allowing the women to be close enough to hear the shouts of their men, yet forbidding them to speak to the men or make any contact with them. To get around this, the women had taken to tying messages to sticks and stones and throwing them over the concrete barrier. They had also organized a makeshift communication system via the toilet drainage system.

They had discovered that the pipes underneath the toilets led into a drain that was common with the one receiving water from the pipes underneath the men's prison. By unscrewing the coverings above the pipes, and lowering themselves down into the opening, they could carry on conversations with the men who did the same thing on their side of the wall. This type of communication could scarcely be called a meaningful substitute for having actual physical contact with husbands and loved ones, but since it was better than nothing, it acted as a morale booster.

Unfortunately, the Japanese guards were always on the lookout for attempts of the male and female prisoners to contact one another, and the punishment they dealt out to those who violated their inhuman rules was fiendish. Women who were caught throwing messages over the wall or maintaining conversation through the underground drain were either tied to a pole and beaten or thrown into solitary confinement. Sometimes they were taken out to see the men they had made contact with—only what they were taken to see was their men being flogged until the blood from their bodies formed pools on the ground.

Women who were kept in solitary sometimes remained there so long they went mad. Only a thin beam of sunlight was allowed to seep through an opening in what served as their solitary cages. Otherwise, all was in darkness. Insects of all sorts crawled into these hot, musty cells. The guard who brought the solitary prisoners their weak soup and water would not talk to them or even look at them. He would simply slip the food through an opening under the cell door and then leave quickly. All day and all night, they had nothing to do except pace endlessly up and down. The world had been shut out from them, and they had no idea when, if ever, they would be allowed to come back to it.

If the commandant thought any of the solitary prisoners was holding out information of any kind, she would be subjected to added tortures. One woman was awakened when she drifted off to sleep at night, dragged to the commandant's office to be insulted and questioned under a white, hot light, then finally thrown back into her cell. The moment she fell off to sleep again, she was slapped awake, dragged out for more of the same inquisition, then thrown back again. This went on for several days and nights at a stretch.

Another woman was tied to a makeshift dentist's chair and forced to remain there for more than seven hours. During this time, a guard pretending to be a dentist smashed a number of her teeth apart by pounding on them with a chisel. To accentuate the agony, he would intermittently drive the chisel against the nerves deep down in the teeth.

A third woman was put through a toenail-cutting ritual—they cut so deeply into the flesh, drawing so much blood and causing so much pain, that she could not walk for days.

Still another who suffered from boils on her body had the boils surgically removed—without anesthesia or painkiller of any kind. The pain was so violent that she fainted several times. After each faint, she would be awakened immediately so she would continue to suffer.

The children, the tradesman said, were not treated as badly, but Changi was a hellhole for them, too. Like the adults, they were suffering from starvation pangs induced by their meager daily diet of watery soup. The tradesman couldn't see how any of the children could survive until the end of the war in this horror camp.

A few days later, the tradesman managed to obtain the information that none of the Chinese children at Changi were the age of Ruth Li's daughter. This latest search for Patsy Li had turned into another wild-goose chase after all.

"You should be glad," the tradesman said. "It's better not to find a child than to find her in Changi."

The Changi incident marked Ruth Li's last attempt to find her Patsy until the end of the war. However, that tenacious mother's intuition which told her her daughter was still alive despite all her tortured missions of failure, still guided her heart and her head. During the last year of the Japanese occupation of Singapore, a couple with several children offered to give a new-born baby girl to Mrs. Li for adoption. They thought that, by giving this child to the grieving mother who had lost her flesh and blood at sea, they would be conferring a great blessing on her.

But they made a stipulation: If they gave their baby away, they wanted Ruth Li to give her unstinted love to it. They wanted her to promise to expend no more of her energies in the search for the lost Patsy. Like D. C. Li, they felt this was a fruitless, senseless, and debilitating process and an utter waste of mother love.

Ruth Li kept the baby for several months. She grew to like her. She taught her to coo and smile. But the vision of a Patsy still alive would not fade. She could not adhere to the stipulation. So she returned the baby.

Now the war was over, and a strange thing had happened. Ruth's sister Katherine, who had spent the war years doing cancer research in New York City, read only one newspaper each day—*The New York Times.* In that one newspaper there had appeared the delayed dispatch by Foster Hailey about the child named Patsy Li, found by the "Padre of Guadalcanal" and saved under dramatic circumstances. Katherine had been struck by the name of "Patsy Li" and had saved the clipping. She had, however, no thought of connecting the child on Guadalcanal with her niece in Singapore. After the war, when communications opened up to the West, she learned in a letter from Ruth about the disaster of the *Kuala.* It was then that she had taken the clipping from her desk and sent it to her sister.

"In action and appearance I am not the religious

type, but deep down in me there is the consciousness of God's guiding hand throughout my trials and tribulations," Ruth Li wrote me in summing up her story. "My stubborn and impractical insistence all through the years that my child did not drown at sea has been based on a deep faith. I am a Protestant and you are a Catholic, but we worship one and the same Being. Does it not seem to you that the same God who has inspired this faith in me should have directed the life of my child into the hands of yourself—one of His disciples on earth? Does it not seem to you that through some miracle, *my* Patsy Li became *your* Patsy Li?

A
Radio,
a
Scar,
and
a
Postcard

11

Ruth Li's story haunted me for days. How I longed to tell this woman who had gone through so much terror and misery what she wanted to hear! Again and again I reviewed in my mind the details of Pao-Pei's life with me on Guadalcanal. Had there been a miracle? Could the thing that Ruth Li believed in so passionately actually have happened without my realizing it or understanding it at the time? Had the good Lord picked me as the catalyst for a phenomenon?

I couldn't believe it no matter how I tried; I just could not accept the beautiful theory that Mrs. Li insisted on putting to me. I was, I told myself, just a humble priest from Brooklyn. I was definitely not the "miracle-worker" type. If God had wanted to create a new miracle worker on earth, He would certainly not have picked me. My capacities were too slim, I told myself, and my achievements too insufficient to warrant my being tapped for so awesome a responsibility.

I ran down to visit with Barney Ross and his lovely wife, Cathy, in Hollywood. Barney had still not recovered completely from his war wounds and his recurrent sieges of malaria. He was trying to regain his health under the baking lamp of the California sun, while he negotiated with the movie studios about a production of his life story. Meanwhile, Cathy was working as a dancer in motion picture musicals. Barney's appearance pained me considerably. He looked almost as bad as he did during those terrible days he spent in the hospital tent on the "Canal." But he waved away talk of his physical condition when he learned I had come to talk to him about Patsy Li.

"What do you make of it?" I asked him, after I had told him Ruth Li's entire story.

"It's one for the books, I'll say that," Barney answered. "Maybe there *is* a chance this is all part of a modern miracle. If the Referee Upstairs did want to pick one of his clergymen to perform a miracle for some sad soul like that Singapore lady, I can't think of a better man than you to get the nod."

"Oh, come on now, Barney, you're an old flatterer," I laughed at him. "It's this Hollywood atmosphere that's got you."

"Where is your little war waif now?" Cathy Ross wanted to know.

"She's in an orphanage in the village of Vila on the island of Efate," I told her. "Efate is part of the New Hebrides group. I left her on the adjoining island of Espiritu Santo, and then she was taken across to this orphanage, which is run by the French Marist nuns. I could advise Mrs. Li to go there, of course, but you must remember that the island is thousands of miles away from Singapore. It's an expensive trip. She used to be well-to-do, but the Japanese robbed her and her family of almost everything they had. How can I encourage her to spend what might be the last of her money to go on a trip that I'm sure would be fruitless? It just can't be the same child. Why, if I'd been wearing a Stetson hat when I went to China as a missionary, I probably would have been known as Father Stetson. Then I would have called our little girl Patsy Stetson, and Mrs. Li would never have written to me at all.

"People have been sending this woman from one place to another looking for her child, and all she's gotten from this is heartbreak. If I encourage her about Patsy, she'll take that long trip to the New Hebrides. Then if nothing comes of it—as I'm sure nothing will—can you imagine how much more heartbreak she will suffer? Why, this could be the straw that pushes her into a complete breakdown. I'd hate to be responsible for that."

Both Barney and Cathy, after much thought and a good deal more talk, agreed with my thinking on that. Barney raised one interesting point; our Guadalcanal waif had surprised us by her delicate, ladylike manner which we felt was out of keeping with a child whose family had presumably lived a primitive island life. It would be in keeping, however, with the background of the Patsy Li child from Singapore who had been brought up in a cultured, highly civilized atmosphere. However, we agreed this was too slender a point on which to justify any real hope that the two children could be one and the same. The arguments against this possibility were too overwhelming.

"Perhaps this Mrs. Li from Singapore would be willing to adopt the girl you called Patsy Li, even though she comes to realize it is not her child," Cathy Ross suddenly pointed out. "Would she settle for that? Would that make her happy?"

"No, it wouldn't," I answered. "She was already offered a child for adoption right in Singapore. She could have given this child the name of Patsy Li if she wanted to, and she would have had a replacement for her own lost child without having to undergo the expense and hardships of a long trip to a far-off island. But you see, she didn't want the adopted child. She gave it back. She wants only her own child, and nothing else will take its place for her."

"Well then, we're back to the original point you made, Father Fred—that is, if you encourage the poor woman to go on what seems like a fool's errand, it would expose her to another damaging emotional blow," said Cathy Ross, summing things up. "You don't want her to be hurt again, so the best idea, I take it, is to gently but firmly discourage any thoughts she has about such an expedition."

I nodded. "That's exactly it," I said. After I left the Rosses, I decided that in addition to again trying to dissuade Ruth Li from her convictions about my war orphan, I would also urge her to write the Marist nun in charge of the Vila orphanage. The Sister, I felt sure, would also stress the point that the girl in her orphanage could not be the child who had been lost in the waters off Singapore. Her letter might seem more convincing to Ruth Li than mine and would go farther toward convincing the grieving mother that she was nourishing false hopes.

How I misread this mother's heart! She wrote the Sister as I suggested, and got the answer I expected. Instead of this answer discouraging her from making plans for a trip to see the child, it acted as the final convincer that she should pack her bags and leave as soon as possible!

"When the Sister wrote me that she was sure the child in the orphanage could not be my child, I am sure she meant to be kind and wanted to spare me the pain and ardor of a fruitless trip," Mrs. Li notified me. "But upon receiving her letter, I decided she had taken it upon herself to foreclose the future of a child whose identity still remains unknown to you who have found her and to those who are keeping her. I decided that no one person, no matter how well-meaning, has the right to irrevocably seal an unknown child's destiny. I have decided it is my solemn obligation to go to Vila, no matter how costly and difficult the trip will be to me, in order to find out for myself whether the child really is mine and whether her future should properly be with me."

Until she made up her mind that she must undertake this trip to Vila and at once, Ruth Li had been preparing to go to Shanghai. Her father, who had suffered a great deal at the hands of the Japanese during the war, had had a second stroke and was believed to be dying. As a devoted and dutiful daughter in a family where duty had always been considered a very important part of the family code, she wanted very much to be at her father's side in his last days and hours. But she felt she had to put that trip aside now because she had a more important obligation to fulfill. She felt her sisters and brother could take her place in Shanghai, but that nobody could take her place in Vila.

The details of the drama that unfolded in Vila did not become known to me for some time afterward, when I learned them from letters sent me by Ruth Li as well as from reports by the Sisters and other eyewitnesses at the orphanage. But I will attempt to reconstruct them now in chronological sequence to make it clear to the reader exactly what happened.

Ruth Li left Singapore in July, 1946, for the New Hebrides. Dr. Albert Lim, another physician who had been a friend of hers and her family for many years, helped arrange the details of her trip. Dr. Lim found that the only ship that traveled to the out-of-the-way island where Patsy was kept left from Sydney, Australia, every three months. These ships made regular cargo stops at many of the little islands strung out across the South Pacific before returning to Australia. In addition to carrying cargo, they also had room for a small number of passengers.

Dr. Lim found that a merchant ship would be leaving Sydney before Mrs. Li could get to Australia if she traveled by sea from Singapore. He therefore made arrangements for Mrs. Li to travel to Sydney by plane. When she arrived, she learned that the ship's regular sailing schedule had been changed, so she had to wait two weeks in a hotel before she finally left on her fateful voyage. The first day on board, she found herself mentally re-living the horror of the *Kuala* sailing. This made her so deathly ill and so prone to seasickness that she spent the entire voyage flat on her back in her bunk.

Her ship pulled into the harbor at Vila on a hot afternoon in August. She stepped slowly down the gangplank, looking weak and wan from her prolonged seasickness, and feeling, as she put it, "a sudden sense of trepidation" that this mission which she had begun with such determination and high hopes would end in tragic failure. "What gave me such a feeling of alarm was the fact that I found myself so terribly alone on a strange island thousands of miles away from the world that I knew," she wrote me.

Suddenly, there was a shout, "Mrs. Li? Is that you, Mrs. Li?"

Startled, Ruth Li looked all around her. Could someone from the convent have decided to meet her at the pier? There were no Sisters in sight, however. About twenty yards away, she saw an Australian coming toward her. "You're Mrs. Li, aren't you?" he called out to her.

"Yes, yes, I am," she answered. "How did you know?" The man gave her a half-salute, and reached for her bags. He was, he said, an assistant to Mr. Bernard Blackwell, the Australian Resident Commissioner on Efate. The New Hebrides group was jointly administered by the French and the Australians so that Mr. Blackwell represented one half the government on the island.

"Mr. Blackwell heard about your trip and sent me to meet you and to welcome you," the man told her. "There's a little hotel close by Mr. Blackwell's official Residency where you can stay. I'll be glad to drive you there."

The courtesy shown her by an official who was a total stranger was so heartwarming to Mrs. Li that her misgivings and fears about her trip seemed to disappear. Shortly after she was settled in the hotel, Mr. Blackwell, a gracious, dark-haired man in his late thirties, came to see her personally. He told her he had already made arrangements with the Sister in charge of the orphanage to have Mrs. Li go there the next day and see the girl who was the object of her trip.

"I will be glad to accompany you there, Mrs. Li, and give you whatever assistance I can," he told her. "I've heard about your story, and I know how much this mission means to you."

"By ordinary standards, my trip would probably be considered foolish and wasteful, but I had to come here and convince myself about this child or I would have no peace for the rest of my life," Ruth Li told him. "If the child is not mine, I will leave here immediately."

"I admire your courage, Mrs. Li," the Commissioner told her. "I only hope that your dreams and your hopes come true."

Early the next day, Mr. Blackwell called for Mrs. Li in his official car. They drove quickly to the old orphanage—which was actually a series of bleak huts—adjoining the little convent of the Sisters. The Sister in charge admitted them to her office. "We have told the girl that a woman is coming from a great distance to see her . . . that this woman thinks she may be her child," the Sister explained. "She has shown no interest or emotion of any kind. But now I will bring her to you and you will see her for yourself."

As the Sister left the office, Mrs. Li suddenly felt faint. She closed her eyes. Mr. Blackwell gripped her arm encouragingly. This seemed to give her strength. She opened her eyes and smiled her thanks at him.

There were footsteps in the hall. Mrs. Li got half-way up out of her chair and stared at the entranceway. A Chinese girl of ten or eleven came in. She seemed tall for her age. She was gawky and graceless. She slouched. Her orphanage uniform hung loosely on her and accented her bad posture. She brought a slight, but disturbing, odor into the room. It was, Mrs. Li learned later, the product of a strong disinfectant used on the girls' clothing to repel insects which sometimes crawled through cracks in the old building. Her hair was stringy.

Her face had no expression, but was strangely blank. Her eyes seemed blank, too, at first. Then they turned sullen.

Behind the girl, the Sister was saying, "This is Father Gehring's Patsy Li."

Mrs. Li uttered a sigh and sank back into her chair. She shook her head from side to side, and then covered her face with her hands. There was dead silence in the room. The girl called Patsy Li turned and stared absentmindedly out the window. Mrs. Li withdrew her hands from her face. Her eyes looked red, and misty, but no tears fell.

"This is not my child," she said in a low voice.

She stood up. The girl looked at the Sister. She seemed to be asking permission to leave. The Sister looked at Mrs. Li, who nodded her head. The Sister gestured toward the door and told the girl in French that she could leave. The girl walked awkwardly out.

Mrs. Li turned to the Commissioner. "I'm prepared to go home immediately—on the first ship that leaves this island," she said.

"No, no," Mr. Blackwell said suddenly. "You have come too far, and gone through too much to give up so quickly. Please stay at my Residency for two or three days. We'll have the child stay there, too, and visit with you for the few days."

"But why?" Mrs. Li asked him. "I am satisfied that I have come on a useless journey. My Patsy was a beautiful, bright little girl with fine, black hair, with charm and poise, with personality in her eyes and in her face. This could not be the same girl. This is not the daughter

I brought up. This is a stranger—a girl given the same name by accident and coincidence."

"Just the same, it will do no harm for you to come with the child to the Residency for a few days," Blackwell persisted. "It'll be a holiday for Patsy, because it'll mean a break in her regular routine. She'll also be waited on and be made to feel like a little queen. I'd like to help make the child happy." He turned toward the Sister. "Would you give your permission for the child to come to the Residency as the guest of Mrs. Blackwell and myself?"

The Sister nodded her head. "If this idea is agreeable to Mrs. Li, I will offer no objections," she said.

Mrs. Li was moved by the unusual compassion the Australian official was showing for this strange Chinese orphan. If he was so desirous of giving the youngster a special treat, how could she not comply with his wishes? "Your invitation is a very kind one, and I accept it," she told him.

The Sister went to call Patsy back. When she had left the room, Blackwell turned to Mrs. Li and said, "Since you are so sure the child is not yours, then I doubt that anything will change your mind, and we will consider this visit with me a little holiday for the child, as I have said. Just the same, I do want you to study her carefully while she is with you. I don't believe you are aware of how orphanage living can change a child—in appearance, in manner, and in attitude. Life is very hard for the children here. There is much washing and cleaning and kitchen work to be done in addition to schoolwork and religious studies. The Marist mission has very limited funds, and the number of foundlings they have to take care of in the orphanage increases every year."

Patsy's attitude was sullen all during the drive to the Residency. Mrs. Li attempted to converse with her in English and got no response. "I'm afraid French is the only language she speaks," Mr. Blackwell explained. "That's the language the children are taught at the convent school. If she ever knew any other language, she doesn't know it now."

Mrs. Li was visibly distressed. "But that means we can't even communicate. . . . I don't speak French," she said.

"I'll interpret for you," Blackwell told her. "I also have two boys about Patsy's age who have been studying French in school. They'll be able to converse with Patsy, play with her, and keep her in good spirits."

Once inside the luxurious Residency, Patsy's eyes roved animatedly over every piece of furniture. She went to the radio, switched it on, and flipped the dial to several different stations. Both Mr. Blackwell and his wife stared at her. They knew there was no radio—or any other modern appliance—at the primitive orphanage, and there had certainly been no such convenience in the little native village on Guadalcanal where the child had lived before the Japanese massacre. Yet Patsy had just shown them she knew exactly how a radio worked.

"Did you ever play a radio before?" Mr. Blackwell asked the girl in French, while gesturing at the radio. She looked startled.

"No, I don't believe so," she answered.

"How is it you knew how to play this one?" he asked her.

She shrugged her shoulders. "I don't know, I just did," she said.

"I assume you had a radio in your home in Singapore," Mr. Blackwell said, turning to Ruth Li.

"Yes, of course we did and my daughter loved to play it," Mrs. Li told him.

For the rest of that day, the Blackwells and Mrs. Li watched the girl from the orphanage closely, while she explored the rest of the large Residency and played games with the two Blackwell boys. They were amazed at the ease with which Patsy handled herself in this home and at her obvious familiarity with the modern, well-appointed furnishings. "This girl lived in a home like this somewhere once—sometime before she ever got to Guadalcanal," Mrs. Blackwell said firmly. She pointed out that the setting at the orphanage was crude and bare by comparison, and that the girl should have been a total stranger to the Residency's surroundings.

"My home was furnished much like yours—in similar style and with the finest of furnishings," Mrs. Li said. But she added suddenly, "It must be just a coincidence again, because as I told you, this is not my child. I would recognize her if she were. And as you can tell, she certainly doesn't recognize me."

"Well, don't think about that for now. We'll just let the child enjoy her visit," the Commissioner said.

He arranged a party for Patsy that evening and invited members of the small Australian and French communities and their families. He also arranged for the girl to sleep with Mrs. Li in a large room in the Residency annex next door. Neither slept very well. There was embarrassment on Mrs. Li's part toward the girl and suspicion on the girl's part toward the visitor. And there was still no communication between them.

The second day was spent again in a careful scrutiny of Patsy at play, at her meals, and in her attitude toward people. Mrs. Li began to see some similarities to her own daughter in the child's mannerisms and her air of restlessness. In the evening, Mr. Blackwell brought Mrs. Li and Patsy into his private office. He asked the child if she had ever seen Mrs. Li before or had any idea who she was. The child shook her head. He asked her if she remembered where she was born and she shook her head. He asked her to tell him about her mother and father, and she said she knew nothing about them.

Finally, he asked her to tell him a little bit about her experiences on Guadalcanal. She looked at him with a strange expression and said, "I have been told by the Sisters that I was found on this island by a priest while a war was going on. I was told that my entire family was lost and that was why the priest brought me here. But I remember none of this myself. The only home I know is the orphanage."

"Don't you even remember Father Gehring and all the American Marines?" Mrs. Li asked incredulously. Patsy stared at her, while Mr. Blackwell translated. When the translation was finished, the girl shook her head at Mrs. Li in answer.

"This is amazing. I cannot understand this child and what has happened to her," Mrs. Li muttered.

"You must remember how close she came to being murdered and what kind of emotional terror she lived with. She may not want to remember that whole period," Mr. Blackwell pointed out.

Patsy asked permission to leave. All these questions were obviously painful to her. The Commissioner nodded his head, but then as Patsy turned toward the door, he suddenly said, "Wait a minute, that looks like a vaccination on your arm." Patsy was wearing a sleeveless blouse, part of the wardrobe Mrs. Blackwell had given her to provide a change from her orphanage uniform. Blackwell got up from his chair and studied a mark on Patsy's left arm high up near the shoulder. "My God, it *is* a vaccination mark," he said with unconcealed excitement.

"Is that important?" Mrs. Li wanted to know.

It was tremendously important, Blackwell told her. He extended the girl's arm forward to Mrs. Li so she could see the vaccination for herself. This was clear-cut proof, he said, that the child did not come from any of the South Pacific islands. "Now we know for sure that she was born elsewhere and was brought to the islands," Blackwell told Mrs. Li.

"I don't understand. What makes you say that? What does the vaccination prove?" Ruth Li wanted to know.

"We don't have any vaccinations anywhere in these islands," Blackwell explained. "Smallpox is no problem out here, so none of the children are ever vaccinated.

She came from the mainland all right. Was your daughter vaccinated?"

"Yes, she was," Mrs. Li told him. She peered at the mark on Patsy's arm. "She was vaccinated in Shanghai before we left there to live in Singapore. Her vaccination mark was just about where this girl's mark is."

"Did she have any other birthmarks that you can remember, or any other unusual characteristics?" Blackwell asked.

Yes, Mrs. Li told him. Her child had a little scar on her left eyelid, something she'd been left with after a siege of childhood sties. She had intended to examine the eyelid of the orphanage girl as soon as she arrived in Vila, but when the girl turned out to be so different from what she'd expected, she hadn't bothered. Now she quickly scanned Patsy's eyelid. The scar was there!

Ruth Li now had what seemed like solid evidence that she had come to the end of her tortuous four-and-a-half-year search. Yet she could not accept this evidence as conclusive. She looked at the Commissioner helplessly, silently pleading with him to help make up her mind for her. "Do you have any other marks or scars on your body?" Blackwell asked Patsy.

Yes, the girl answered. She rolled down her stocking and pointed to a discoloration on her left leg. The Sisters had told her it was a birthmark, she said.

Blackwell turned quickly to Mrs. Li. She was already shaking her head. Her child had never had such a birthmark. Was she sure, the Commissioner wanted to know? She was absolutely sure, she answered. She could not possibly have forgotten something like that.

Mrs. Li was now so distraught that Blackwell sent the girl out to play with his sons. To soothe his guest, he said, "I'm going to arrange to extend the child's visit here. I know what kind of agonizing dilemma this is for you, and I don't want you to rush into any decisions. I'm also going to contact Espiritu Santo and find out which doctor examined and treated the child after Father Gehring first brought her to our islands. In view of all those terrible wounds she suffered on Guadalcanal, I'm sure Père Jean must have had some doctor look her over. That doctor may be able to clear up the mystery for us."

"But that doctor—if there was a doctor—may have left the islands long ago," Mrs. Li pointed out.

Blackwell patted her arm. "Even if he has, I'm sure I can find out just where he's gone," he told her. "I'll try to contact him by radio. If necessary, we may be able to make arrangements to bring the child to him. I'm going to do everything I can for you to be able to go home either with your daughter, or with your mind completely satisfied that your daughter was never here."

The next three days presented a new kind of torture for Ruth Li—the torture of indecision. The birthmark apparently ruled out the possibility that the two Patsy Lis were one and the same, yet what about the vaccination and the scar from the sties? Then again, could one accept a vaccination, an obvious familiarity with luxurious furnishings, and a tell-tale scar as proof if neither sullen girl nor grieving mother could recognize each other? Again and again, conflicting thoughts swirled through Ruth Li's mind, so that she found herself scarcely able to eat or sleep, or do anything save watch the girl constantly and think about her.

On the fourth day, Mr. Blackwell brought important news. There *had* been a French doctor named Pouliquen who had carefully examined the Guadalcanal waif soon after I brought her to Espiritu Santo. What's more, for the past year that doctor had been practicing right in Vila. He had been interested in seeing this child again, but had never gotten around to visiting the orphanage. He had known from the vaccination and from other physical characteristics that the child was not a native of the islands and had a markedly different origin than Père Jean, the Sisters, or I suspected. But since he believed the child had lost her family, he had felt there was no point in bringing this up.

Dr. Pouliquen came to the Residency that same afternoon. He brought with him a medical and dental record of his first examination of the girl I named Patsy Li. When Patsy was brought into the Commissioner's office to see the doctor, he stared at her the same way Mrs. Li had done the first day she came face to face with her at the orphanage.

"I have known how orphanage life changes the appearance of young children, yet the change in this particular girl is almost unbelievable," the doctor told Mrs. Li and the Commissioner.

"Do you see anything in her that you recognize?" Mrs. Li asked him.

"Just from looking at her, I don't recognize her at all as the girl I saw on Espiritu Santo. I would not believe it was the same girl if you hadn't told me."

The doctor's examination of Patsy took more than a half-hour. When he finished, he told Mrs. Li, "She is Father Gehring's Patsy Li, all right. My examination makes that quite certain. And I am quite certain, too, from what I see in this girl and from the evidence of the scar on the eyelid, that she is your Patsy Li as well. I have no idea how she got from the waters off Singapore to Guadalcanal, which is more than four thousand miles away, as you know. But I imagine that a Japanese ship heading toward Guadalcanal picked her up. Once she got to the island, I suppose the Japanese dumped her off on some native family."

"But what about the birthmark on her leg?" Ruth Li asked.

There was no birthmark, the doctor assured her. She had never had that mark until she came to Guadalcanal. It was a powder burn, a remnant of the injuries inflicted on her by the Japanese.

Ruth Li was still not satisfied. "If she is my child, why doesn't she recognize me by now?" she demanded.

"She has had a loss of memory about the early years of her life," he explained. The memory loss was quite understandable, he said. Here was a child who had been parted from her mother after a terrifying bombardment of the ship she was sailing on, and after she had been literally flung into the open sea. She had been a child gripped with unspeakable fear, and with the belief that her mother had abandoned her. After she had been picked up and taken to Guadalcanal to live with other people, this new family of hers had been massacred, and she herself had been beaten into unconsciousness. Saved from death, she found herself again forsaken, by the people who had sheltered her and kept her. Then when she found new kindness and shelter from a strange man in a chaplain's uniform, this man too had suddenly taken her away to another unknown place where he had —in her mind—followed the pattern of ruthlessly and cruelly casting her off.

"Has ever a child in the history of this globe been treated as this poor child has?" the doctor pointed out. "She has lived through such tragic adventures as would defy the pen of a Zola or a Conrad. You do not have to be a psychiatrist to understand why she would want to blot out of her mind the memory of every single thing that happened to her before she finally found herself in an institution where she knew what was going to happen to her every day; and where after a time she could tell herself with reasonable certainty that there would be no more volcanic disturbances in her life—no more episodes of violence, terror, and abandonment."

All the elements in the Patsy Li mystery jigsaw puzzle now seemingly fitted into place. And yet a cloud of doubt still lingered over Ruth Li. "In my head, I am convinced that this child must be mine, and yet in my heart, I cannot be sure," she said.

The next night, the Blackwells went off to a naval party which was being held on an Australian gunboat offshore. Mrs. Li remained at the Residency, moodily observing Patsy at play in the parlor with the Blackwell children. The children were busy making colored drawings and tracing pictures from a magazine. Suddenly,

Mrs. Li remembered a postcard her sister Katherine had sent her just before she left for the New Hebrides. It had been written by her daughter Patsy to Katherine in New York in 1941, when the child was first learning to write English.

It was the only evidence she had of her child's handwriting. Everything else Patsy had ever written and indeed every souvenir that Ruth Li had ever possessed had been lost when the Japanese razed her house in the last days of their Singapore occupation. Ruth had enclosed the postcard in a folder and packed the folder in turn in one of her suitcases. She now rushed over to her room in the annex, searched quickly through the luggage, and dug out the card. Patsy had been taught to print her English words in block letters, rather than write them. She also had a special fault—she always inverted her "E's." The precious card read:

DƎAR AUNT KATHƎRINƎ
WƎ ARƎ ALL WƎLL. HOW ARƎ YOU?
I LOVƎ YOU.
PATSY

Back in the Residency parlor, Ruth Li seated the children around a table and gave them pencils and paper. "We're going to play a little writing game," she told them.

"Will we write in English or in French?" one of the boys asked. It would be an English message, Mrs. Li explained, but Patsy could play too, even though Patsy didn't know the language. Mrs. Li would call out some English words to them letter by letter and they would write down the letters as she called them.

Breathing so deeply the children thought she was gasping, Ruth Li spelled out the postcard message letter by letter. "D-e-a-r . . . A-u-n-t . . . K-a-t-h-e-r-i-n-e . . . ," she started. Obediently, the children followed her, setting down the words on paper. She was almost afraid to look at how Patsy was writing, so she kept her eyes focused on the wall behind the table. Midway through her reading, she had a frightening thought. What if this child was really hers, but had been re-trained by the Sisters to use the running continental script? How could she satisfy her doubts then?

She finished reading the postcard message. Patsy put aside her pencil, and looked up at her with a frown to indicate she didn't understand what she had written. Ruth Li stared down at the paper. Patsy had not used a continental script. She had printed block letters! Every letter was the exact duplicate of what was on the postcard and every "E" was inverted!

Ruth Li knew now in heart as well as mind—and handwriting experts confirmed this later beyond all question—that the thing which had not seemed rational or conceivable had come to pass. Later that evening, in the annex room she shared with Patsy, she had the girl write the fateful postcard greeting again and again. Each time the result was the same. When the girl fell asleep, Ruth remained awake. From time to time, she reached over to touch Patsy's head, her hair, her fingers, her legs, and her toes. She studied the girl's restless movements in sleep and marveled at how they became more and more familiar to her.

In the morning, emotions surged through her natural wall of reserve. She ran out of the annex room toward the Residency building shouting for Mr. Blackwell. When he came out, she cried over and over again, "She *is* my child! Oh, my God, she *is* my child!"

I was in San Francisco again when the news came to me from Ruth Li by cablegram. I ripped open the envelope and read these words: "You have been the architect of a miracle, for I have found my Patsy Li. . . ." I could read no further. Suddenly I felt as though I were floating weightlessly, dizzily, in air. Instinctively, with my fingers locked about the cablegram, I groped my way to the chapel on the Naval base. I flung myself down in front of the altar.

"Thank you, oh, Mary," I cried, "for having given Ruth Li the strength to ignore the words of fools like me who would have stopped her from completing her mission of faith. Thank you for teaching me that there is no power greater than mother love—that mother love can still flatten mountains, turn the earth upside down, and make the wildest dreams of mortals come true."

"Will
You
Take
Patsy
Li?"

12

If this story were fiction, the saga of my Guadalcanal waif would have ended right there, but in dealing with human lives, one finds that they have their own surprising way of making new chapters for themselves. And when you have new chapters and new developments, they also make for unexpected twists in endings. So it was to be with the girl I called Patsy Li who turned out to *be* Patsy Li.

At first the wonder of discovery overshadowed everything. I had no way of knowing that the very surprise—and shock—of discovery would produce new whirlpools that would have to be bridged and new pitfalls that would have to be circumvented.

When the news about Patsy's reunion with her mother came out, I was deluged with so many letters from the members of our "Guadalcanal Alumni Society" that I found the mere process of answering them took almost all my waking and thinking time. Needless to say, the boys were thrilled at the turn of events surrounding our little war mascot. They wanted me to flesh out the bare bones of the "miracle story" with all the human interest details of Ruth Li's search and her manner of identification of her lost child. Some of the boys were so staggered by the news they just couldn't accept it at first. Did it really happen the way the reports said, they wanted to know. How in the world did Patsy ever cross the thousands of miles of water from the site where the *Kuala* was bombed to our embattled island?

I assured them that, in this case, truth indeed had proved stranger than blarney, and that all of us "foster parents" of sad-eyed Patsy could take personal pride in the fact that we had kept her alive and safe so she could later achieve the joy of family reunion. I told them that the mystery of how Patsy traveled to Guadalcanal would probably never be completely cleared up, but that we already had a pretty good idea of what had happened. After the story of Ruth Li's recovery of her child was reported in Australian and Far East newspapers, two British seamen came forward to report that they had plucked a Chinese child answering Patsy's description out of the waters near the burning *Kuala*. These seamen had not gone ashore at Pom Pong as had other survivors of the Japanese bombing attack, but had drifted to another island. Thus they knew nothing of Ruth Li's search for Patsy or her desperate—and seemingly futile—hope that her child had been saved.

The seamen had been swimming in the water and had put the Chinese child aboard a small boat. Apparently, the boat was sighted and picked up by a passing Japanese ship. A study of Japanese shipping records showed that the Japanese were at this time sending both warships and supply ships from various bases in the area to the Solomon Islands. The idea advanced by the French doctor at Vila—that the Japanese ship had dumped the child at a native village—has always seemed to me the most logical explanation of how our war waif came to be living in the village which subsequently was massacred.

Patsy's memory of her early years never returned, except for one faint flash of remembrance of her drifting around and around in open water. But in addition to what the Sisters had told her about the Marines and myself, Mrs. Li told her a good deal more. When Patsy started to learn English again, I began to get little letters from her. Mostly, they were simple messages thanking me for having sheltered and protected her, and asking about America and Americans. I wrote her long letters in turn, told her I would always regard her as "my little girl," and that I hoped to see her again some day. I explained that I had been a missionary in her part of the world before the war, and that I hoped to return again, at which time we'd have a gay reunion. I told her, too, that if she were ever able to come to America, all her old

Marine and Navy guardians would join me in seeing to it that she had the time of her young life.

Apparently, she'd been taken to at least one movie that had a South Pacific theme and starred Robert Montgomery, for she wrote me one day, "I hope Mr. Montgomery will recognize me when he sees me again!"

I kept up a correspondence with Ruth Li, too. Surprisingly, her letters didn't say very much about Patsy, other than that she was "all right" and was "getting along."

Following my discharge from active duty in the Navy, I was put on the reserve list. I thought I might resume my mission work in China, but as the Communists there gained ground, our missionary activities in the field had to be reduced rather than expanded. My superiors assigned me temporarily to administrative work for the Vincentian Missions at our mother-house in Germantown, Pennsylvania.

I kept hoping, of course, that the Communist tide could be reversed in China, but it didn't work out that way. That ominous cry of hate that the Communists had sounded when I was in China—"Tao-tsao-de-ku-chu-nee. Tao-tsao Jesu Chao" ("Down with foreign imperialism! Down with Christianity!")—had now become their victory slogan all over this ancient country. Mobs were thundering it at public meetings, children were being taught to use it as an epithet against the missionaries, and it was being painted in huge red letters on every church the Reds took over to garrison their troops. On one mission compound, the words were written in human blood.

For me, the worst blow came when I learned that the Reds had overrun all of Kiangsi Province and had occupied the missions where I had served for seven years. Sisters and priests were evicted from the orphanages, schools, and hospitals, and some were thrown into jail on trumped-up charges. From letters that were smuggled out to us, we learned that many of the ailing youngsters in the orphanages and in the hospitals had died for lack of care. I remembered the many little "Patsy Lis" I had played with in the orphanage at Kanchow, and I shuddered at what was happening to them.

The Red rulers maintained that they would not interfere with "strictly religious" practices, but this statement became a mockery with the arrest of our beloved Bishop John O'Shea. He had just started Mass one winter morning in Kanchow, assisted by my old associate, Father Frank Moehringer, when Red soldiers burst in. They seized the Bishop, lined him up outside with five others from the hospital and school staff, and read a long indictment accusing "Ho Jo-wan"—the Bishop's Chinese name—of being a spy of the "imperialist" American government. He was also charged with being the organizer of the "Legion of Mary" in Kiangsi Province. The Legion, they said, wasn't really interested in religion, but instead was a "subversive force."

Bishop O'Shea was taken to the local jail and put into solitary confinement. His cell was tiny, about five by eight feet. Two of the walls were made of logs with three-inch chinks between them. The openings allowed gusts of cold air to come in. His jacket and coat were taken away, and he was ordered not to do any walking around in the cell, but rather to sit quietly. Only one thing comforted him. His jailers searched his pockets and trousers carefully, but somehow failed to locate a small Miraculous Medal which lay in his watch pocket. The Medal stayed with him and helped sustain him during seven months of imprisonment.

Every night, the Bishop was subjected to an inquisition by the agents of the local politburo. They demanded that he confess to the spy charges. They also accused him of having murdered thousands of Chinese children. Pagan families in Kanchow traditionally threw their blind, seriously ill, and crippled children out of their houses and left them to die. The Daughters of Charity would take these children to their hospital and try to save them. Many were indeed saved, but some of course proved to be beyond help and were buried in the mission cemetery. These were the children Bishop O'Shea was supposed to have murdered!

When he refused to confess at his nightly inquisitions, the Bishop would be reviled and threatened by the politburo men. The next day, a jailer would come around with honeyed words and assure him he would be treated kindly if he only signed the statements the Communists had prepared for him. When the Bishop insisted he wouldn't prostitute the truth in any case, he was told that this "incorrigible" attitude was senseless—it would only doom him to the firing squad.

Because of his great popularity with the people of Kanchow, the Communists wanted to put Bishop O'Shea on public trial, where he would be accused of nefarious crimes by a group of witnesses. But despite all the threats they made against the Chinese who had worked or helped out at the mission compound, not a single one of them would agree to give false evidence or false testimony. So no trial was held. The Bishop remained in his cell, getting steadily weaker from the poor food, the biting cold, and the rain that poured in through the open chinks and soaked his cell and his bed. He finally came down with fever, which was diagnosed as pneumonia.

The Communists did not want the public to blame them for killing him without cause, so he was put into a hospital. His pneumonia was cured, but the ravages of malnutrition had reduced his weight to 98 pounds. Put back in jail, he continued to waste away. It seemed obvious that he was dying, and the Communists didn't want him to perish in their jail. So they released him and let him go to free Hong Kong. They felt he would die there and the "imperialists" would have to assume the responsibility. But he hung on to life. Later, he came back to us at Germantown and regained enough of his strength to resume his work for the Church in Connecticut.

Although I was thrilled at the fact that our heroic Bishop had been saved, his report of the manner in which the Communists were solidifying their grip on the country I had learned to love was very depressing. My already dim hopes of returning to the Far East as a missionary were becoming well-nigh invisible. So were my hopes of a sentimental reunion with my little miracle girl, Patsy Li.

Then suddenly, under circumstances that were as astonishing as the manner in which Patsy came to me in the first place, I found myself bound up in her life all over again. This new chapter in our relationship began in 1949 with another dramatic letter from Ruth Li. Written in the lucid and forthright style that reflected her cultured background, it nevertheless laid bare a fresh picture of human anguish. It was a painful revelation of how even "miracles" can founder on the rock of human frailties.

The letter came from Shanghai, not Singapore, where Patsy was living. This was its first surprise. But most surprising of all was the request the letter put to me. For Ruth Li wanted to know whether I would be willing to bring Patsy to America, and take her once again under my care. This would be not only for the duration of a reunion visit or for a summer of educational sightseeing, as I had envisioned in my letters to Patsy. Incredible as it seemed, the mother who had gone through years of heartbreak and had turned the world upside down to find her child was now proposing a permanent separation from that child.

What had happened between mother and daughter? From Ruth Li herself and from a very perceptive Australian woman named Frances Hogan, who was traveling in Singapore and who sought out Patsy at my behest, I learned that the difficulties began on Efate not more than two days after the miracle of discovery was consummated. Late on that second day, as Patsy was looking out the window of the room in the Residency annex which had been turned over to her mother, she saw the youngsters from her orphanage go marching past. Suddenly, she burst into tears. When Ruth rushed over to soothe her, she shrank from her mother's touch. That evening, at dinner with the Residential Commissioner, she scarcely touched her food. She would not look at her mother, and when Ruth Li pressed a plate of ice cream on her, she pushed it away and ran sobbing out of the room.

Her face white, her eyes clouded with pain, Ruth Li turned to the Commissioner. "You see, she doesn't want me after all," she said. "I went through so much to find her and now she rejects me."

The Commissioner urged patience. Ruth Li would have to face certain realities, he said. Patsy was a highly emotional child who had reacted to all her ordeals of terror by blocking out the memory of her early life. The only life she knew was in the orphanage. The orphanage, the children who lived there, and the Sisters who ran it, represented security to her. When she saw the orphans pass by and realized she was going to be cut off from the only security she knew, she had been overcome with fear. It had been exciting at first for Patsy to be told that a long-lost mother had found her and would take her to her real home, but it was no surprise that this excitement had worn off very quickly.

"The child is now reminding herself that the woman we say is her mother is a total stranger to her, and that she is going to take her to a great unknown," the Commissioner said. "Patsy is thinking, 'Who knows what terrible things will happen to me in this unknown world?' So she feels a surge of resentment toward you, and she is panic-stricken for herself. This will pass, as you show her kindness and understanding, and she finds a new security. She will love you again . . . but give it time."

A special cargo ship, the *Morinda,* was due to touch at Efate within a few days. It was heading for Australia, though it would make stops at several other islands along the way. Ruth Li made a quick decision to arrange for passage for herself and Patsy on the ship. She felt that if they remained on Efate longer, it would only give the child more time to think and brood. They would be the only passengers on the ship and thus could spend long hours getting to know each other better.

With the Commissioner's help, all the documents necessary to transfer Patsy to her mother's legal custody were quickly prepared. But Patsy's final good-bys to the orphanage people erupted in an orgy of sobbing, and the slow trip to Australia proved a nightmare.

The small cargo ship heaved and rolled, so that Patsy became violently seasick and cried constantly. The strain between mother and daughter was intensified because they could not communicate with each other. Mrs. Li's languages were English and Chinese. Patsy spoke only French. An Australian woman, Mrs. John Boulton, who taught the Commissioner's children, had tried to teach Patsy some English during the girl's stay at the Residency, but the stay had been too brief and hectic for any lessons to sink in. At the Residency, there had been helpful interpreters; on the boat there were none.

Mrs. Li expected to leave for Singapore soon after she arrived in Sydney, Australia. However, she changed her mind after she got to Sydney and remained in Australia with Patsy for nine months. A Mr. Le Mothe, who was an old friend of her Singapore neighbor, Dr. Albert Lim, put Ruth and Patsy up for a few days. He also introduced her to a woman who taught English to foreigners. Mrs. Li decided that Patsy would be able to adjust to her future life in Singapore and make friends there more readily if she were already able to converse in English when she got there. So she hired the teacher to give Patsy daily private lessons in English. She also sent Patsy to a ballet school to learn grace, and arranged for lessons in music.

This whole educational program was put on an intensive basis, with Mrs. Li herself supplementing the English teacher's efforts by working with Patsy on her language every evening. Ruth Li had been brought up in an atmosphere where strict discipline was enforced and where painstaking work habits and an all-consuming interest in the pursuit of knowledge were demanded of every child. Her father, a pioneer eye surgeon and a distinguished medical scholar, set these standards, and his children had accepted them without question. He felt this was the only way for his children to become outstanding. The fact that they had all finished at or near the top of their classes in college, and that his son and three of his daughters had achieved notable success in the medical profession, seemed to have proved his thesis.

Ruth Li now applied these selfsame standards to

Patsy's education and upbringing. She sincerely felt that what had proved right under her parents' roof would prove right for her daughter. She herself had gone into teaching, rather than medicine, and in this way had been a disappointment to her father. She had disappointed him again by marrying someone he did not like, and she disappointed him a third time when she had gone to Efate instead of answering his summons to his deathbed. He had died while she and Patsy were on the boat taking them to Australia, and she felt his loss keenly. She had already determined that she would try to honor his memory by training the daughter she had found on Efate for a career in medicine. Retraining the child in a new language would place an extra handicap in shaping this career, but Mrs. Li felt that with special effort and sacrifice it could be done.

For these reasons, Patsy was placed under a strict regimen of work and more work, with little time for play or pranks. Coming on top of her difficulty in adjusting to a strange environment, this heavy pressure on rapid learning seemed unbearable to her. The lack of easy communication between mother and daughter also made it difficult for Patsy to grasp the idea that this program was intended for her future benefit. She felt only that the strange woman who had taken her away from her old life was a harsh taskmaster. She thought that Ruth Li had taken her only out of a sense of obligation. Her mother, she told herself, didn't really want her and was punishing her for being a burden. All right, if that was the case, she would show her mother she didn't care for her either.

She had a bright mind, as Ruth Li knew, and as the Sisters in Efate had discovered, but she had no intention of making full use of it. Instead of cooperating with her mother's plans, she rebelled. She progressed at toadlike speed in her lessons. The more her mother worked on her to speed up, the more she balked and the more she tried to frustrate both teacher and parent. When her mother used a parent's prerogative to discipline her sternly or send her to bed without supper for disobedience, she threw tantrums.

Mrs. Li knew nobody in Sydney aside from the Le Mothe family, and Patsy had no real friends her own age. They were living in a small city apartment. The unhappy contrast between this atmosphere and the open environment and the many friends she had had on Efate added to the child's feelings of antagonism.

The daughter Mrs. Li had lost was pretty, well-mannered, and graceful. The girl she had found was at the awkward age, and awkward in appearance. In primitive surroundings, she had taken on more of the habits and attitudes of a coolie girl. The ballet school and Mrs. Li's home instructions in grooming and behavior were designed to put Patsy back in the Li mold. Patsy seemed to like the ballet school; but she sensed her mother's anxiety to change her quickly and she construed this as more pressure. So she resisted anew. She was willing to develop grace and charm in school, but at home she lapsed back into a slouch walk and sloppy habits. This drove Mrs. Li to distraction.

From
Singapore
to
Virginia

13

Ruth and Patsy Li returned to Singapore a little over five years after they left it together aboard the ill-fated *Kuala*. Publicly, it seemed like a joyous homecoming, but privately the two principals were unhappily aware that there was a gulf between them. The mother felt unwanted by her daughter; the daughter had the same feeling about her mother. Events in Singapore did not improve the situation.

I had known from what Ruth Li told me in her account of the bombing of the *Kuala* and its aftermath, that a rift had developed between herself and her husband. I did not know just how serious the rift was, however, and I was flabbergasted to learn from Ruth Li's detailed letter from Shanghai that she had obtained a divorce shortly before leaving on her trip to the orphanage. The bitter feelings that were spawned as a result of the couple's tragic loss of their children at sea had finally led to a break-up. During the period the Lis spent under Japanese occupation in Singapore, they had lived apart both physically and psychologically. Mrs. Li said she had asked for, and received, a divorce after she learned that her husband was seeing other women.

She was frank to say that she had not told me or the people on Efate of the divorce because she felt this might prejudice her chances of securing the return of the child. She had also avoided bringing up this painful subject in her occasional letters to me from Singapore, but now she wanted me to have the complete facts. She had used the money from the divorce settlement to finance her trip to the New Hebrides and her stay in Australia. D. C. Li had signed over to her custody of their child in the event that the girl Patsy Li *did* turn out to be theirs. D. C. Li had considered the trip foolish. Indeed, he—and others—had regarded Ruth Li's frantic insistence that Patsy was alive to be a ridiculous and unhealthy obsession.

Ruth's friends in Singapore hoped that her return with Patsy would lead to a reconciliation with her husband, but it was not to be. D. C. Li visited Patsy, acknowledged her as his daughter, and gave her gifts. But as Patsy later told me, "he showed no real interest in me and no love for me." Mrs. Hogan was to tell me, "he regarded her as part of a world that no longer concerned him."

Thus, though Patsy was now returned to a home of her own, it was a broken home. She felt underprivileged compared to other children who had both mothers and fathers. At this crucial juncture in her life, paternal love and guidance would have been very beneficial to her. Because it was lacking, Ruth Li felt she had to be both mother and father to the child, and that it was incumbent on her to continue the doctrine of strict discipline. Patsy answered with more rebellion. In her classes in the Singapore school, she lagged behind the others. This made Ruth Li feel all the more frustrated in her efforts to make her daughter "outstanding."

The bitterness between her parents was made apparent to Patsy on the few occasions when her father came to see her. This aggravated her feelings of unhappiness. There were financial problems at home, too. D. C. Li, who had returned to his insurance business, said he would contribute to Patsy's support, but Mrs. Li told me his payments were few and insufficient. Her own property and private funds had been lost to the Japanese. She did some private teaching, but it brought in only a small amount of money.

Two years after her return to Singapore, Ruth Li fell in love with and married a salesman for a Chinese export firm. He had been assigned to the firm's Singapore office, but soon after the marriage he received transfer orders to their Shanghai office. Naturally, he expected his wife to accompany him. In his new job, her husband was to work only part of the year out of the

Shanghai office, and would spend the other part traveling around the Orient. He wanted her to join him on at least some of these trips. This posed a tremendous problem for Mrs. Li. Patsy flatly refused to leave Singapore to go to another strange city. Mrs. Li had to admit that another move would be unhealthy for a child who desperately needed roots and security. In Shanghai, too, Chinese, not English, was the principal language, and if Patsy were to live there, she would have to be reeducated in this difficult tongue. This would now be an all-but-impossible task.

Patsy had made friends with some girls in Singapore who were attending a Methodist boarding school. She said she wanted to enroll there. Mrs. Li agreed. Mrs. Li's old friends and neighbors, Dr. Albert Lim and his wife, told her they would be glad to have Patsy with them on weekends. They had five children who could provide companionship. Patsy's father consented to pay for part of the tuition at the boarding school.

Mrs. Li left Singapore with a feeling of trepidation, but also with a feeling that, all things considered, this was the best arrangement for Patsy for the time being. In view of the personality conflict between herself and her daughter, a temporary separation might even spur the girl to improve herself.

Mrs. Li's hopes, however, did not come to fruition. Patsy did not like the school. She liked the kind Lims, but she was always aware that she was an extra person in a crowded household. She felt she'd been deserted again and resented it. Though she had not gotten along with her mother, she did not appreciate the separation.

At the end of her school term she did not pass, and was told she would have to repeat the term—her last term in grade school—all over again.

This episode came as a final, stunning jolt to Ruth Li and inspired her letter to me. Patsy had often told her of her desire to come to see me, and had expressed a strong interest in going to an American school. Because of my letters to Patsy in which I had described her as the "sweetheart of the U. S. Marine Corps and Navy," she thought of herself as a part of America. Shanghai may have seemed like a foreign, disagreeable world to her, but America represented a fascinating dream.

Mrs. Li was well aware of the advantages an American education could bring to Patsy. But most of all, she felt that in America Patsy might find the happiness that had eluded her in the country of her birth. Mrs. Li could perhaps force her husband to leave his position in Shanghai and return with her to Singapore, but her candid opinion was that it would not help Patsy.

"It is with a great feeling of distress that I have to confess that I cannot do what I hoped to do with Patsy," she said. "Reeducating her to the point where she can take her proper position in life and find personal fulfillment and happiness has proved beyond my talents. Her feelings toward me and my efforts are too deeply antagonistic. It will be heartbreaking for me to let my daughter go out of my life again, but we are at the point where I can see that America represents her only chance for a happy future. If your generous spirit and your devotion to the child you once saved moves you to reach out again to help her, I will be forever grateful."

My heart, of course, went out to Patsy. I had promised the child that if she ever needed me, I would be Johnny-on-the-spot, and it was a promise I was going to keep. But I wanted to make sure the child did indeed need—and want—my help. So I wrote her directly asking if she wanted to come to the United States to attend both high school and college here and perhaps remain permanently. She told me this would make her the happiest girl in the world.

When I learned that Mrs. Hogan, an old friend of our Vincentian missions and a woman with much experience in the family relations field, was in Singapore, I enlisted her services. She sought out Patsy, the Lims, and other people who knew the Li family, and confirmed the frank report Ruth Li had given me. Patsy was a troubled and difficult child. She needed a fresh start, under different auspices, and in an atmosphere that held a great attraction for her. What touched me most of all was Mrs. Hogan's report that when she spoke to Patsy, the child broke down and cried, "I once had a mother and a father, but neither of them wanted me." I would be well advised, Mrs. Hogan said, to get the child to America as quickly as possible.

My first job was to get Patsy into a good school. I knew the Sisters of Mercy had just opened a new academy for girls of high-school age, so I flew to their mother house at Merion, Pennsylvania, and sought out Mother Bernard, the head of the Order. She promised me that in view of the special circumstances, she would arrange for Patsy to attend the school on a scholarship. It is called Walsingham Academy and is located in Williamsburg, Virginia. "The climate is very much like Singapore's, and many of the students are children whose parents have traveled around the world," she said. "It seems like the setup would be ideal for your Patsy. There are Protestant girls there as well as Catholic, and she can continue to have her own religion."

I intended to watch over Patsy with a fatherly eye, but as a priest I could not serve as her legal guardian. So now all I had to do was find that guardian; get a student visa from the proper government officials; fill out dozens of papers to send to Singapore; arrange the transportation of my protégé, and finally pay the bill.

Well, the Chinese had once taught me that every journey, no matter how many miles, starts with a single step. Step Number One was to find that guardian, and almost before I knew it, I had the right person. "Lady" Eleanor Bumgardner, whom I had first met aboard the *Coolidge* traveling to the Orient in 1933, had never married though she had had many suitors over the years. She was living alone in a doll-like home in the Georgetown section of Washington, D.C., and told me she would be delighted to make Patsy her legal ward. Lady had served Frank Murphy as confidential secretary from his days as Mayor of Detroit until his untimely death as Justice of the Supreme Court. She was still working at the Court as roving secretary to the other Justices. She was a woman of charm and wit and broad understanding; she had traveled widely and had many friends in social and government circles. She could—and would—help Patsy immeasurably.

The visa problem was taken out of my hands by

Bruce Mohler, director of the National Catholic Welfare Council's Bureau of Immigration. And the money problems relative to bringing Patsy over and getting her settled proved easy to lick, too. All I did was spread the word among our Guadalcanal Navy and Marine "alumni" that I needed some financial help to bring our "miracle girl" over.

A few days before Christmas, 1950, I received a cable from Singapore: PATSY LI LEAVING VIA PAN-AMERICAN FOR LOS ANGELES. She arrived, fatefully enough, on Christmas Day. Lady was waiting at the airport for her and the two went to church to pray for the youngster's happy future in her new country. Two days later, Patsy's plane landed at La Guardia Field, New York, where I was waiting for her along with several members of my family. As she stepped out into the slush and cold of a New York winter morning, she was stunned by an explosion of flash-bulbs. The newspapers had been alerted that the "Miracle Girl of World War II" was arriving for a reunion with her old friend, and they were out in force.

The blinding lights frightened Patsy and she shrank back. I hurried forward to comfort her. My first impulse was to take her in my arms as I had done those many nights when we lived through more dangerous explosions. But as I came up to her, I stopped. This, of course, was not the tearful clinging orphan of the foxholes, but a serious-looking Chinese girl of fifteen who bore no resemblance to the child I had known. So I just held out my hand like a clumsy schoolboy and said, "Welcome, Patsy." She held out her hand just as awkwardly and said in British-accented English, "I'm very glad to be here." We stood there uncomfortably, murmuring platitudes, till a photographer happily broke the tension by shouting, "This girl is probably thinking, 'Why did I pick such a cold, slushy city to come to? Why didn't I go back to nice, hot Guadalcanal?' "

The next few days were a dizzy romp. My cousin, Frank Gehring, a prosperous textile merchant, had booked a hotel suite for Patsy and Lady, and prepared a gala party. Under Frank's Christmas tree, there was a pyramid of gifts for the Singapore girl. Playing the role of Santa Claus was Al Landes, my old chaplain's assistant. As he cavorted for Patsy, her face lit up like a neon sign. Remembering all his fruitless efforts on Guadalcanal to get her to show a glimmer of pleasure, he whispered to me, "Thank God, the kid's finally learned how to smile!"

There was also a tour of Manhattan's bright spots, a luncheon with Cardinal Spellman, an appearance on the "We the People" television show, radio interviews, long-distance calls from Barney Ross, Gene Markey, Robert Montgomery, Joe Foss, Captain Jack Leonard, Dr. Joel White, and many other Guadalcanal alumni, and, in all, more than enough to take a youngster's breath away. Then finally, we were on a train heading toward Virginia and the end of Patsy's ten-thousand-mile hegira from the Orient.

Now the girl sitting between Lady and myself was strangely quiet and tense while I chattered like a magpie about the good times she would be having at the Academy. Knowing Patsy's background, and aware of her fears and insecurities, I felt I had to keep assuring her that she would be entering an atmosphere of warmth and good will. But my chattering was also a method of convincing myself that I had done the right thing by Patsy. I had to admit that I knew very little about her character and the person she had become. What if the school and the girls she was to live with turned out to be all wrong for her and she all wrong for them? What if it developed that it was beyond my power to make Patsy a happier and better-adjusted individual than she had been in Singapore? How could I then justify my action in bringing her to America and having her burn her bridges behind her?

My anxiety about the reaction of Patsy's American schoolmates lessened appreciably when we arrived at Walsingham. All the students were lined up at the front entrance of the picturesque, sun-dappled Academy building. Waiting with them were Mother Bernard and Sister Constance, the head of the school. As Patsy was introduced to each girl, she received a greeting of such obvious warmth it touched both her and myself. One girl brought on a gust of laughter by squealing, "She comes all the way from Asia and yet she speaks English!"

Patsy noted quickly that she was the only Chinese girl there, but it was also apparent that the girls were welcoming her as one of them. Blessings on Mother Bernard and Sister Constance—they had done their job of preparation well!

A charming, red-headed little miss named Drury Price, who seemed to be the leader of the student group, now stepped up and offered to take us on a guided tour. Lady and I, and Bill McComb, a government official and friend of Lady's who had come down with us, fell into step behind the girls. With Drury animatedly pointing out the high spots, we trooped from room to room and hallway to hallway until we came to the third floor dormitory where Patsy would now live. Each cubicle had a mirrored dresser with various pennants and feminine knickknacks that individualized the student assigned to it. The space that was awaiting Patsy was right in the middle, rather than at either of the ends. It was another thoughtful little gesture to emphasize that the girl from afar was being accepted as an intimate member of the "gang."

When it was time to go, I took Sister Constance aside and told her I had a request to make about Patsy. "Sister, I know there will be times when you will have to scold Patsy, but may I ask that you do it in private, rather than in front of her fellow boarders," I said. "You see, the Chinese are frightfully self-conscious and they don't like to lose face." Sister Constance fixed me with a merry glint and said softly, "Around here, Father, we try not to let even the American girls lose face." As she turned away, I could hear her chuckle, "Ah, these oversolicitous guardians."

For Patsy, I had a good-by blessing, and this time the paternal hug and kiss I had been too bashful to bestow at La Guardia Field. The last time I had said my good-bys to her, in 1942, I had left her shaken with panic and hysteria. There were no hysterics this time—the tears that welled in her eyes were tears of joy. "I owe you so much for bringing me to America that I want to do everything to make you proud of me," she confided.

"My child, Lady and I want and expect you to do your best," I told her. "Do that, and that's all we'll ever ask from you."

I realized that the first weeks at Walsingham, under the discipline and routine of daily lessons and boarding-school life—and far removed from the hoopla of the New York reception—would be a crucial measure of Patsy's adjustment. Back at my mission headquarters in Germantown, I kept telling myself to expect early reports of problems and difficulties, and to clothe myself in patience until the kinks smoothed. But when the reports came, they were so good I felt like the undersized soul who suddenly becomes nine feet tall. Patsy was being given an intensive cram course to bring her up to the scholastic level of her contemporaries, and she was responding beautifully. There were no fits of obstinacy, no spells of laziness and aimlessness. The warm camaraderie that the girls of Walsingham had shown the stranger that first day showed no signs of chilling.

Thus, the mold for Patsy's new life in America was set, and as the months rolled by, it hardened into permanence. The child who had been so troublesome in Singapore and could not pass her courses was getting 90's and 95's in a school with high standards. The girl who had resisted all attempts to school her in the arts and graces was an eager volunteer learning the fine points of the piano, the dance, the drama, and the paint brush, and signing up for class plays and choral singing. Introduced to such non-Asiatic pursuits as basketball, softball, and gymnastics, she was even displaying a surprising skill in these directions. The brooding introvert was knocking down all the fences she had built for herself and was sunning herself in the open pasture.

What had happened, plainly and simply, was that Patsy Li had found love. The girl's native intelligence and basic good qualities had come to the fore the moment she stopped telling herself she was an unwanted child. Now there was no longer reason to strike out against imagined tormentors, to sulk, to resist, to do the opposite of what was asked of her. Feeling the healing potion of love on all sides, she too wanted to love, and to do the things that cheered those who cheered her.

The months were very full for Patsy. She spent many of her weekends in an active swirl of Washington activities, expertly and devotedly shepherded by Lady—or "Aunt Eleanor," as she now called her. I would hurry down to see her and counsel her as often as I could, and burn up the telephone wires when I couldn't. She had trips to New York and Philadelphia, and I arranged for her summer vacation to be spent at a beautiful outdoor camp in New York State run by the Grey Nuns. When, at year's end, it came time for Patsy to go to her first dance, I temporarily usurped Aunt Eleanor's function as supervisor and provider of the girl's wardrobe by producing a long gown from a Philadelphia shop. As I arrived on the scene, somewhat breathless from a hurried train trip and bearing my festooned clothes box, Aunt Eleanor eyed me with the same merry glance I had gotten from Sister Constance and muttered, "Behold, the Father of the Bride!"

From time to time, my superiors would send me around the country to speak before religious groups and help raise funds for the missions. I had remained in the Navy as a Reserve officer, and found myself addressing so many military functions and civic and patriotic dinners that George Jessel, the "Toastmaster General" who crossed my path on occasion, insisted I was the only man in America who ate home less than he did.

When I told stories about the meaning of faith and how we managed to nourish its flame in the blackest hours on Guadalcanal, I always brought in the dramatic episode of Patsy Li. Now that she was blooming in America, I was able to make her the pièce de résistance of my little speeches. Frequently, I would get letters from people who had been dogged with misfortune, and I would use the example of Patsy's story to help infuse them with fresh hope and courage.

*The
Return
of
Ruth
Li*

14

Patsy's happy romance with America continued throughout the fifties. She was graduated from Walsingham with high honors and many treasured memories, was awarded a scholarship to Gwenyd Mercy Junior College, and then went on to Catholic University in Washington, D.C. She had by now converted to the Catholic faith, though I had assured her that her scholarship was not predicated on her religious affiliation, and that the love we all had for her was independent of her faith.

In college, her grades continued in the top level and

she began work toward a degree in nursing science. She wanted to heal bodies, she told me, the way her own had been healed on Guadalcanal.

She had developed poise, charm, and good looks. She exuded warmth and a talent for cultivating and maintaining friendships. Through Lady's boundless generosity, she was able to take many trips around the country. As she traveled and met new streams of people, she broadened her range of human understanding. Her school chums began to turn to her as their counselor when they had troubles at home or with their boy friends.

When I was transferred out of my mission headquarters for a new assignment as student counselor at St. John's University, I told Patsy she ought to have my job. "You're putting me out of business," I told her. "I'm supposed to be counseling you and other young people, and here you are acting as mother hen to your own brood of chicks."

Patsy laughed and assured me she was still an amateur. If she was a satisfactory mother hen, she said, it was only because she had lived so many lives in her young years and experienced so much—both good and bad—that she seemed like a fount of wisdom to her less-seasoned confreres.

There remained one aspect of Patsy's new life that troubled me: her relationship with her mother. Patsy was completely open with me about virtually all her inner feelings and desires, but this was one area where she discouraged exploration. The ready wit and facile conversation she could summon up at a moment's notice to deal with the small problems of her chums failed her when I tried to probe her own larger problem. I knew she wrote Ruth Li very rarely, and then perfunctorily. Indeed, at times she would let a whole year go by without sending a note. When I prodded her about this, she became very troubled. Finally, she confessed to me her feeling that her mother had deserted her and that therefore she owed her no more filial obligations.

She wanted, too, to forget the world she had left behind in Singapore and the unpleasantness that went with it. This attitude became apparent even in her social relationships. There was a Chinese-American Society in Washington which sponsored many dances for young people. The offspring of Chinese diplomats and of prominent Chinese-Americans attended these socials, and both Lady and I encouraged Patsy to go. Invariably, she refused. She went to other socials with her girl friends instead. These were mostly dances for servicemen, and from time to time she would date the GI's she met there. She explained her preference for these socials to the total exclusion of the other affairs by saying that the "American" dances were conducive to her present happy life and personality, while the others had an association with the past that she wanted put into limbo.

Lady and I tried, as gently as we knew how, to show Patsy she was mistaken in her feelings toward her mother and the past, but we didn't succeed. I then put the matter in a mental pigeonhole on the theory that Patsy would acquire a different perspective as she grew older. Meanwhile, I kept up my own correspondence with Ruth Li, and Lady did the same. Patsy's complete turnabout in the scholastic world, the manner in which she had been accepted in America, and her decision to go into a field related to medicine had thrilled her mother. Her daughter, she wrote me, was fulfilling all the dreams she had had for the child she lost at six and found again at ten. She was most generous in her praise of Lady and myself. We had done what she had proved incapable of doing, she said, and she hoped Patsy would always realize the debt she owed us.

Ruth's deep sadness over Patsy's estrangement from her was evident from many of the things she wrote me. Yet she said she did not want to cry over it, first because crying was not part of her proud Chinese heritage, and second, because she felt no mother had the right to cry over a child's success, even if that success was not shared with her.

Her resolute defenses finally broke down, however, when Foster Hailey crossed her path in 1955. Ruth and her husband had escaped from Shanghai after the Red takeover of that city, and had gone on first to Hong Kong and then to Formosa. Foster, coincidentally, had been assigned to cover Formosa for his paper at the same time. Ruth Li's first meeting with the correspondent whose story had provided the vital link in her search for Patsy proved such an emotional strain she could not hold back the sobs. Knowing how much this meant to Mrs. Li in terms of "loss of face," Foster felt deeply for her.

Ruth Li confided to him that in her soul-searching over her failure with Patsy, she had come to realize that her own inflexibility and overstrictness were primarily responsible. But as Foster pointed out to me, how could any of us condemn a mother who had acted in the light of her own family tradition and who had sincerely felt she was doing right by her child?

In 1957, Ruth Li's longing for her daughter reached such a point that she broached to me for the first time the possibility of coming to America herself. Her husband, she said, preferred to remain in Asia, but was willing to make the move if it meant so much to her. I encouraged her to come, and pointed out that our government had liberalized its quota system to aid Chinese who had been driven from the mainland by the Communist government

Ruth, her husband, and her boy Billie, born of this second marriage, were able to get visas and come to this country a few months later. Ruth's sister, Dr. Katherine Li, who had read the fateful Hailey story, was no longer here, but she had another sister living in San Francisco. This sister made a temporary home for her. Patsy had a vacation period from school not long afterward, and I made arrangements for her to fly to San Francisco.

Patsy was reluctant to go, but Lady and I prompted her in the cherished hope that a face-to-face meeting between mother and child would break down old barriers and lead to a warm reconciliation.

It didn't work out that way. Patsy made it plain to her mother that she had come only out of a sense of duty. Ruth Li, in turn, still couldn't communicate to her daughter the deep feelings she had for her. Patsy cut her visit short. Furthermore, when she returned east, she told Lady and myself that one of the GI's who had dated her had asked her to marry him. He was leaving the service to return to his home, a small town in the rural midwest. To accept his proposal, Patsy would have to leave college without completing her scholarship, and give up her plans to join the nursing service at Providence Hospital in Washington after graduation. Yet she was seriously thinking of saying "Yes."

This news came as an unwelcome shock. Lady and I knew how much Patsy wanted to finish college and follow through on plans she herself had made. From what we knew of our ward, we could tell that she had suddenly magnified a liking for someone into an illusion of love.

"We don't want you to act on impulse," we cautioned Patsy. "We don't intend to take on the roles of the hard-hearted guardians who tell their daughter to 'go chase that fellow and never let him darken our door again.' But at the same time, we want you to give yourself a great deal of time to think. We don't want you to rush into anything. If you're looking at this proposal simply as another means of cutting yourself off from your mother and your background, then you should forget it."

Our little sermon made a deep impression on Patsy. She promised Lady and myself she would make no decision until she had thought the subject through from every angle. A few weeks later, she told us with a shy smile that her tentative engagement to her admirer had been called off. He was a nice boy and all that, but there was no real love and no basis for marriage.

There still remained the festering sore of the daughter-mother relationship. I kept telling myself there must be some way to convince Patsy that Ruth Li had always loved her. I felt that was all that was needed to knock down the block that separated child from parent. Religion had become a very important thing to Patsy since her conversion, and Biblical stories were particularly meaningful to her. I decided to find an appropriate story which could prove my point to Patsy by analogy, and discuss it with her heart-to-heart at a propitious moment.

I combed my storehouse of memory, made notes to myself about Bible stories that had a relation to the subject at hand—and then threw them away. Somehow, none that came to mind seemed quite germane. I was still wrestling with the idea when a rabbi came to my rescue.

The occasion was Patsy's spring vacation in 1959, which we spent in part at the huge Grossinger's resort in New York's Catskill Mountains. When he was lying wounded and ill in the hospital tent on Guadalcanal, Barney Ross had jestingly promised he would take my little war waif to his favorite resort someday to "fatten her up." At the time, of course, it was highly doubtful that any of us would ever see Patsy Li again, but now Barney wanted to make good on his old pledge and he arranged this holiday for us.

Jennie and Harry Grossinger set aside rooms in their own cottage for Patsy, Lady, and myself, and we spent a few glorious days riding, playing tennis, and swimming in a king-sized indoor pool. On our last evening, we sat around after dinner with the Grossingers, Barney and his wife, Eli Epstein, the tennis pro, Bob Weitman, a top executive of Metro-Goldwyn-Mayer, and Rabbi Harry Stone. The rabbi not only conducted services at the resort but was also a delightful raconteur.

The talk got around to the Passover holiday, which was to be celebrated in a few days. Rabbi Stone made the cogent point that the age-old story of the Lord's deliverance of the Hebrews from Egyptian slavery had much modern significance with peoples all over the world striving to burst out of feudal bondage. Then, in recalling the history of Moses, who led the Hebrews to freedom, he alluded to the sacrifice of Moses' mother. The Egyptians were killing many Hebrew boys and Moses' mother felt her child was not safe with her. One morning, she left the child in a waterproof cradle at the river bank, where he was found by an Egyptian woman willing to rear him in safety. Ironically, the woman who brought up Moses was the Pharaoh's own daughter.

I felt something akin to an explosion in my head as the rabbi was talking, and I told myself, "Fritzie, you dolt, why didn't you remind yourself of the story of Moses' mother before? It's just the kind of story that would have real meaning to Patsy."

Later on, as we walked slowly back to our cottage, Patsy seemed eager to discuss this wonderful story. "You see," I said gently, "there can be times when a mother deserts a child—or seems to desert it—for very good reason. Moses' mother left her youngster in an act of love. I'm not saying your case is exactly the same as that, but I do believe there is an important parallel. Your mother's 'desertion' of you was an act of love, too. She was confessing that due to various circumstances, she could not do for you what others could do.

"Your mother has never lost her love for you, Patsy. She has told me that many times, and even though she finds it hard to get this across to you, I have never doubted her."

Patsy said nothing, and I didn't press the point further. But the next day she told Lady and myself she had written Ruth Li a long letter. "Not gushy, you understand, just friendly," she explained. She swiftly had a long letter in turn, and then there were more letters. The time was fast coming for Patsy's graduation. It would, of course, be a memorable day in her life, and Lady and I were anxious that she should have her mother there. Two weeks before the big day, we received good news from Ruth Li herself. She wrote that Patsy had invited her to the ceremonies and she would be there "with bells on."

On June 7, 1959, with the proper pomp, ceremony, and circumstance, and in the measured cadence of the graduation march, the Baccalaureate Procession of the Catholic University of America filed out of the college gymnasium and onto the campus. Ruth Li, Lady, and I stood there on the green turf, warmed by the sun and the whole glowing spectacle of commencement. We were waiting for our girl, and as the procession broke ranks to be swept up in a proud sea of mothers and fathers, we strained for a look at her.

She came slowly at first. In her left hand was her degree, Bachelor of Science in Nursing. In her right were various certificates attesting to scholarship. Perched on her head like a regal bouquet was her graduation hood of gold velvet, with gold-and-white lining and trimming. As the sunshine flecked her face and her long, dark hair, and dramatized the poise and attractiveness of this 23-year-old graduate, I found it hard to remember the battered little piece of human flotsam who had come to me adrift in a raging war.

Suddenly, she spotted us, waved, forgot her poise, and started running. In a few seconds, she was in Ruth Li's arms. And in that moment, I recognized the child again. Only this was not the child of tragedy and tears. This was a happy child who had found her mother—for the second time.

"You know, Fritz, when you think about it, there have been four miracles in your Patsy's life." It was Mother talking one winter night in our cozy, if antique, edifice on Willoughby Avenue. Mother was in her nineties now, and there were times when she stumbled over her decades and had FDR in the White House instead of that gallant ex-PT Boat commander who used to go whipping around our Solomon Islands. There were other times, however, when her dear head would suddenly shuck off the fluttering web of confusion and grasp everything with luminous clarity again. This was a night of clarity.

"Four miracles," Mother repeated. "The first miracle came when she somehow survived the bombing of her ship off Singapore. Everybody but Mrs. Li thought she had drowned, but instead she was saved. Then there was

the second miracle, when the Japanese butchered her
and left her to die. She came back to life in your tent.
That made it two times the Japanese had apparently
killed her, and two times she came back from the brink.

"The third miracle was when you gave her the name
that had been yours in China, and that turned out to be
her real name. And the fourth miracle—well, it certainly seems like another miracle to me—was the one
that brought her together with her mother again after
the years of separation.

"I doubt that there has ever been a girl like this one!
When she first came to you, you pitied her as a poor
orphan left alone in the world. But she not only became
the sweetheart of all your Marines and Navy boys, but
also grew up to have two mothers—her own mother, and
Lady Eleanor, who has assuredly been a second mother
to her. This girl has been able to make the sun, the
moon, and the stars stand still for her. The good Lord
and the little fairies have touched her so often I imagine
there can't possibly be any more wonders in her lifetime."

Mother, however, had underestimated my Patsy Li.
Just about the time we were having our little chat, Patsy
was finishing a long day at Providence Hospital and
hurrying over to join the final hours of a dance at the
Chinese-American Society. There, she met a young man
named Joe. He asked her for a dance, and they danced
and danced. He was a graduate of the University of
Maryland, a native of Baltimore, a veteran of the National Guard, and a mathematician employed by one of
the defense plants. His father, who came to this coun-

try as a poor Chinese immigrant, had worked his way up to the ownership of a well-known restaurant in Baltimore.

Joe had come to the social hoping to meet a good-looking girl who was intelligent, witty, musically-inclined and "not the bashful kind." He had found her. There followed many calls from Baltimore, letters, and months of dating.

Mrs. Li and Lady and I came to meet the young man. We liked what we saw. And we agreed that something cheerful was brewing here. In November 1961 I got a call from Lady asking me to come down to Washington the next night for a "special party." I asked for a postponement on the grounds that this was the night we were going to celebrate the installation of an eminent Vincentian named Father Edward Burke as the new president of my college. There were whispers at the other end between Lady and Patsy, and no doubt a follow-up call to Baltimore. At any rate, the night was switched, and at the appropriate time I presented myself at Lady's place. I had my fiddle in tow because I suspected that I would be called on to play a few love songs.

The place was buzzing. There were Patsy's friends from school, girl friends from Washington like Joan Cuddihy Krecks, and Reba and Mary Ellen Ransom, Ann Crowley, the former star of "Oklahoma!", and many of Lady's friends in diplomatic and government circles. Then as Patsy and Joe came in—fashionably late —Patsy waved her hand to show us a diamond engagement ring, and the number "True Love" burst forth from my violin in a tempo so loud and excitable it made the fiddle sound like a clatter of trumpets.

The wedding was planned for spring, but there was nearly no spring for Joe. One night, a bus boy in his dad's restaurant took sick and Joe offered to drive him home. Two thugs jumped them in front of the boy's house and took their wallets. Then they announced they were going to take the car. Joe tried to stop them. One thug grabbed his arms, but he fought him off. Then the other hoodlum took out a long knife and cut Joe's throat.

An ambulance picked Joe up out of a puddle of his own blood and raced for the hospital. He was on the critical list for several days, but he managed to pull through.

On May 12, 1962, the Right Reverend Monsignor John B. Roeder of the St. Thomas the Apostle Church in Washington, D.C., greeted me in his cathedral-like structure and then turned it over to me. This was Patsy's wedding day, and though it had begun with a gloomy, overcast morning, the sun broke through the clouds just before the ceremony. The sudden change from darkness to brightness seemed to me to be symbolic of the whole pattern of Patsy's life.

The pews filled quickly. The Epistle side of the church, where the groom's parents, relatives, and friends were seated, was a pageant of colorful Oriental finery. On the Gospel side, traditionally reserved for guests of the bride, were many of Washington's young social set.

Promptly at two, the ushers rolled out the white runners along which the bridal party would march. As the first notes of the wedding music sounded, Joe entered through the side door, flanked by his best man. He was still pale from his ordeal, but as he stood waiting for his bride I felt almost paternally proud of the fine appearance he made. In his bearing could be seen the intelligence, gentleness, and sense of responsibility that I knew Patsy would always be able to rely on and love.

Now the bridesmaids, like a slowly rising sea of chiffon and blossoms, made their procession toward the altar. Then came Patsy. Proudly borne on the arm of my cousin Frank Gehring, she was dressed in shimmering white satin, and as Frank lifted her veil to kiss her before presenting her to her bridegroom, I could see that she had never known a happier moment. Could there ever be a happier moment than this? As I wondered, I found myself so close to tears that I began to understand why women always cry at weddings. I looked at the front pews, and, sure enough, women on both sides were shamelessly wiping their eyes.

During my thirty-two years in the priesthood I have, of course, married countless couples, but never had there been a wedding like this one! Even as I spoke the words of holy union, my thoughts kept darting back to the child of twenty years before. She had come to us on Guadalcanal a living symbol of war's worst horror—frightened, hungry, homeless, loveless children. But she had survived to teach us that hope and love are still the only answers to the problems of life in this world.

Now the couple turned to each other and pronounced their vows of faith and fidelity. I pressed their hands together and said loudly, if rather huskily, *"Tien chu pao-iu"*—"God be with you, now and forever."

One of the doctors who had attended the groom at the hospital was at the ceremony. "That blade missed Joe's jugular vein by the tiniest fraction of an inch," he confided to me. "If the knife had gone just a little bit farther, the boy would have been dead."

But the knife had gone no farther. And Patsy had her fifth miracle.

Oh, I almost forgot to mention Joe's last name. It's L-E-E, Americanized from the Chinese "Li," but pronounced exactly the same. Thus, the child of miracles who was named by destiny will carry that name for the rest of her days.

"The End Is Not Yet"

Seventeen years have now passed since several of the miracles noted in this book took place. The battlegrounds of the Southwest Pacific have become again lush tropical islands. Yet even now, remnants of the defeated foe are still emerging from out of jungle hiding places, first learning that the conflict ended long ago. Discoveries are continually being made of the fierce avidity with which the Japanese defended their usurped possessions on the atolls from which they boasted they would step into the White House to dictate the surrender of the United States Forces.

Since the present persists in unfolding evidences in the Southwest Pacific of people and things associated with World War II, it may well be that the publication of *A Child of Miracles* will bring to light material that will illuminate certain of the miracles. With this expectancy, the author deems it fitting to advise the reader that "the end is not yet." Should the future reveal a need for a further exploration of the Miracles, another volume will be forthcoming.

—Rev. Frederic P. Gehring, C.M.

October, 1962